Paris

WHAT'S NEW | **WHAT'S ON** | **WHAT'S BEST**

www.timeout.com/paris

Contents

Don't Miss

Sights & Museums 8
Eating & Drinking 14
Shopping 21
Nightlife 26
Arts & Leisure 30
Calendar 34

Itineraries

Revolutionary Road 42
Meet the Moderns 47
Vintage on a Vespa 50

Paris by Area

Champs-Elysées & Western Paris 56
Map 58
Opéra to Les Halles 70
Map 72
Montmartre & Pigalle 87
Map 89
North-east Paris 95
Map 97
The Marais & Eastern Paris ... 100
Map 102
The Seine & Islands 116
Map 117
The 7th & Western Paris 122
Map 123
St-Germain-des-Prés & Odéon 129
Map 131
The Latin Quarter & the 13th .. 141
Map .... 143 & 151
Montparnasse 153
Map 155
Worth the Trip 158

Essentials

Hotels 164
Getting Around 182
Resources A-Z 186
Vocabulary 189
Index 190

Published by Time Out
4th Floor
125 Shaftesbury Avenue
London WC2H 8AD
Tel: + 44 (0)20 7813 3000
Email: guides@timeout.com
www.timeout.com

Editorial Director Sarah Guy
Group Finance Manager Margaret Wright

Time Out Guides is a wholly owned subsidiary of Time Out Group Ltd.

© **Time Out Group Ltd**
Chairman & Founder Tony Elliott
Chief Executive Officer Tim Arthur
Chief Financial Officer Matt White
Publisher Alex Batho

Time Out and the Time Out logo are trademarks of Time Out Group Ltd.

This edition first published in Great Britain in 2014 by Ebury Publishing
A Random House Group Company
Company information can be found on www.randomhouse.co.uk
Random House UK Limited Reg. No. 954009
10 9 8 7 6 5 4 3 2 1

Distributed in the US and Latin America by Publishers Group West (1-510-809-3700)

For further distribution details, see www.timeout.com

ISBN: 978-1-84670-339-3

A CIP catalogue record for this book is available from the British Library.

Printed and bound in Germany by Appl.

MIX
Paper from
responsible sources
FSC™ C004592
www.fsc.org

Penguin Random House is committed to a sustainable
future for our business, our readers and our planet.
This book is made from Forest Stewardship Council®
certified paper.

Paris Shortlist

The **Time Out Paris Shortlist** is one of a series of guides that draws on Time Out's background as a magazine publisher to keep you current with everything that's going on in town. As well as Paris's key sights and the best of its eating, drinking and leisure options, the guide picks out the most exciting venues to have opened in the last year and gives a full calendar of events. It also includes features on the important news, trends and openings, all compiled by locally based editors and writers. Whether you're visiting for the first time in your life or the first time this year, you'll find the *Time Out Paris Shortlist* contains all you need to know, in a portable and easy-to-use format.

The guide divides central Paris into ten areas, each containing listings for Sights & Museums, Eating & Drinking, Shopping, Nightlife and Arts & Leisure, and maps pinpointing their locations. At the front of the book are chapters rounding up these scenes city-wide, and giving a shortlist of our overall picks. We also include itineraries for days out, plus essentials such as transport information and hotels.

Our listings give phone numbers as dialled within France. From abroad, use your country's exit code followed by 33 (the country code for France) and the number given, dropping the initial '0'.

We have noted price categories by using one to four euro signs (€-€€€€), representing budget, moderate, expensive and luxury. Major credit cards are accepted unless otherwise stated. We also indicate when a venue is NEW .

All our listings are double-checked, but places do sometimes close or change their hours or prices, so it's a good idea to call a venue before visiting. While every effort has been made to ensure accuracy, the publishers cannot accept responsibility for any errors that this guide may contain.

Venues are marked on the maps using symbols numbered according to their order within the chapter and colour-coded as follows:

❶ Sights & Museums
❶ Eating & Drinking
❶ Shopping
❶ Nightlife
❶ Arts & Leisure

Map Key	
Major sight or landmark	
Hospital or college	
Railway station	
Park	
River	
Autoroute	
Main road	
Main road tunnel	
Pedestrian road	
Arrondissement boundary	
Airport	✈
Church	✚
Métro station	Ⓜ
RER station	Ⓡ
Area name	LES HALLES

Time Out **Paris** Shortlist

EDITORIAL
Editor Dominic Earle

DESIGN & PICTURE DESK
Senior Designer Kei Ishimaru
Group Commercial Senior Designer
 Jason Tansley
Picture Editor Jael Marschner
Deputy Picture Editor Ben Rowe
Freelance Picture Researcher
 Lizzy Owen

ADVERTISING
Jinga Media Ltd (www.jingamedia.com)

MARKETING
Senior Publishing Brand Manager
 Luthfa Begum
Head of Circulation Dan Collins

PRODUCTION
Production Controller
 Katie Mulhern-Bhudia

CONTRIBUTORS
This guide was researched and written by the writers of *Time Out Paris*.

PHOTOGRAPHY
Pages 2 (top left), 8, 11 ppl/Shutterstock.com; 2 (bottom left), 40 Marko Kudjerski/Wikimedia Commons; 2 (bottom right), 13, 41, 42, 43, 44 (bottom) Kiev.Victor/Shutterstock.com; 3 (top left), 119 (middle) Luciano Mortula/Shutterstock.com; 3 (top right), 172 Martine Houghton; 3 (bottom left), 134 Jean-François Dréan; 7, 109 Danielle Rubi; 21, 47, 52, 105 Oliver Knight; 25, 181 (left) Olivia Rutherford; 28 David Monniaux/Wikimedia Commons; 29 atm2003/Shutterstock.com; 30 Ateliers Jean Nouvel; 34 Radu Razvan/Shutterstock.com; 35 Yoann MORIN/Shutterstock.com; 36 Crobard/Shutterstock.com; 38 photogolfer/Shutterstock.com; 39 Erik Tomasson; 44 (top) Dmitry Brizhatyuk/Shutterstock.com; 45 NeydtStock/Shutterstock.com; 48 Colros/Wikimedia Commons; 49, 144 (bottom right) Tupungato/Shutterstock.com; 51 Karl Blackwell; 55 © JAKOB + MACFARLANE; 56 vichie81/Shutterstock.com; 63 © Fondation Louis Vuitton/Nicolas Borel; 66 © La Pâtisserie des Rêves; 70, 95 bjul/Shutterstock.com; 75 (top) Adrien Chevrot © Jeu de Paume; 75 (middle and bottom) Arno Gisinger © Jeu de Paume; 79 Virginie Garnier; 84, 125 Lilyana Vynogradova/Shutterstock.com; 87 Nattee Chalermtiragool/Shutterstock.com; 90 ilovebuvette; 100 pio3/Shutterstock.com; 114 (top left) Vincent Fillon; 114 (top right and bottom) Maria Spera/CRT PIdF; 116 Vladimir Sazonov/Shutterstock.com; 119 (top) Heloise Bergman; 119 (bottom) bensliman hassan/Shutterstock.com; 122 Dafinka/Shutterstock.com; 129, 153 Rrrainbow/Shutterstock.com; 141 zprecech/Shutterstock.com; 144 (top) Alan Kraft/Shutterstock.com; 144 (bottom left) abxyz/Shutterstock.com; 146 (top) Annabelle Schachmes; 146 (bottom) © www.tibo.org; 158 ToucanWings/Wikimedia Commons; 161 Nathalie Prébende; 163, 164, 169 Christophe Bielsa

The following images were supplied by the featured establishments: 2 (top right), 3 (bottom right), 14, 22, 26, 50, 93, 139, 156, 176, 181 (right)

Cover photograph: Susanne Kremer/4Corners

MAPS
JS Graphics (john@jsgraphics.co.uk).

About **Time Out**

Founded in 1968, Time Out has expanded from humble London beginnings into the leading resource for those wanting to know what's happening in the world's greatest cities. As well as our influential what's-on weeklies in London and New York, we publish nearly 30 other listings magazines in cities as varied as Beijing and Mumbai. The magazines established Time Out's trademark style: sharp writing, informed reviewing and bang up-to-date inside knowledge of every scene.

Time Out made the natural leap into travel guides in the 1980s with the City Guide series, which now extends to over 50 destinations around the world. Written and researched by expert local writers and generously illustrated with original photography, the full-size guides cover a larger area than our Shortlist guides and include many more venue reviews, along with additional background features and a full set of maps.

Throughout this rapid growth, the company has remained proudly independent, still owned by Tony Elliott four decades after he started Time Out London as a single fold-out sheet of A5 paper. This independence extends to the editorial content of all our publications, this Shortlist included. No establishment has been featured because it has advertised, and no payment has influenced any of our reviews. And, for our critics, there's definitely no such thing as a free lunch: all restaurants and bars are visited and reviewed anonymously, and Time Out always picks up the bill.
For more about the company, see www.timeout.com.

Don't Miss

What's best: **Sights & Museums**   8

What's best: **Eating & Drinking**   14

What's best: **Shopping**   21

What's best: **Nightlife**   26

What's best: **Arts & Leisure**   30

What's on: **Calendar**   34

WHAT'S BEST
Sights & Museums

A decade ago, a weekend for many in the French capital would have meant a quick dash round the Louvre and Musée d'Orsay, a hike up the Eiffel Tower and a twilight cruise on the Seine, followed by *steak-frites* and a carafe of Bordeaux in a cramped, smoky St-Germain bistro. Fast-forward to today and the Louvre is now home to a dramatic subterranean Islamic Arts Gallery (see p74), the Musée d'Orsay has had a dynamic revamp (see p126), the Palais Galliera (see p61) is a feast of fashion once again, the Palais de Tokyo (see p61) has tripled in size, and the Eiffel Tower (see p122) has a spectacular new glass floor. And thanks to Bertrand Delanoë's courageous Berges de Seine project, the river has had a makeover too, with a stretch of the Left Bank between Musée d'Orsay

and the Pont de l'Alma converted into a pedestrian promenade with play areas, cafés and bars.

Come 2015, there will be more new or good-as-new cultural treats awaiting arts-lovers, including two much-delayed delights – a renovated Musée Picasso (see p106) and the new Fondation Jérôme Seydoux-Pathé showcase of film memorabilia.

Paris, of course, already reigns supreme when it comes to sights and museums, with three of the world's top ten most visited art museums within its clutch – the Louvre holds an unassailable lead with more than nine million visitors per year, some three million ahead of its closest rival the British Museum, while the Pompidou (see p100) and newly revamped Musée d'Orsay squeeze in at no.8 and no.10 respectively. Across the rest of the city, the list of sights worth your time is almost endless – from iconic treasures such as the Arc de Triomphe (see p56) to lesser-known gems such as the Musée Fragonard (see p160). All this, and much more that we haven't yet mentioned, in a city that's a manageable size and boasts one of the best transport networks anywhere in the world.

Neighbourhood culture

As well as all these wonderfully exciting revamps in central Paris, culture is also migrating around the capital. Western Paris is home to the Musée Belmondo (see p162) – not an *hommage* to the Nouvelle Vague heartthrob, but rather to Jean-Paul's father, Paul, one of France's most important 20th-century sculptors. Up north, meanwhile, Larry Gagosian (www.gagosian.com) and Thaddaeus Ropac (www.ropac.net) have both headed out to the *banlieue* to open galleries with the sort of space they could only have dreamed of in the Marais. Also worth a mention is the new Musée de la Grande Guerre du Pays de Meaux (www.museedelagrandeguerre.eu), just half an hour by train from the Gare de l'Est and a fitting tribute to the horrors of 1914.

The lie of the land

Parisians identify parts of their city by two systems: there are the named districts, whose frontiers aren't always clear – the Marais, the Latin Quarter, Montparnasse and so on – and the 20 numbered arrondissements that spiral out, clockwise and in ascending order, from the Louvre. Together they comprise an urban jigsaw. Each piece has a particular connotation or function: the fifth is academic;

SHORTLIST

Best new/revamped
- Eiffel Tower (see p122)
- Musée du Louvre Islamic Arts Gallery (see p74)
- Musée National Picasso (see p106)
- Musée d'Orsay (see p126)
- Musée Zadkine (see p132)
- Palais Galliera (see p61)

Best secret
- La Collection 1900 (see p70)
- Musée Valentin Haüy (see p126)

Best art
- Centre Pompidou (see p100)
- Musée du Louvre (see p74)
- Musée d'Orsay (see p126)
- Musée de l'Orangerie (see p74)
- Palais de Tokyo (see p61)

Best dead
- Cimetière du Montparnasse (see p153)
- Cimetière du Père-Lachaise (see p101)

Best outdoors
- Bois de Boulogne (see p162)
- Jardin du Luxembourg (see p130)
- Parc des Buttes-Chaumont (see p96)

Best views
- Arc de Triomphe (see p56)
- Cathédrale Notre-Dame de Paris (see p118)
- Eiffel Tower (see p122)
- Institut du Monde Arabe (see p142)
- Sacré-Coeur (see p88)
- Tour Montparnasse (see p154)

DON'T MISS

The most comfortable and modern boats in Paris

vedettes de paris

The sightseeing cruise of Paris
Get the best in 1 hour
www.vedettesdeparis.com

Location:
At the foot of the Eiffel Tower
Port de Suffren, 7th district + 00 33 (0)1 44 18 19 50
M° Bir-Hakeim & Trocadero; RER C Champ de Mars

This Parisian sightseeing cruise has to be at the top of your list of things to do when you are in the French capital.

Ideally located at the foot of the Eiffel Tower, its charming boats enhance the pleasure of a guided cruise on the Seine.

Listed by UNESCO as World Heritage, the river banks offer you some of the most well-known monuments such as the Eiffel Tower, the Louvre, the Orsay Museum and Notre Dame Cathedral amongst others.

Recorded multilingual commentary and a bar service on board.

Departures :
Everyday every 30/45min from 11am to 10pm. Times vary depending on the season. Check out our website for exact times.

Sightseeing or «by Night» cruise:
€14: Adult; €6: Children 5-12s; free under 4s

Exclusive :

from €19 to €23

Sparkling cruise

The magic of Paris by Night

Snacking cruise

Get a sample of the best monuments

Exclusive: a bar on board

Palais Garnier

the sixth is arty and chic; the 16th is wealthy and dull; while the 18th, 19th and 20th arrondissements are riotously multicultural. Residents are frequently assessed, on first meeting at least, by their postcode, and as a consequence often develop a fierce sense of local pride. Indeed, many will inform you that the French capital isn't so much a city as a jumble of villages.

We've divided this book into areas, though not necessarily into shapes that residents would recognise; we've imagined the city as a series of visitor-friendly concentrations of shops, sights, restaurants and bars. The Champs-Elysées & Western Paris section has the famous avenue as its spine, lined with high-end shops. It also contains fashion's most glamorous thoroughfare, avenue Montaigne, which is almost matched in terms of lustre and allure by rue du Fbg-Saint-Honoré.

Montmartre & Pigalle has, at its northern end, picture-postcard Montmartre with its vertiginous flights of steps, narrow winding streets and the massive bulk of Sacré-Coeur (see p88). To the south lies Pigalle, famous for the Moulin Rouge and its strip clubs and scuzzy bars (though it's a considerably more salubrious proposition today than it once was).

Opéra to Les Halles used to be the centre of royal power in Paris, and you can get a sense of this by taking a stroll around the Palais-Royal (see p74). Today, however, it's the city's commercial and cultural powerhouse: it's home to the Les Halles shopping complex, to the jewellers and fashion houses of place Vendôme, and to the Louvre, the Palais Garnier (see p86) and Monet showcase the Musée de l'Orangerie (see p74).

North-eastern Paris is the area visitors from the UK are likely to see first: Eurostar trains terminate at the Gare du Nord (see p95) in the tenth arrondissement. The area is on the up, with its main artery, the charming Canal St-Martin, lined with boutiques and cafés. Further north and east of here is the magnificently odd Parc des Buttes-Chaumont (see p96), a warren of cliffs and grottoes carved out of a former quarry. Marais, Bastille & Eastern Paris is barfly territory, especially along rue Oberkampf, rue Jean-Pierre Timbaud and rue St-Maur. The ever-trendy Marais is chock-full of independent galleries and quirky shops, and is also the centre of gay life in Paris.

The Islands – the Ile de la Cité, the oldest part of the city and home to Notre-Dame Cathedral (see p118),

and the more elegant Ile St-Louis – are essential ports of call. Notre-Dame celebrated its 850th anniversary in 2013 with a set of nine new, sweetly tuned bells.

Undeniably, the main attraction of the affluent 7th & Western Paris area is the Eiffel Tower, universal emblem of the French capital. Its ironwork is most alluring at night, when it is lit up by thousands of shimmering lightbulbs. This is also the best time to climb it, because the queues are at their shortest.

For many years, St-Germain-des-Prés was the intellectual heartland of the city. But these days it's more about fashion than philosophy, and the cafés are no place for starving writers. The city's most beautiful park, the Jardin du Luxembourg (see p130), won't cost you a *sou*, however; and the Musée d'Orsay is still excellent value, and gleaming after its revamp. Due east, the Latin Quarter is home to several august academic institutions, including the Sorbonne. And to the south, Montparnasse, although no longer the artistic stronghold it was in the 1920s, still boasts excellent cafés and restaurants, and the resting place of some of France's most illustrious dead, the Cimetière du Montparnasse (see p153).

Vélib'

Getting around

Vélib', the municipal bike hire scheme that puts some 20,000 bicycles at the disposal of residents and visitors, continues to flourish. Emboldened by the bikes' runaway success, Bertrand Delanoë launched another green transport innovation: an eco-friendly car hire system, which began operating in December 2011. Dubbed 'Autolib', the project allows subscribers to pick up and drop off a car at any one of approximately 700 stations. The scheme has a fleet of 1,800 green (100 per cent electric) cars, and each vehicle is tracked in real time. When drivers have finished their hire period, they are guided to the nearest available parking spot.

If you don't feel confident about your chances in Paris traffic, the métro and RER are extensive and reliable, and buses are clean and cheap. Some of the bus routes are worth riding just for the sightseeing opportunities they offer: no.24 takes you through St-Germain-des-Prés and the Latin Quarter; no.69 runs all the way from Gambetta in the east, via the Louvre, to the Champ de Mars in the west; and no.73 connects the Champs-Elysées to the futuristic concrete jungle of La Défense.

But when all is said and done, you really can't beat walking for getting around the capital. Paris is compact enough to be navigated fairly easily on foot, and this is the best way to hear the heartbeat of the city.

For a selection of fascinating self-guided tours around the city, check out the Itineraries section of the guide (pp42-53).

DON'T MISS

Lazare

Eating & Drinking

A surprising number of new restaurants are thriving in the difficult economic climate, from snob-free gastronomy at Cobéa (see p155), to station brasserie style at Eric Frechon's Lazare (see p91) in the eponymous station. Except for the simplest restaurants, it's wise to book ahead. This can usually be done on the same day as your visit, although top-notch establishments require bookings well in advance.

Bistro boom

Thankfully, the French continue to love classic bistro style. Many are old favourites, but the last few years have also seen the rise of the neo-bistro scene, updated for a new generation. At the very centre is Le Chateaubriand (see p108), the *coeur d'artichaut* of this dining trend, which the categorisers call 'bistronomy' (not a word necessarily embraced by the chefs themselves).

So, what are the magic ingredients of the bistronomy boom? First, take the same flair long associated with Parisian gastronomy but use a little less finesse and significantly more innovation; next, add world-beating raw ingredients of thoroughly researched provenance and chefs who are generally young auto-didacts enjoying success with their first business (Inaki Aizpitarte, Le Chateaubriand's Basque chef-owner was previously a *paysagiste*, his sommelier an actor, his olive oil supplier a tight-rope walker). Finally, sprinkle with reasonable prices and an atmosphere that's relaxed and intentionally unbourgeois.

The Chateaubriand's kitchen buys many of its delectable treats locally.

The olive oil comes from La Tête dans les Olives (2 rue Ste-Marthe, 10th, 09.51.31.33.34, www.latetedanslesolives.com), a tiny shop in a pretty street. Owner Cedric Casanova goes to Sicily every six weeks, where he organises and advises 26 farmers on how to make the fruit of their 20,000 olive trees attractive to the Paris market. Should you wish to sample more of his Sicilian products, including pasta made by his fishing buddy, Cedric has opened a restaurant with one table next door. It only seats six and works out at roughly €30 per head. Booking is by email and there's a three-month waiting list to enjoy his tomatoes, figs and extraordinarily heady oregano.

Aizpitarte's other big opening is the Rem Koolhaas-designed Le Dauphin (see p108), a tapas-style restaurant/bar a few doors down at 131 avenue Parmentier, where dishes include *magret séché* and *tempura de gambas*. As at Le Chateaubriand, sourcing is all-important. Bread comes from Du Pain et des Idées (see p99), voted best baker in Paris a few years ago.

Such is the hoopla that Aizpitarte has created, there is inevitably talk of a new scene in the 11th: the proprietors of *branché* Chez Jeanette and Chez Justine chose a site opposite Le Chateaubriand and Le Dauphin for their new catering venture, Le Floréal (see p110) – an American-style diner serving up hamburgers and cupcakes.

Another Chateaubriand success story of the past couple of years has been former sommelier David Loyola's Aux Deux Amis (45 rue Oberkampf, 11th, 01.58.30.38.13). This tiny bar is permanently packed with a hipster crowd, but it's a different vibe from the student hangouts around the Oberkampf metro nearby. Vodka caramel is *interdit* – instead, customers enjoy

SHORTLIST

Best recent openings
- Buvette Gastrothèque (see p88)
- Cobéa (see p155)
- Frenchie Bar à Vins (see p77)
- Lazare (see p91)
- Miss Kô (see p64)
- Verjus (see p80)

Best value
- Le Camion qui Fume (see p19)
- L'Encrier (see p108)
- Le Hangar (see p110)

Most glamorous
- Alain Ducasse au Plaza Athénée (see p62)
- Café de la Paix (see p76)
- Jules Verne (see p127)
- Lapérouse (see p135)
- Le Meurice (see p78)

Bars with character
- Café Charbon (see p107)
- Chez Jeanette (see p96)
- Chez Prune (see p96)
- La Fourmi (see p91)
- La Palette (see p136)

Cocktail classics
- Café Marly (see p76)
- Candelaria (see p107)
- Le Crocodile (see p147)
- Le Fumoir (see p77)
- Lizard Lounge (see p111)

Best for nighthawks
- L'Alimentation Générale (see p106)
- Harry's New York Bar (see p77)
- Le Tambour (see p78)

Bistronomic stars
- Le Chateaubriand (see p108)
- Frenchie (see p77)
- Granterroirs (see p64)
- La Maison Mère (see p91)

DON'T MISS

organic wines and simple dishes such as *tortilla de Jeannine*.

And if you're headed up to the Marché aux Puces de St-Ouen, don't miss out on Starck bistro Ma Cocotte (www.macocotte-lespuces.com), perfect for a post-browse brunch.

Brasserie classics

The spectacle of sitting amid art nouveau extravagance, as waiters in black and white rush between tables serving platters of oysters and choucroute, comes at a price, but is cheaper at lunchtime or late at night. Bofinger (see p107) and La Coupole (see p155), both part of the Flo chain, pull in locals and tourists. The Costes brothers set the standard for the modern brasserie experience with stylish restaurants such as Georges (6th floor, Centre Pompidou, 19 rue Beaubourg, 4th, 01.44.78. 47.99); they have also taken over a few old bistros, such as Chez Julien (1 rue du Pont Louis-Philippe, 4th, 01.42.78.31.64).

Top tables

To crank it up a notch, you could opt for a spot of all-out luxury in one of the city's haute cuisine restaurants. And it doesn't come much more haute than Jules Verne (see p127), Alain Ducasse's classy venue perched in its eyrie on the second floor of the Eiffel Tower. For once, the food is as good as the views, with dishes such as turbot with champagne zabaglione. Other sumptuous dining experiences are to be had at Le Meurice (see p78) and the Plaza Athénée (see p62).

Restaurants where you can easily spend €200 or more a head often have lunch menus for €75-€80 – still a lot of money, but for this you are treated to a full-blown experience from *amuse-bouches* to *mignardises*. Ordering the lunch menu often

means having a more limited choice of dishes, but staff are likely to draw on the freshest ingredients from the market. A notch down from haute cuisine, restaurants such as Le Restaurant (see p136) and Pétrelle (see p92) offer sumptuous dining experiences for less than €100 per person.

In the mix

Having lagged behind London and New York for years in the cocktail stakes, Paris is now being flooded with a host of cool new mixology bars. The trend was started by the Experimental Cocktail Club a few years ago, and the new wave includes the likes of Sherry Butt, Candelaria and L'Entrée des Artistes, all run by ex-Experimental bartenders. Each has its speciality – Candelaria (see p107) is a taqueria specialising in tequila cocktails; Sherry Butt (20 rue Beautreillis, 4th, 09.83.38. 47.80, www.sherrybuttparis. com) favours a whisky base, as its name subtly suggests; and L'Entrée des Artistes (8 rue de Crussol, 11th, 09.50.99.67.11) is embracing the aged cocktails trend started by molecular pioneer Tony Conigliaro.

What they all have in common is that they are small, tucked away and packed with a new breed of imbiber who approaches cocktails as if they were fine wines. The icing on the cake is the fact that Conigliaro himself, star of the London cocktail scene, has now opened a bar in Paris, Le Coq (12 rue du Château d'Eau, 10th, 01.42.40.85.68, www.barlecoq.com).

There are some wonderful wine bars in the capital as well, and two of the best for a tipple are cult *cave à manger* Le Verre Volé (see p98) and Frenchie offshoot Frenchie Bar à Vins (see p77), a good pick when you can't get a table at the wildly oversubscribed original.

the moose
canadian sports bar & grill

sundays
american style brunch
11:30am - 3:30pm

monday-friday
happy hour
4:00pm - 8:00pm

open 11am - 2am daily

16 rue des quatre vents 75006
paris metro odeon   tel 01 46 33 77 00

www.mooseparis.com

Café culture

While Paris excels when it comes to café culture, from sitting out on the terrace of the Café de Flore (see p132) to popping into your local for a *grand crème* and croissant, until now that culture has not extended to the quality of the coffee itself. All that's changing fast, though, with a new generation of cafés opening up, many run by Australian and American baristas who take their espresso skills very seriously.

Caféothèque (52 rue de l'Hotel de Ville, 4th, 01.53.01.83.84, www. lacafeotheque.com) is where the coffee revolution in Paris kicked off a few years ago, created by the doyenne of 'coffeeology' Gloria Montenegro. At the moment, Caféothèque stocks and roasts coffee from 23 countries. Other fresh brews include the Coutume Café (see p127) and Télescope Café (see p78), essential spots for coffee purists.

The Marché d'Aligre has become the hottest weekend rendezvous for foodies, and there's no shortage of trendy hangouts for coffee-lovers. But to feel the authentic pulse of Aligre, and taste some great coffee, nothing compares to stopping off at tiny Café Aouba (30 rue d'Aligre, 12th, 01.43.43.22.24). Opened in 1938 by a Portuguese butcher, this is the ultimate market bar, packed with stallholders, shoppers and curious tourists. The friendly *patronne* flits between making coffee for everyone, checking her beans on the big coffee roaster, and selling everything from artisan honey to homemade jam. Don't expect any sort of designer deco here, just a red Formica counter with elbow room for half-a-dozen customers, and a shining Faema espresso machine. While the house brand is a mixture of beans from Colombia and Brazil, there are also brews from Cuba, Mexico, Kenya and Uganda.

If you're after something stronger, the tenth and 11th, especially around rue Oberkampf, continue to be the most happening areas for bars. Café Charbon (see p107), both a restaurant and a pre-club cocktail bar, and L'Alimentation Générale (see p106), whose excellent concerts give stage space to up-and-coming musicians, are places to be seen. Also worth a trip is the area of St-Blaise, in the 20th.

Breton and beyond

There are several decent crêperies around Montparnasse, where the Bretons originally settled, or you could try gourmet crêperie Breizh Café (109 rue Vieille-du-Temple, 3rd, 01.42.72.13.77, www.breizh cafe.com) in the Marais.

The streets around Belleville (20th) and the southern end of the 13th are crammed with decent Chinese, Vietnamese and Laotian restaurants; the second, around rue Ste-Anne, is flourishing with Japanese eateries, including the excellent Kaï (see p77). Rue des Rosiers in the Marais is a centre for Jewish cooking, and Italian, Indian, Moroccan and Lebanese cuisines can be found across the city. US food has been getting a look-in, too, with gourmet burger van Le Camion qui Fume (www.lecamionquifume.com) setting the pace, and burger joints Blend (see p76), Big Fernand (see p88) and La Maison Mère (see p91) fuelling the trend.

In the know

Many venues close for their annual break during August. All bills include service charge, but a tip of a few euros (for the whole table) is polite unless you're unhappy with the service. Finally, avoid anywhere displaying a sign saying '*menu touristique*' or 'We speak English'.

Diptyque

WHAT'S BEST
Shopping

Paris shopping has never been in better shape. Where else in the world can you find so many independent boutiques and specialist shops, right in the middle of some of the most picturesque areas of the city? Whether you're tasting cheeses at Alléosse (see p65), sniffing candles at Diptyque (see p149) or selecting a pair of Tropézienne sandals for summer at K Jacques (see p113), shopping in the French capital is a sensual pleasure based around quality, not quantity. Where we have window-shopping, they have window-licking (*lèche-vitrine*).

And now, even the chain stores are looking pretty fly with a slew of mainstream fashion brands – Banana Republic, Levi's, Hugo Boss, Abercrombie & Fitch (see p65) and even Marks & Spencer – opening new flagship stores on the Champs-Elysées, luring Parisians back to their long-neglected heartland of consumer chic.

Different areas of the city have different specialities. There are clusters of antiques shops in the seventh arrondissement, and second-hand and rare book outlets in the fifth; crystal and porcelain manufacturers still dot rue de Paradis in the tenth; furniture craftsmen as well as children's clothes shops inhabit rue du Fbg-St-Antoine; bikes and cameras are clustered on boulevard Beaumarchais; and the world's top jewellers can be found on place Vendôme. The historic covered passages in the second and ninth are also fun places in which to shop, with chic stores mixed in with philatelists and booksellers.

Colette

Family-run food shops have thankfully not been eroded by supermarket culture, and tend to cluster in 'market streets' such as rue des Martyrs and rue Mouffetard, as well as around the many covered and open-air food markets. Here, everything from a vintage bottle of armagnac to a single praline chocolate is lovingly presented, served and wrapped. Informed discussion is still very much part of the purchasing process, and beautiful, old-style shops, which have remained unchanged for decades, add to the pleasure.

Green, organic and ethical have also become sexy concepts to the French: not-for-profit concept store Merci (see p113) offers guilt-free clothes shopping, and hipster optician Jimmy Fairly (see p112) has a 'buy one, give one' policy – for every pair of glasses sold, it donates a new pair to someone in need.

metropolitan, glamorous but down-with-the-kids Colette (see p81); bobo I-probably-care-more-about-my-home-than-my-wardrobe Merci; and sophisticated, avant-garde L'Eclaireur (see p112). And then the smaller ones such as Loulou Addict (25 rue Keller, 11th, 01.49.29.00.61, www.loulouaddict.com). But what they all have in common is a product range that is both entertainingly diverse and seductively scarce.

At Colette, you can find Zippo lighters a few feet away from Smythson diaries, a few feet away from Ladurée macaroons, all one flight of stairs away from Alexander Wang and Valentino. At Merci, perfume and porcelain sit happily alongside each other on the main floor. And in Loulou Addict, a mini 2CV in lacquered wood by Vilac nestles next to a 1970s maroon purse with orange flowers by Blafre.

Concept kings

The concept shop trend is a central feature of the scene, crossing the boundaries between clothes, music and product design. The capital's concept kings have very different personalities. There's cosmopolitan,

Boutique chic

The stretch of rue St-Honoré and rue du Fbg-St-Honoré from the Hôtel Costes to the Hôtel Bristol is wall-to-wall fashion boutiques, with Givenchy and Lanvin (see p82) two major highlights.

Nearby rue Boissy d'Anglas has a branch of L'Eclaireur with its Fornasetti café (10 rue Boissy d'Anglas, 8th, 01.53.43.03.70, www.leclaireur.com).

Avenue Montaigne's headliners include Fendi at no.22, the Roberto Cavalli flagship at no.53 and, next door at no.52, Ralph Lauren's three-floor womenswear store. The small streets criss-crossing the Golden Triangle also have a few surprises.

Palais-Royal & around

If you're visiting Colette, don't miss a detour to the Marché St-Honoré. This former food market, rebuilt in glass by Ricardo Bofill, combines bistros and boutiques, with Marc by Marc Jacobs (see p83) a big attraction.

Easily reached on foot from here, the Palais-Royal gets better and better. On the eastern side, galerie du Valois has Stella McCartney (see p85), cult Swedish brand Acne Jeans at no.124, and the covetable and racy gloves of Maison Fabre at no.10. Opposite, with the idyllic gardens in between, is galerie de Montpensier, containing Marc Jacobs (see p83) and vintage wear from Didier Ludot (see p81), as well as Martin Margiela in the road behind (see p83). Also in the area is Kitsuné (52 rue de Richelieu, 1st, 01.42.60.34.28, www.kitsune.fr), the record label now selling its own-brand clothing.

Further east, the Etienne-Marcel area is the centre for club and streetwear, with boutiques and chains such as All Saints (49 rue Etienne-Marcel, 1st, 01.44.88.91.30) and Kiliwatch (see p82).

Marais mode

From second-hand T-shirt bargain bins to vintage designer pieces for hundreds of euros, the Marais is

SHORTLIST

Best recent openings
- Causses (see p92)
- Jimmy Fairly (see p112)
- Storie (see p157)

Best concept stores
- Colette (see p81)
- L'Eclaireur (see p112)
- LE66 (see p67)
- Merci (see p113)

Best hand-picked fashion
- L'Eclaireur (see p112)
- Kokon To Zai (see p82)

Best for accessories
- Colette (see p81)
- Marc by Marc Jacobs (see p83)

Best for posh frocks
- Lanvin (see p82)
- Yves Saint Laurent (see p140)

Best souvenirs
- Arty Dandy (see p137)
- Diptyque (see p149)

Best food and wine
- Alléosse (see p65)
- Gâteaux Thoumieux (see p128)
- Lavinia (see p83)
- Du Pain et des Idées (see p99)
- Pierre Hermé (see p140)
- Première Pression Provence (see p113)

Literary life
- La Hune (see p138)
- I Love My Blender (see p112)
- Shakespeare & Co (see p149)

The classics
- Le Bon Marché (see p18)
- Galeries Lafayette (see p82)
- Printemps (see p83)

the place to head for everything pre-loved. The cavernous Kilo Shop (69-71 rue de la Verrerie, 4th, 09.67.13.79.54, www.kilo-shop.fr) sells bags, shoes, furs, knits and more by weight; Vintage Bar (16 rue de la Verrerie, 4th, 01.42.74.56.95), complete with decommissioned beer taps, stocks scarlet-soled Louboutins; Plus Que Parfait (23 rue des Blancs Manteaux, 4th, 01.42.71.09.05) sells on your unwanted threads for a commission.

Going Gauche

St-Germain tends to be more conservative, but is increasingly offering a mirror image of the Right Bank, with brands insisting on a presence on both sides of the Seine. These include Vanessa Bruno (see p140), plus a stunning Hermès store (see p138) set in an old swimming pool. Shoe heaven is found along rue de Grenelle with all the top brands. Other highlights include bobo bags in colourful fabrics and denim from the former prêt-à-porter designer Jérôme Dreyfuss (1 rue Jacob, 6th, www.jerome-dreyfuss.com); and multi-brand shop Kyrie Eleison (15 carrefour de l'Odéon, 6th, 01.46.34.26.91) with lush creations by Orla Kiely, Eros-Erotokritos and La Fée Parisienne.

On the luxury scene, opium-coloured walls and lacquered ceilings provide a showcase for Stephane Pilati's creations at Yves Saint Laurent (see p140), while at Sonia Rykiel's St-Germain flagship (see p140) black mosaics, smoked glass and multiple mirrors evoke a '70s nightclub. And if you're in the market for jewellery, head to Marie-Hélène de Taillac's store (see p138).

Further south, new Montparnasse shop Storie (see p157) is drawing curious, creatively bent shoppers to the area, offering an eclectic mix of homewares from around the world.

Edible delights

The layout of Fauchon (24-26 pl de la Madeleine, 8th, 01.70.39.38.00, www.fauchon.com), with different areas (pâtisserie, bakery, fruit and vegetables, etc) and chefs on hand at each to offer advice and recipes, provides an excuse to indulge at this luxury store. Food markets are found in all arrondissements – two of the most popular are the historic Marché d'Aligre in the 12th, and the Marché des Enfants Rouges in the 3rd, which focuses on organic produce. Near the Marché d'Aligre, pop into Première Pression Provence (see p113), an olive oil paradise. Causses (see p92), SoPi's (South Pigalle) new *alimentation générale extraordinaire*, is well worth a visit.

Practicalities

Shops generally open from 10am to 7pm Monday to Saturday. Sunday opening is found in the Marais, on the Champs-Elysées, at Bercy Village and the Carrousel du Louvre.

Causses

Wanderlust

WHAT'S BEST
Nightlife

Serious party people may have migrated long ago to more happening cities such as London, New York and Berlin, but the French capital is fighting back with a string of leftfield Left Bank venues pumping out everything from gypsy jazz to electro-tropical candomblé to the Seine-side party crowds.

Go early if you want to avoid the queues, but bear in mind that Parisians tend to go out clubbing late and most venues will be pretty empty if you turn up before midnight. Also look out for flyers, join the MySpace and Facebook groups of your favourite venues, and most importantly, make friends with people in the places you go to: it's the best way to hear about cool underground parties coming up. Many of these new nightlife stars double up as gig venues, too, giving much-needed stage space to the city's up-and-coming bands.

Nightclubs

The 13th is Paris's new nightlife central. The long-delayed Cité de la Mode et du Design on the quai d'Austerlitz has opened its doors, and its on-site clubs are setting tongues wagging. Wanderlust and Nüba have joined the likes of Petit Bain and Batofar (for all, see p152) along the banks of the Seine, making the 13th arrondissement the undisputed clubbing capital. Spread across a vast space, Wanderlust includes a wooden terrace perfect for sunset drinks, an open-air cinema, art installations and a restaurant run by TV chef Benjamin Darnaud with dishes such as *steak-frites* and poached cod with lemongrass.

Running the venue is the ultra-hip Savoir Faire team (the brains behind Le Social Club and Silencio), so it should come as no surprise that the dress code is designer, the bouncers are unforgiving and the queues are long (come very early or late). You'll also find ping pong tables, weekend yoga lessons and chill-out areas dotted with chaises longues. Music is minimal techno and house on a top-notch sound system, getting the crowd going to the point where, if you're outside, you can watch a sea of well-dressed backsides gyrating together in the club's street-level bay windows.

The big name on Paris's nightlife scene in the past few years has been André Sareiva. Having gone from underground street artist to head of a multinational brand, he has redefined the meaning of cool in under a decade. Much hype surrounded L'Appartement, an ephemeral project launched by Sareiva and Lionel Bensemoun, aka La Clique. Hidden away in a Left Bank *hôtel particulier*, invite-only L'Appartement allowed the chosen few to party in a 3,000 sq ft flat, with everything arranged to make them feel at home: you could pour your own drink, tuck into a gourmet buffet and rifle through the collection of old vinyl. The only rule was to keep the address a secret and let the rumour spread.

La Clique's latest project, Nüba, is again grabbing the hip headlines with its rooftop clubbing and relaxed vibe. The terrace offers a panoramic view over the surrounding quays, a wooden DJ booth playing chillout world music, deckchairs, big communal tables and table football. Inside, coloured lights reveal rooms done out in copper and stone. There are gigs in the evenings, punctuated by clubby electro sets and inventive dance shows from the House of Drama collective.

SHORTLIST

Best new/revamped
- Nüba (see p152)
- Wanderlust (see p152)

Best bands
- Le Bataclan (see p115)
- L'International (see p115)
- Point Ephémère (see p99)

Best sound systems
- Panic Room (see p115)
- Rex (see p86)

All night long
- Batofar (see p152)
- Mix Club (see p157)

Best for chanson
- Les Trois Baudets (see p94)

Perfect for posing
- Le Baron (see p67)
- Le Montana (see p140)
- Silencio (see p86)

Best for star DJs
- Rex (see p86)

Seine-side partying
- Petit Bain (see p152)
- Wanderlust (see p152)

Best gay club
- Queen (see p69)

Best for jazz
- Caveau de la Huchette (see p149)
- Au Duc des Lombards (see p85)
- New Morning (see p99)

Killer cocktails
- Panic Room (see p115)

Life is a cabaret
- Le Lido (see p69)
- Moulin Rouge (see p94)

If it's more big-room clubbing you're after, Queen (see p69) is a gay-friendly club known for its wild disco nights, while Rex (see p86) offers up mainstream and experimental electro on one of the best sound systems in Europe.

If you prefer your clubbing cosy, plenty of bars around Bastille, Oberkampf and Grands Boulevards are willing to oblige. Panic Room (see p115) is one of the hippest, with a stream of French electro nights. Traditionalists can choose their poison too; a host of school disco-type nights where the DJ is no superstar take place at the twice-monthly Bal at Elysée Montmartre (72 bd de Rochechouart, 18th, 01.44.92.45.36), and salsa and world music get a good hammering at Le Divan du Monde (see p94).

Because Paris clubs don't really get going until 2am, people usually hit a DJ bar before, and diehards finish their evening at an 'after' on Sunday morning. Free passes can be found on various flyers (see www.flyersweb.com). Other good sites are www.radiofg.com and www.lemonsound.com. Also look out for one-off events in venues like Rex and Point Ephémère (see p99).

The last métro leaves at around 12.45am (1.45am on Friday and Saturday), and the first gets rolling at 5.45am; in between you'll have to use a night bus, Vélib or taxi.

Rock, roots & jazz

Paris's music scene is bubbling with talent, and the emergence of some great new bands speaks volumes about the creativity of today's up-and-coming artists. The capital is brimming with authentic gig venues, and concert halls such as L'International (see p115) give precious stage space to those on the way up the ladder.

Chanson française is still going strong, helped by the revival of Les Trois Baudets (see p94), a government-subsidised *chanson* hall in the heart of Pigalle. Jazz is having a mini revival too: after the disappearance of old flames like Le Slow Club, Le Bilboquet and Les 7 Lézards, a handful of new joints have opened up, while flagship clubs Au Duc des Lombards (see p85), New Morning (see p99) and Le Sunset/Le Sunside (60 rue des Lombards, 1st, 01.40.26.46.60) continue to book top-notch acts.

Batofar p26

Moulin Rouge

Paris is also a European leader for world music, particularly African and Arab acts. And every 21 June, the city turns into one giant music venue for the Fête de la Musique.

The weekly magazine *Les Inrockuptibles* is a decent resource. Alternatively, try bi-monthly gig bible *Lylo*, free in bars and branches of Fnac. The Fnac (www.fnac.com) ticket office also displays details of up-and-coming concerts.

Prices for gigs vary according to a group or artist's pulling power, but several excellent venues, like La Bellevilloise (19-21 rue Boyer, 20th, 01.46.36.07.07), host regular free nights – ideal if you're feeling adventurous and/or are on a budget. For concerts, it's best to turn up at the time stated on the ticket: noise curfews mean that times are adhered to pretty closely.

Cabaret

The promise of busty babes slinking across the stage in nothing but frilly knickers has turned glamour cabarets into some of the hottest spots around. The Moulin Rouge (see p94) popularised the skirt-raising concept during the 19th century, and since then venues such as Le Lido (see p69) have institutionalised garter-pinging.

These days, a cabaret is an all-evening, smart-dress affair, with a pre-show meal and champers. The Moulin Rouge is the most traditional revue and the only place with cancan. Toulouse-Lautrec posters, glittery lamp-posts and fake trees lend tacky charm, while 60 Doriss dancers cover the stage with faultless synchronisation.

For sheer space go to Le Lido. With 1,000 seats, this classy venue is the largest cabaret: high-tech touches optimise visibility. The slightly tame show, with 60 Bluebell Girls, has boob-shaking and wacky costumes. For a more risqué performance, try Crazy Horse (12 av George V, 8th, 01.47.23.32.32, www.lecrazyhorseparis.com).

Artist's impression of the new Philharmonie

WHAT'S BEST
Arts & Leisure

A number of major cultural developments and innovations, and several new sites, have given a significant lift to Paris's cultural scene in the last few years. The revamped Théâtre de la Gaîté Lyrique (see p115) reopened in 2011 after a ten-year renovation as the capital's first digital cultural centre, and the completion of the extension of the Palais de Tokyo (see p61) in early 2012 tripled its size and created the largest contemporary art centre in Europe.

Construction has also finished on the Cité du Cinéma (www. citeducinema.org) in the northern suburb of St-Denis, nicknamed Hollywood-sur-Seine. Backed by maverick French film director Luc Besson, the enormous complex houses eight studios and promises to give the national film industry a massive boost – not that it really needs much of a boost after the raging success of *The Artist* and *Intouchables*. Between them, they garnered a raft of awards and hugely impressive box office takings.

Another major building project is the much-vaunted Philharmonie, which is rising near the Cité de la Musique. Architect Jean Nouvel's 2,400-seat concert hall is now due to open in 2015 and will give the city a major venue for the classical repertoire, as well as hosting jazz and world music.

What's especially good about the arts here is the accessibility: there are any number of festivals and discount promotions on offer throughout the year, many organised by the city council, that bring what the Brits often consider to be 'elitist' art forms within reach of the public.

Film

Cinema-going is a serious pastime in Paris. In any given week there's a choice of some 350 movies – not including the numerous festivals (see pp34-40), many of which offer free or discounted entry. The city houses some 90 cinemas and around 400 screens, almost a quarter of which show nothing but arthouse. Even the multiplexes regularly screen documentaries and films from Eastern Europe, Asia and South America. This vibrant scene is constantly evolving, with new multi-screen complexes under construction and classic picture houses constantly under renovation.

Visiting one of the city's many picture palaces is an experience in itself – from the glorious faux-oriental Pagode (see p128) to the innovative surroundings of the Forum des Images (see p86). And 2013 saw the reopening of the revamped Louxor (see p94) in all its glorious Egyptian-inspired art deco glory.

Opera & classical

The Opéra National de Paris (see p86) continues to thrive under director Nicolas Joel, who came to the capital after 18 years with the Toulouse Opera. With a reputation for traditional values, Joel favours a classical repertoire, while music director Philippe Jordan offers some youthful energy. Major recent productions include *Madama Butterfly* and *La Traviata*. The Théâtre National de l'Opéra Comique (see p86), meanwhile, continues to capitalise on new financial security following its promotion to National Theatre status and will no doubt be celebrating its 300-year anniversary in style in 2015.

Elsewhere, at the Châtelet (see p86) director Jean-Luc Choplin's

SHORTLIST

Wonderful settings
- Louxor (see p94)
- Palais Garnier (see p86)
- Théâtre des Champs-Elysées (see p69)
- Théâtre Marigny (see p69)

Most innovative
- International opera at Festival d'Automne (see p34)

Most romantic
- Candlelit recitals for the Festival Chopin (see p38)
- Lovers' seats at MK2 Bilbliothèque (see p99)

Best bargains
- €3.50 film tickets, Printemps du Cinéma (see p37)
- Free concerts at Paris Jazz Festival (see p39)

Best alfresco
- Cinéma en Plein Air (see p40)
- Festival Classique au Vert (see p40)
- Fête de la Musique (see p38)

Best film venues
- Forum des Images (see p86)
- Louxor (see p94)
- La Pagode (see p128)

Best opera venues
- Palais Garnier (see p86)
- Théâtre National de l'Opéra Comique (see p86)

Original creations
- Gaîté Lyrique (see p115)
- Théâtre Paris Villette (see p161)

Culture after dark
- Nuit Blanche (see p35)
- Nuit des Musées (see p37)
- Palais de Tokyo (see p61)

DON'T MISS

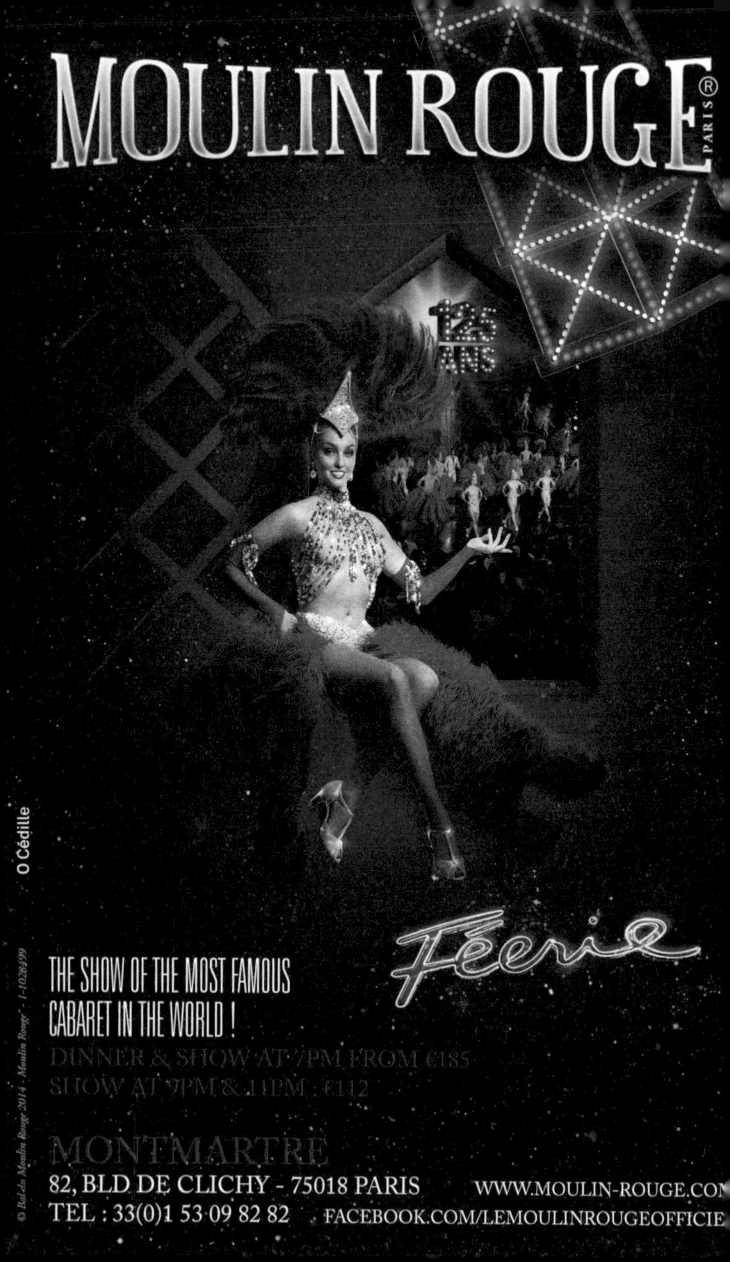

MOULIN ROUGE®
PARIS
125 ANS
Féerie
THE SHOW OF THE MOST FAMOUS
CABARET IN THE WORLD !
DINNER & SHOW AT 7PM FROM €185
SHOW AT 9PM & 11PM : €112
MONTMARTRE
82, BLD DE CLICHY - 75018 PARIS
TEL : 33(0)1 53 09 82 82
WWW.MOULIN-ROUGE.COM
FACEBOOK.COM/LEMOULINROUGEOFFICIE
© Bal du Moulin Rouge 2014 - Moulin Rouge® - 1-1028499
O Cédille

populist programming has included a string of retro musicals recently, including big-hitters *West Side Story* and *Carousel*.

The main musical provider in summer is the Paris Quartier d'Eté festival (01.44.94.98.00, www.quartierdete.com), with concerts in gardens across the city. The Festival de Saint-Denis (01.48.13.06.07, www.festival-saint-denis.com) also offers top names in a spectacular setting.

Many venues offer cut-rate tickets to students (under 26) an hour before curtain-up. During the Fête de la Musique (21 June) all events are free, and freebies crop up at the Maison de Radio France and the Conservatoire de Paris.

Dance

Paris is home to a thriving dance scene, with some sumptuous ballet productions at the Palais Garnier and international companies at Châtelet. Recent highlights at the Palais Garnier have included Gluck's *Orphée et Eurydice* and John Cranko's adaptation of *Onéguine*.

The Centre National de la Danse (1 rue Victor-Hugo, 93507 Pantin, 01.41.83.27.27, www.cnd.fr) is an impressive headquarters for France's 600-plus regional dance companies. Every season sees some kind of contemporary dance festival in or near Paris; the Festival d'Automne (see p34) has been a star fixture on the circuit for more than 40 years.

Theatre

French-speaking theatre buffs can choose from some 450 productions every week: from offbeat shows in small, independent venues to high-brow classics in grandiose auditoriums like the Comédie Française (2 rue Richelieu, 1st, 08.25.10.16.80, www.comedie-

francaise.fr), whose staple shows feature the giants of French drama. A new shining star on the theatre scene is the freshly reopened Théâtre Paris Villette (see p161) in the 19th, one of the city's most avant-garde stages.

Fortunately for Anglophones, the Paris theatre scene is becoming ever more international, with translations of English and American plays firmly in vogue. The restored and re-baptised Odéon Théâtre de l'Europe (pl de l'Odéon, 6th, 01.44.85.44.00, www.theatre-odeon.fr) offers plays in a number of languages, including at least one per season in English. Anglophone performances are occasionally programmed at the Théâtre des Bouffes du Nord (37bis bd de la Chapelle, 10th, 01.46.07.34.50, www.bouffesdunord.com), while the cutting-edge MC93 Bobigny (1 bd Lénine, 93000 Bobigny, 01.41.60.72.72, www.mc93.com) regularly hosts international companies performing in their mother tongue.

Meanwhile, the Improfessionals (www.improfessionals.com) stage regular improvised performances in English, and Shakespeare in English is performed every summer at the Bois de Boulogne's Théâtre de Verdure du Jardin Shakespeare by London's Tower Theatre Company (www.towertheatre.org.uk).

What's on

For listings, the best sources are the weekly magazines *L'Officiel des Spectacles* and *Pariscope*. When it comes to films, be sure to take note of the two letters printed near the title: VO (*version originale*) means a screening in the original language with French subtitles; VF (*version française*) means that it's been dubbed into French. Cinema seats can be reserved at www.allocine.fr.

WHAT'S ON
Calendar

Le Tour de France p39

This is our pick of the best annual events in Paris. On public holidays, or *jours feriés*, banks, many museums, most businesses and a number of restaurants close. New Year's Day, May Day, Bastille Day and Christmas Day are the most piously observed holidays.

Autumn

Early Sept **Jazz à la Villette**
Cité de la Musique & various venues
www.jazzalavillette.com
The first fortnight in September brings one of Paris's best jazz festivals. There's also a series of Jazz for Kids concerts alongside the main festival.

Early Sept-mid Oct **Festival Paris Ile-de-France**
Various venues
www.festival-ile-de-france.com
Each year, the Paris Ile-de-France festival offers a brilliantly varied programme of music from classical to contemporary, traditional and folk to cutting-edge electronic, at venues ranging from central Paris to Vincennes via Fontainebleau.

Mid Sept **We Love Green Festival**
Parc de Bagatelle,
Bois de Boulogne, 16th
www.welovegreen.fr
This three-day eco festival is held in the verdant surroundings of the Parc de Bagatelle. It's a bucolic celebration of music and nature, and the audience is positively expected to dance barefoot in the grass.

Mid Sept **Techno Parade**
Various venues
www.technoparade.fr
The Saturday parade (which finishes up at Bastille) is followed by several late, late club nights around the capital.

Mid Sept **Journées du Patrimoine**
All over France
www.journeesdupatrimoine.culture.fr
Embassies, ministries, scientific establishments and corporate headquarters open their doors to the public.

Mid Sept-mid Jan **Festival d'Automne**
Various venues
www.festival-automne.com

This major annual arts festival focuses on bringing challenging contemporary theatre, dance and modern opera to Paris. Apart from its exceptional length, the Festival d'Automne also has enormous means at its disposal and an exceptionally high quality line-up.

Late Sept **Fête de la Gastronomie**
Various venues
www.fete-gastronomie.fr
This recently launched nationwide festival is aimed at celebrating the wonders of French cuisine. The inaugural theme was 'terroir', with more than 3,000 events across the country.

Early Oct **Mondial de l'Automobile**
Paris-Expo, pl de la Porte
de Versailles
www.mondial-automobile.com
The biennial Paris Motor Show features cutting-edge design from all over the world. The next shows are due to pull into Paris-Expo in 2014 and 2016.

Early Oct **Nuit Blanche**
Various venues
http://nuitblanche.paris.fr
Nuit Blanche is a free dusk-to-dawn carnival of arts and culture inspired by St Petersburg's 'White Nights'.

Early Oct **Prix de l'Arc de Triomphe**
Hippodrome de Longchamp,
Bois de Boulogne, 16th
www.prixarcdetriomphe.com
France's richest flat race meeting attracts the elite of horse racing for a weekend of pomp and ceremony. The big race gallops off on Sunday afternoon.

Early Oct **Fête des Vendanges
de Montmartre**
Rue des Saules, 18th
*www.fetedesvendanges
demontmartre.com*
Although the vines produce an average of just 1,000 bottles a year, the modest harvest is the pretext for a long weekend of Bacchanalian street parties.

Mid Oct **FIAC (Foire Internationale
d'Art Contemporain)**
Various venues
www.fiacparis.com
International contemporary art fair featuring more than 180 galleries, along with a series of outdoor installations in the Jardin des Tuileries.

Early Nov **Festival des
Inrockuptibles**
Various venues
www.lesinrocks.com

Nuit Blanche

Famous indie cultural journal *Les InRockuptibles* has changed a lot during its 25-year history, but this annual rock festival has always kept its spirit alive. Expect folk, soul and electronica too.

11 Nov **Armistice Day**
Arc de Triomphe, 8th
To commemorate French combatants who served in the World Wars, the President lays wreaths at the Tomb of the Unknown Soldier underneath the Arc de Triomphe. The *bleuet* (a cornflower) is worn.

Late Nov-late Dec **Africolor**
Various suburbs
www.africolor.com
This music and dance festival has been running for more than 20 years, featuring artists from all across Africa.

Late Nov **Fête du Beaujolais Nouveau**
Various venues
www.beaujolaisgourmand.com
The third Thursday in November sees cafés and wine bars buzzing as the young red *vin de primeur* Beaujolais nouveau is released on to the market. Just six to eight weeks old, the wine is intended for immediate consumption.

Winter

24-25 Dec **Noël (Christmas)**
Christmas is very much a family affair in France, with a dinner on Christmas Eve (*le Réveillon*), normally after mass.

31 Dec-1 Jan **New Year's Eve/New Year's Day**
Jubilant crowds swarm along the Champs-Elysées. Nightclubs and restaurants hold expensive New Year's Eve soirées, and on New Year's Day the Grande Parade de Paris brings floats, bands and dancers.

6 Jan **Fête des Rois (Epiphany)**
Pâtisseries sell *galettes des rois*, cakes with a frangipane filling in which a *fève*, or tiny charm, is hidden.

Jan **Mass for Louis XVI**
Chapelle Expiatoire,
29 rue Pasquier, 8th
On the Sunday closest to 21 January – the anniversary of the beheading of Louis XVI in 1793 – right-wing crackpots mourn the end of the monarchy.

Jan/Feb **Nouvel An Chinois**
Around av d'Ivry &
av de Choisy, 13th

Noël (Christmas)

Lion and dragon dances, and lively martial arts demonstrations to celebrate the Chinese New Year.

Early Feb **Paris Face Cachée**
Various venues
www.parisfacecachee.fr
Quirky and educational, Paris Face Cachée is in the same vein as autumn's Nuit Blanche. A huge variety of venues and activities lift the lid on places you might never have known existed, and give participants a chance to experience Paris at work behind the scenes.

Feb-Mar **Six Nations**
Stade de France, 93210 St-Denis
www.rbs6nations.com
Paris hosts two huge rugby weekends during the spring. Log on to the website at least three months in advance to be in with any chance of getting tickets.

Spring

Mar **Le Printemps des Poètes**
Various venues
www.printempsdespoetes.com
This long-running national poetry festival featured 'Au Coeur des Arts' as its theme in 2014.

Mid Mar **Printemps du Cinéma**
Various venues
www.printempsducinema.com
Film tickets at a variety of cinemas all across the city are cut to a bargain €3.50 for this popular three-day bonanza.

Early Apr **Marathon de Paris**
Av des Champs-Elysées, 8th, to av Foch, 16th
www.parismarathon.com
One of the world's most picturesque marathons, with up to 40,000 runners heading off from the Champs-Elysées. If you fancy joining them, registration begins in the previous September.

Apr **Banlieues Bleues**
Various venues in Seine-St-Denis
www.banlieuesbleues.org

Festival of French and international jazz, blues, R&B, soul, funk, flamenco and world music.

Good Friday **Le Chemin de la Croix**
Square Willette, 18th
A crowd of pilgrims follows the Archbishop of Paris from the bottom of Montmartre up to Sacré-Coeur as he performs the Stations of the Cross.

Apr-May **Foire du Trône**
Pelouse de Reuilly, 12th
www.foiredutrone.com
France's biggest funfair runs for nearly two months. At the weekends the Mairie runs a free bus from Bercy and Nation.

1 May **Fête du Travail**
Various venues
May Day is strictly observed. Key sights (the Eiffel Tower aside) close, and unions march in eastern Paris via Bastille. Sweet-smelling posies of lily of the valley (*muguet*) are sold on every street corner.

Mid May **Le Printemps des Rues**
Various venues
www.leprintemps-desrues.com
This two-day street-theatre festival takes place along the Canal St-Martin and has a distinctly experimental vibe.

Mid May **La Nuit des Musées**
All over France
www.nuitdesmusees.culture.fr
During this one-night culture fest, museums open their doors late for special events and entertainment, including concerts, dance, lectures, unique access and special exhibitions.

Mid May-early June **Festival Jazz à Saint-Germain-des-Prés**
Various venues
www.festivaljazzsaintgermainparis.com
This two-week festival of jazz and blues celebrated its 13th anniversary in 2013 with everything from piano cruises on the Seine to gigs in the Eglise St-Germain-des-Prés.

Marche des Fiertés

End May **Art Saint-Germain-des-Prés**
Various venues
www.artsaintgermaindespres.com
Nicknamed the 'block party', more than 50 galleries get together to showcase their top artists.

Late May-early June
French Tennis Open
Stade Roland-Garros,
2 av Gordon-Bennett, 16th
www.frenchopen.org
Paris plays host to the most prestigious clay court competition in the world.

Summer

June **Festival de St-Denis**
Various venues in St-Denis
www.festival-saint-denis.com
The Gothic St-Denis basilica and other historic buildings in the neighbourhood host four weeks of top-quality classical concerts.

Early June **Fête du Vélo**
Across Paris
www.feteduvelo.fr
Thousands of cyclists meet up at various points in the suburbs and pedal to Paris en masse. During the two-day festival visitors can also try in-line skating, as well as bicycles specially designed for children and people of reduced mobility.

Mid June **Prix de Diane**
Hippodrome de Chantilly, 16 av du Général-Leclerc, 90209 Chantilly
www.prix-de-diane.com
The French Derby draws the cream of high society to Chantilly, sporting silly hats and keen to have a flutter.

21 June **Fête de la Musique**
All over France
www.fetedelamusique.culture.fr
Free gigs, encompassing all genres, take place across the country and around the world as part of this festival on the summer solstice.

End June **Marche des Fiertés (Gay Pride)**
Various venues
www.centrelgbtparis.org
Outrageous floats and flamboyant costumes parade towards Bastille; then there's an official fête and various club and nightlife events.

Mid June-mid July
Festival Chopin à Paris
Bois de Boulogne, 16th
www.frederic-chopin.com

Organised by the Chopin Society, these candlelit evening recitals of the composer's works are performed in the idyllic Parc de la Bagatelle.

June-July **Paris Jazz Festival**
Bois de Vincennes, 12th
www.parisjazzfestival.fr
Two months of free jazz weekends take place in the Parc Floral.

End June **Solidays**
Longchamp Hippodrome
www.solidays.org
A three-day music festival, for the benefit of AIDS charities. The 2014 event welcomed more than 170,000 festival-goers and saw performances from the likes of Franz Ferdinand.

Early July **Paris Cinéma**
Various venues
www.pariscinema.org
Premieres, tributes and restored films make up the programme at the city's excellent summer filmgoing initiative.

14 July **Le Quatorze Juillet (Bastille Day)**
All over France
France's national holiday commemorates the storming of the Bastille in 1789. The evening before the holiday, Parisians dance at place de la Bastille. At 10am on the 14th, large crowds line up along the Champs-Elysées as the President reviews a full military parade. By night, the Champ de Mars fills for the fireworks display.

July **Le Tour de France**
Av des Champs-Elysées, 8th
www.letour.fr
The ultimate spectacle in cycling is reserved for the end of July, when the world's biggest bike race arrives in Paris. After three weeks of racing, the battle for the leader's famed yellow jersey is all but over, and the final stage usually climaxes in a mass sprint with everyone finishing together. It's an incredible spectacle as the riders propel themselves at speeds of up to 65 km/h (40mph) around nine laps of a four-mile finishing circuit that takes in the Champs-Elysées and Tuileries area.

July **Etés de la Danse**
Théâtre du Châtelet, 1st
www.lesetesdeladanse.com
Every year, the sumptuous Théâtre du Châtelet brings a major dance company from overseas to the capital. Most theatres in Paris take a break over the summer, so it's one of July's few opportunities to see classical ballet.

Etés de la Danse

Mid July–mid Aug
Paris, Quartier d'Eté
Various venues
www.quartierdete.com
Global in outlook, ambitious in scope, citywide and often free, the Quartier d'Eté festival offers a fantastic summer programme of dance, theatre, concerts and circus. Previous years have seen open-air films, gypsy music, ballet by Merce Cunningham, and an opera by Youssou N'Dour.

Mid July–mid Aug **Paris-Plages**
Various venues
www.paris.fr
Back in 2002, Bertrand Delanoë began the tradition of lining the banks of the Seine with sand, deckchairs, food stalls and volleyball nets, creating a series of city beaches for those stuck in town during the long, hot months. Since 2007, the project has extended along the length of the canal in Bassin de la Villette, making an idyllic landscape of boules, picnicking, sunbathing and watersports.

Mid July–end Aug
Le Cinéma en Plein Air
Parc de la Villette, 19th
www.villette.com

Outdoor moviegoing at its finest, with films screened for free at sundown in Parc de la Villette, the architectural, music and art hub that's a big part of the recent buzz around north-east Paris.

Aug-Sept **Festival Classique au Vert**
Bois de Vincennes, 12th
www.classiqueauvert.fr
Free classical music recitals in a park setting every weekend during August and September.

15 Aug **Fête de l'Assomption**
Cathédrale Notre-Dame de Paris, pl du Parvis Notre-Dame, 4th
www.cathedraledeparis.com
This is a national holiday. Notre-Dame becomes a place of religious pilgrimage for Assumption Day.

End Aug **Rock en Seine**
Domaine National de St-Cloud
www.rockenseine.com
The city's premier rock festival, Rock en Seine has been held in the Domaine National de Saint-Cloud every last weekend in August since 2003. For the best experience, buy a three-day pass and camp in the historic park grounds.

Paris-Plages

Itineraries

Revolutionary Road   42

Meet the Moderns   47

Vintage on a Vespa   50

Place de la Concorde

Revolutionary Road

If you can keep your head while those around you are losing theirs, get on the blocks for our promenade through the goriest spots of regicidal fever. You'll need some stout shoes and a fervent imagination.

START: On **place de la Concorde** (see p74). The key date here is 21 January 1793. Since 8am the gates of Paris have been locked, the shutters barred. A crowd of 20,000 has assembled in place Louis XV, renamed place de la Révolution. At 10am there is a drum roll, Louis XVI is strapped to a plank and pushed towards the guillotine. The device slices through his neck, the crowd roars and clamours to soak their hankies in the monarch's blood. But to see how the nation reached this bloodthirsty state, we have to step back in time.

Walk through the gates from Concorde into the **Jardin des Tuileries** (see p71). The palace that used to stand on this spot was the scene of repeated revolutionary fracas. On 13 July 1789, the eve of Bastille Day, a crowd ransacked the royal *garde-meubles* for weapons. This was only a taster of what was to come, though. On the night of King Louis' arrest in 1792, 600 of his Swiss Guards were murdered, their genitals hacked off and fed to dogs.

Turn right on to rue de Rivoli and walk to the **Palais-Royal** (see p74). The Duc d'Orléans' pleasure palace was a revolutionary hotbed as nobles and plebs mingled among the coffee shops and sideshows.

Walk through the arch in the Louvre's north wing to place du Carrousel, where the guillotine briefly stood. Cross Pont des Arts and head down rue Bonaparte. On your left you'll see the **Ecole des Beaux-Arts** (see p130), where

Palais-Royal

Alexandre Lenoir tried to save France's heritage from the mob – he threw himself on the grave of Richelieu and took a stab in the back for his pains.

Rue de l'Abbaye was the site of one of the revolution's worst atrocities, in September 1792, when 115 priests were trapped in the garden and butchered. The red brick Abbot's Palace is now the Institut Catholique. Take rue Garancière past St-Sulpice to the **Palais du Luxembourg** (see p130). The palace was commandeered as a prison and housed, among others, activists Danton and Thomas Paine. Take rue Rotrou through place de l'Odéon, where influential pamphleteer Camille Desmoulins lived at no.2, and follow rue de l'Odéon, where Paine, having escaped the guillotine, lived at no.10. Cross boulevard St-Germain to **Café Procope** at 13 rue de l'Ancienne Comédie. A favourite slugging ground of Voltaire, Rousseau, Danton and Marat, it contains Voltaire's desk.

Head back across boulevard St-Germain and take **rue de l'Ecole de Médecine**, where the Cordeliers' Club met at no.15 in the former Couvent des Cordeliers. No.18 was the scene of pamphleteer Marat's infamous demise, when Charlotte Corday stabbed him in the bath with a kitchen knife.

Follow the road east and cut up rue St-Jacques and rue Dante until you meet rue Galande. By the time the Terror started, every available space was being used as a prison. At no.52, the **Caveau des Oubliettes** jazz club gets its name from a gory death sentence whereby prisoners were thrown into cells and 'forgotten'.

At Pont St-Michel, cross to Ile de la Cité and call in at the **Conciergerie** (see p120). This 'vast antechamber of death' was one of the most appalling prisons of the revolution, where prisoners slept in their own excrement. Not so Marie-Antoinette, who had a bed and wallpaper.

Cross the Seine again and you'll find yourself in front of the

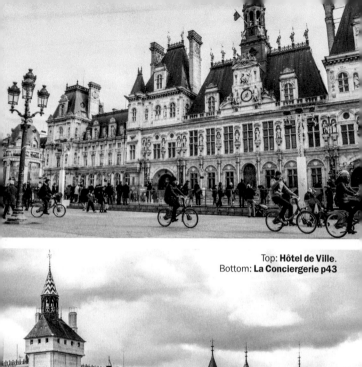

Top: **Hôtel de Ville**.
Bottom: **La Conciergerie p43**

Hôtel de Ville (see p101). In October 1789, a mob of some 3,000 fishwives and others commandeered guns and cannon from here before marching to Versailles to lynch the King. They returned with the severed heads of two guards.

Take rue du Temple, the road of no return for Louis XVI, turn right into rue Ste-Croix-de-la-Bretonnerie and left into rue Vieille-du-Temple. Now take rue des Francs-Bourgeois, which will bring you to the **Musée Carnavalet** (see p104) with its fine collection of revolutionary history.

Follow rue de Sévigné south to the church of St-Paul-St-Louis on rue St-Antoine, from which the hearts of Louis XIII and XIV were seized and sold to a painter. Take boulevard Henri IV and notice the brown bricks in the road as you approach **place de la Bastille** (see p106). These mark the spot where the Bastille prison stood; similar marks can be seen on rue St-Antoine, where no.5 is the site of the main gate and the famous 'storming' on 14 July 1789. On place de la Bastille, in June 1794, the guillotine claimed 73 victims in three days.

Finally, walk east to **place de la Nation** (or hop on a bus if you're flagging). Nation, formerly place du Trône, was the guillotine's last stand before the murderous device moved back to Concorde to give Robespierre the chop.

ITINERARIES

Place de la Nation

Castel Béranger

Meet the Moderns

In stark contrast with its current rather snooty image (the area is the epitome of thorough bourgeois respectability), during the early 1900s the 16th arrondissement was a veritable hotbed of avant-garde architecture and experimentation, and is today home to some of the capital's seminal modernist buildings. This walk explores the artists' studios, apartment blocks and luxury villas that sprang up in a district that had only recently been incorporated into Paris proper.

START: On rue La Fontaine at **Castel Béranger** (no.14), the art nouveau masterpiece of Hector Guimard, before dropping in for an early coffee break at the whimsically pretty **Café Antoine** (no.17, 01.40. 50.14.30), inserted into another Guimard building with clever wraparound corners. Next admire the rampart tendrils sprouting out from the wrought-iron fence of the

Hôtel Mezzara at no.60, which was also designed by Guimard, for textile manufacturer Paul Mezzara. Further along at no.65, don't miss the 1920s Studio Building designed by modernist maverick Henri Sauvage.

Turning right into avenue Mozart, you'll stumble across Guimard's former home at no.122, where he lived with his American artist wife, Adeline Oppenheim. On the corner as you turn left into rue Jasmin stands an imposing Beaux Arts-style apartment building – exactly the sort of neo-Renaissance frippery against which Guimard was rebelling.

Turn right into rue Henrich Heine, then left on rue du Dr Blanche. Here you'll find the **Fondation Le Corbusier** (8 square du Dr Blanche, 01.42.88.75.72, www. fondationlecorbusier.fr), which is housed in two villas designed by the architect in 1923. The interior reveals his mastery of multiple

Houses by Robert Mallet-Stevens

La Rotonde

viewpoints, fluidity of space and surprising use of colour.

Just off rue du Dr Blanche, turning right into Rue Mallet-Stevens, stand a series of six exclusive Cubist houses by Robert Mallet-Stevens, the glamorous architect and designer who best combined the elegance of art deco with the rigours of modernism. Back at 5 rue du Dr Blanche are artists' studios by Pierre Patout, who also decked out the luxury cruise liner *Normandie* (art deco was known as '*le style paquebot*').

Head right down rue de l'Assomption, then turn left on to avenue Mozart and right on to rue de Passy at La Muette métro station, with glitzy art deco brasserie **La Rotonde** (12 chaussée de la Muette, 16th, 01.45.04.01.32) on the corner. Next to the Passy covered market, take rue Duban, then rue Singer down towards the river on to rue Raynouard. Nos.51-55 were designed by Auguste Perret in reinforced concrete, cunningly tinted golden yellow to match the traditional Paris stone. Best known for housing the **Théâtre des Champs-Elysées**

(see p69), this building contained apartments and Perret's architectural offices. Turn left on rue Raynouard, past the Maison de Balzac, and cross place du Costa Rica into rue Benjamin-Franklin.

There's more Perret at no.25bis (a) where, behind the leaf motif tiles, the 1904 building was one of the first to be constructed around a concrete frame. The revolutionary structure freed up the floor plan from load-bearing walls, creating the light, airy spaces associated with modernism – as well as giving all the occupants a view of the Seine. The walk ends at Trocadéro with the **Palais de Chaillot**, a prime example of gigantesque 1930s state classical revival. It was designed by Léon Azéma, Louis-Hippolyte Boileau and Jacques Carlu for the 1937 Exposition Universelle, with two curved wings, giant bronze sculptures by Henri Bouchard and Pommier, and quotations by Paul Valéry. Pop into the **Cité de l'Architecture** (see p57), in the east wing, for a more thorough tour of French architecture past, present and future.

Left Bank Scooters

Vintage on a Vespa

Vintage shops in London and New York have been adding retro flair to wardrobes for years, but it has taken Paris – the city of 'serious' haute couture – a little longer to jump on the bandwagon. Today, though, the city is dripping in everything your vintage heart could desire, from rare 1920s Chanel accessories and art deco lighting to '60s rock LPs and '80s kitten boots. And the good news is that many of the capital's best vintage boutiques are condensed on the Right Bank between Palais-Royal and Faidherbe Chaligny (east of Bastille) – an easy distance to cover in one well-planned afternoon.

To really look the part, and for whizzing between the shops for maximum rifling time, hire a vintage-style Vespa from **Left Bank Scooters** (06.78.12.04.24, www.leftbankscooters.com; over-20s only). There are two models to choose from,

each with a handy compartment for stashing your shopping: the metallic green, 1955-style Vespa LXV 125cc with chrome trimmings and leather seats (€80 a day) or the red Vespa S 50cc (€70 a day), which is based on the 1962 Primavera model. Both can be delivered to and picked up from your hotel at no extra cost.

French law now stipulates that you need a motorcycle licence to drive a 125cc scooter, but your standard driving licence will do for the 50cc. And don't worry too much about parking. Where possible, look out for parking bays for motorbikes (*parking moto*). But if you can't find room under the official parking sign, the traffic police are generally pretty lenient, as long as you don't block the road or pavement.

START: Park your Vespa at the *parking moto* area on the corner of rue Paul Bert and rue Faidherbe, 11th (M° Faidherbe Chaligny).

Bistrot Paul Bert

Most vintage boutiques on this tour only open in the afternoon, so start things off with a retro lunch on rue Paul Bert. If you're looking for a touch of old-school Paris, **Bistrot Paul Bert** (see p107) never fails to deliver, with its zinc bar, 1930s tiles and lip-smacking dishes such as suckling pig with potato gratin. Alternatively, for a mix of hippy chic and slabs of Argentinean steak, try **Unico** (15 rue Paul Bert, 11th, 01.43.67.68.08, www.resto-unico.com), a former 1970s butcher's shop that has kept its original orange and white tiles.

After lunch, leave your Vespa and walk down rue Faidherbe, stopping off briefly to admire **Les Années Scooter** (23 rue Faidherbe, 11th, 01.46.59.47.90, www.lesanneesscooter.com), a den of mid 20th-century scooters, table lights, clocks, jukeboxes and street signs. Philippe, the passionate owner, can tell you the story behind every piece on display. A few doors further down, **Restaur'Bronze** (41 rue Faidherbe, 01.43.71.44.25, www.restaurbronze.com) is one of the last places in Paris to specialise in metal objects from the 1930s and '40s, including some show-stopping art deco lights, all perfectly restored by owner Marc Arguence, who learned the trade from his father.

One thing's for sure: you can't scoot around town with a 1932 crystal candelabra in tow, so head back to your Vespa. Drive back down rue Faidherbe and turn left down rue de Charonne. Park up opposite the Bistrot du Peintre café (where you'll be coming back for coffee in a while) – there are usually a few free *moto* spots available. Take a right down bohemian rue Keller, lined with galleries, bars and emerging clothes designers.

Turn left on to rue de la Roquette and walk to **Adöm** (35 & 56 rue de la Roquette, 01.48.07.15.94), which is split into two small boutiques. Girls head to no.56 for 1970s and '80s jeans and '60s shift dresses, while boys drop into no.35 for 1950s baseball jackets, cowboy boots and a decent selection of sneakers.

Noir Kennedy

Continue along rue de la Roquette, then turn right into rue Saint-Sabin. **Born Bad** (11 rue Saint-Sabin, 11th, 01.43.38.41.78, www.bornbad.fr) is an Aladdin's cave of second-hand new wave, soul, 1950s rock and '60s surf LPs and CDs that attracts music-savvy Parisians through the door from across town.

Now retrace your steps to the art nouveau surroundings of **Le Bistro du Peintre** (116 av Ledru-Rollin, 11th, 01.47.00.34.39, www. bistrotdupeintre.com), where you can peruse your purchases over a fortifying *café au lait*.

Sustenance over, the boutique-filled Haut Marais beckons. Return to your Vespa and head south down av Ledru-Rollin, then right on to car-clogged rue du Faubourg-St-Antoine. At place de la Bastille, take a right up bd Beaumarchais and park up near St-Sébastien Froissart métro station.

During the last few years, this previously forgotten northern stretch of the Marais has been transformed into one of Paris's hottest shopping areas, with numerous one-off boutiques – including two wonderful vintage finds. The first is aesthete William Moricet's tiny **Studio W** (6 rue du Pont-aux-Choux, 3rd, 01.44.78. 05.02), a sparsely stocked vintage shop where quality is king. There are clothes – mostly rare designer vintage dresses by YSL and Chanel – but it's the accessories that shine: 1970s boots, '80s stilettos and enough dinky '60s leather clutch bags to make your heart swoon.

The second shop, **Matières à Reflexion** (19 rue de Poitou, 3rd, 01.42.72.16.31, www.matieres areflexion.com), is the ultimate vintage bag-maker – a place where old leather jackets and clothes are crafted into one-off bags and satchels that fasten with aged brass hardware.

From here, hop back on the bike and whizz down rue du Pont-au-Choux, turn left on to rue de Turenne and then right on to rue St-Antoine. Park up somewhere near St-Paul métro station. Walk up rue Pavée and turn left on to rue du Roi de Sicile, and you'll find two classic vintage hotspots. For a slice of punky London retro style, head for **Noir Kennedy** (see p113), which is chock full of leather coats, lumberjack shirts, ripped jeans and funky 1980s T-shirts. If '40s fashion is more your style, try **Mam'Zelle Swing** (35 rue du Roi de Sicile, 4th, 01.48.87.04.06, www.mamzelle-swing.com), where Bérénice stocks well-selected pieces, many with price tags under €100.

Back on your Vespa, drive all the way down rue de Rivoli, turn right up rue de l'Echelle and right down rue St-Honoré, then park wherever you can at Palais-Royal. From here, take a stroll under the arcades of the Palais-Royal gardens to Paris's ultimate temple of luxury vintage, **Didier Ludot** (see p81). You just have to catch a glimpse of the window displays to see there is something rather special about Ludot's pieces, many of which look like they could easily have been cast-offs from Audrey Hepburn or Marilyn Monroe.

If you're daring enough to go in, you'll find outfits by today's up-and-coming designers too – or the vintage pieces of tomorrow, as the owner likes to call them.

Shopping over for the afternoon, head back east for a fittingly retro-style dinner at red- and white-checked **Astier** (44 rue Jean-Pierre Timbaud, 11th, 01.43.57.16.35, www.restaurant-astier.com), where Cyril Boulet and Nicolas Frezel revive vintage French dishes such as smoked herring, braised Charolais beef, and vanilla cream with sophisticated flair.

Paris by Area

Champs-Elysées & Western Paris | 56
Opéra to Les Halles | 70
Montmartre & Pigalle | 87
North-east Paris | 95
The Marais & Eastern Paris | 100
The Seine & Islands | 116
The 7th & Western Paris | 122
St-Germain-des-Prés & Odéon | 129
The Latin Quarter & the 13th | 141
Montparnasse | 153
Worth the Trip | 158

Arc de Triomphe

Champs-Elysées & Western Paris

In truth, '*la plus belle avenue du monde*' is not especially beautiful and it heaves with cars and crowds at pretty much any time of the day. The hordes aren't here for beauty, though. They're here for the shops, which the avenue, after years in the retail doldrums, now supplies in abundance. Fortunately, amid all this rampant consumerism are a good number of museums covering such cerebral topics as architecture, human evolution and life on the ocean waves, plus a greatly extended Palais de Tokyo that now lays claim to the title of Europe's largest contemporary art centre.

The western end of the Champs-Elysées is dominated by the Arc de Triomphe towering above place Charles-de-Gaulle, also known as L'Etoile. Built by Napoleon I, the arch was modified to celebrate the Revolutionary armies. From the top, visitors can gaze over the square (commissioned later by Haussmann), with 12 avenues radiating out in all directions. South of the arch, avenue Kléber leads to the monumental buildings of the Trocadéro.

Sights & museums

Arc de Triomphe

Pl Charles-de-Gaulle, 8th (01.55.37. 73.77). M° Charles de Gaulle Etoile. **Open** *Oct-Mar* 10am-10.30pm daily. *Apr-Sept* 10am-11pm daily. **Admission** €9.50; free-€6 reductions. **Map** p58 B2 ❶ The Arc de Triomphe has long been one of the capital's quintessential landmarks. But until recently, the interior was unimpressive, having changed little since the 1930s. After a revamp by architect Christophe Girault and artist Maurice Benayouna, a new museum opened with interactive screens and multimedia displays allowing visitors to look at other arches around the world, as well as screens exploring the Arc's tumultuous 200-year history. But the main reason to head up here is the view, one of the finest in the city.

Bateaux-Mouches

Pont de l'Alma, 8th (01.42.25.96.10, www.bateaux-mouches.fr). M° Alma-Marceau. **Tickets** €12.50; free-€5.50 reductions. **Map** p58 C4 ❷

If you're after a whirlwind tour of the sights and don't mind tourists and schoolchildren, this, the oldest cruise operation on the Seine, is a good option.

Cinéaqua

2 av des Nations Unies, 16th (01.40. 69.23.23, www.cineaqua.com). M° Trocadéro. **Open** 10am-7pm daily. **Admission** €19.90; free-€15.90 reductions. **Map** p58 B5 ❸

This aquarium and three-screen cinema is a wonderful attraction and a key element in the renaissance of the once moribund Trocadéro.

Cité de l'Architecture et du Patrimoine

Palais de Chaillot, 1 pl du Trocadéro, 16th (01.58.51.52.00, www.cite chaillot.fr). M° Trocadéro. **Open** 11am-7pm Mon, Wed, Fri-Sun; 11am-9pm Thur. **Admission** €8; free-€6 reductions. **Map** p58 A4 ❹

Opened in 2007 in the east wing of the Palais de Chaillot, this architecture and heritage museum impresses by its scale. The ground floor is filled with mock-ups of cathedral façades and heritage buildings, and interactive screens place the models in context. Upstairs, darkened rooms house full-scale copies of medieval and Renaissance murals and stained-glass windows. The highlight of the modern architecture section is the walk-in replica of an apartment from Le Corbusier's Cité Radieuse in Marseille.

Galerie-Musée Baccarat

11 pl des Etats-Unis, 16th (01.40.22. 11.00, www.baccarat.fr). M° Iéna. **Open** 10am-6pm Mon, Wed-Sat. **Admission** €5; free-€3.50 reductions. **Map** p58 B3 ❺

Philippe Starck has created a neo-rococo wonderland in the former mansion of the Vicomtesse de Noailles. See items by Georges Chevalier and Ettore Sottsass, services made for princes and maharajahs, and show-off items made for the great exhibitions of the 1800s.

Galeries Nationales du Grand Palais

3 av du Général-Eisenhower, 8th (01.44. 13.17.17, www.grandpalais.fr). M° Champs-Elysées Clemenceau. **Open** times vary. **Admission** prices vary. **Map** p59 E4 ❻

The Grand Palais was built for the 1900 Exposition Universelle and the design was the work of three different architects. During World War II, it played the role of reluctant host to Nazi tanks. In 1994, the glass-roofed central hall was closed when bits of metal started falling off. After major restoration, the Palais reopened in 2005 and now hosts major exhibitions.

Musée d'Art Moderne de la Ville de Paris

11 av du Président-Wilson, 16th (01.53. 67.40.00, www.mam.paris.fr). M° Alma Marceau or Iéna. **Open** 10am-6pm Tue-Sun. **Admission** free. *Temporary exhibitions* €5-€11; free-€5.50 reductions. No credit cards. **Map** p58 B4 ❼

This monumental 1930s building, housing the city's modern art collection, is strong on the Cubists, Fauves, the Delaunays, Rouault and Ecole de Paris artists Soutine and van Dongen.

Musée Jacquemart-André

158 bd Haussmann, 8th (01.45.62. 11.59, www.musee-jacquemart-andre. com). M° Miromesnil or St-Philippe-du-Roule. **Open** 10am-6pm daily (until 8.30pm Mon & Sat during exhibitions). **Admission** €11; free-€9.50 reductions. **Map** p59 D2 ❽

A stern pair of stone lions usher visitors into this grand 19th-century mansion, home to a collection of stately *objets d'art* and fine paintings. The

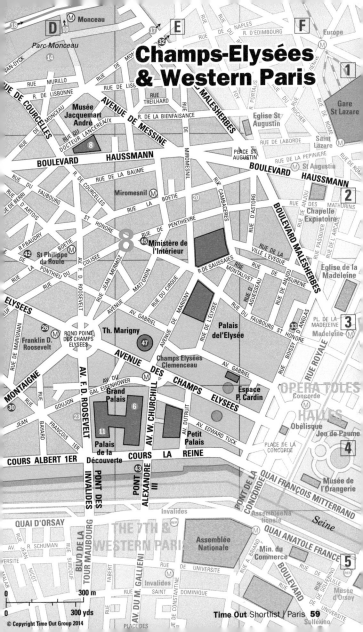

Champs-Elysées
& Western Paris

© Copyright Time Out Group 2014

BATOBUS
PARIS

RIVER-BOAT SHUTTLE SERVICE

1 PASS / 8 STOPS
to discover Paris by boat

HOP ON, HOP OFF as you please...

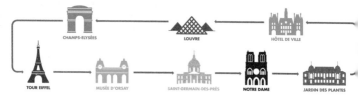

CHAMPS-ELYSÉES   LOUVRE   HÔTEL DE VILLE

TOUR EIFFEL   MUSÉE D'ORSAY   SAINT-GERMAIN-DES-PRÉS   NOTRE DAME   JARDIN DES PLANTES

Batobus shows you a different view of Paris...
Your ticket is a pass: you can get on and off the boat where you like,
when you like for 1 day, 2 days or a year.

0 825 05 01 01 (0,15€/mn) - www.batobus.com

collection was assembled by Edouard André and his artist wife Nélie Jacquemart, using money inherited from his rich banking family. The mansion was built to order to house their art hoard, which includes Rembrandts, Tiepolo frescoes and paintings by Uccello, Mantegna and Carpaccio.

Musée National des Arts Asiatiques – Guimet

6 pl d'Iéna, 16th (01.56.52.53.00, www. museeguimet.fr). M° Iéna. **Open** 10am-6pm Wed-Sun. **Admission** €7.50; free-€5.50 reductions. **Map** p58 B4 ⑨

The museum houses 45,000 objects from Neolithic times onwards, in a voyage across the diverse Asian religions and civilisations. Lower galleries focus on India and South-east Asia, centred on Hindu and Buddhist Khmer sculpture from Cambodia. Don't miss the Giant's Way, part of the entrance to a temple complex at Angkor Wat. Upstairs, Chinese antiquities include mysterious jade discs. Afghan glassware and Moghul jewellery also feature.

Musée National Jean-Jacques Henner

43 av de Villiers, 17th (01.47.63.42.73, www.musee-henner.fr). M° Malesherbes. **Open** 11am-6pm Mon, Wed-Sun (until 9pm 1st Thur of mth). **Admission** €5; free-€3 reductions. **Map** p59 D1 ⑩

The Musée Jean-Jacques Henner traces the life of one of France's most respected artists, from his humble beginnings in Alsace in 1829 to his rise as one of the most sought-after painters in Paris. On the first floor, Alsatian landscapes and family portraits are a reminder of the artist's lifelong attachment to his native region. What brought the artist most acclaim (and criticism), however, was his trademark nymph paintings. The museum is closed until 1 April 2015.

Palais de la Découverte

Av Franklin-D-Roosevelt, 8th (01.56. 43.20.21, www.palais-decouverte.fr). M° Champs-Elysées Clemenceau or *Franklin D. Roosevelt.* **Open** 9.30am-6pm Tue-Sat; 10am-7pm Sun (last entry 30mins before closing). **Admission** €8; free-€6 reductions. *Planetarium* €3. **Map** p59 D4 ⑪

This science museum houses designs dating from Leonardo da Vinci's time to the present day. Models, real apparatus and audio-visual material bring the displays to life, and exhibits cover astrophysics, astronomy, biology, chemistry, physics and earth sciences. There are shows at the Planetarium, and 'live' experiments take place at weekends and during school holidays.

Palais Galliera

NEW *10 av Pierre 1er de Serbie, 16th (01.56.52.86.00, www.palaisgalliera. paris.fr). M° Alma Marceau or Iéna.* **Open** 10am-6pm Tue, Wed, Fri-Sun; 10am-9pm Thur. **Admission** varies. **Map** p58 B4 ⑫

Since the reopening of the Palais Galliera, it's been hard to decide whether to be more impressed by the building or the clothes on show inside. This extraordinary mock-Renaissance folly, as only the 19th century knew how to do them, has been brought back to its full glory of Pompeian red walls, black woodwork, mosaic floors and vaulted ceilings painted with grotesqueries and arabesques. As before, the Galliera is dedicated solely to temporary exhibitions – due to the fragility of the fabrics, clothes can only be exhibited for four months at a time under strictly controlled lighting – but the shows manage to provide a decent glimpse of the Palais' incredibly rich collection, which stretches from late 17th-century period costume, via the birth of haute couture, to the creators of today.

Palais de Tokyo: Site de Création Contemporaine

13 av du Président-Wilson, 16th (01.81. 97.35.88, www.palaisdetokyo.com). M° Alma Marceau or Iéna. **Open** noon-midnight Mon, Wed-Sun. **Admission** €10; free-€8 reductions. **Map** p58 C4 ⑬

PARIS BY AREA

Paris's most happening major art space since it opened in 2002, the Palais de Tokyo has now virtually tripled in size to become the largest contemporary art centre in Europe. The organisation is known for its highly international approach, and for blurring boundaries between art, music, science and politics – as well as for its artist-designed Tokyo Eat restaurant and Black Block shop. Architects Lacaton & Vassal, who transformed the 1937 building in 2002, have now tackled the remaining spaces, many of them unused for over 30 years.

Parc Monceau

Bd de Courcelles, av Hoche, rue Monceau, 8th. M° Monceau. **Open** Nov-Mar 7am-8pm daily. Apr-Oct 7am-10pm daily. **Admission** free. Map p59 D1 ⑭

Monceau is a favourite with well-dressed children and their nannies. It was laid out in the 18th century for the Duc de Chartres in the English style, with a lake, lawns and follies: an Egyptian pyramid, a Corinthian colonnade, a Venetian bridge and sarcophagi.

Eating & drinking

Les 110 de Taillevent

195 rue du Faubourg Saint-Honoré, 8th (01.40.74.20.20, www.taillevent.com). M° Ternes. **Open** 12.15-2.30pm, 7.30-10.30pm daily. **€€€**. **Brasserie**. Map p58 C1 ⑮

Elegant design and French cuisine go hand in hand at the Gardinier brothers' brasserie, with 110 wines from the Taillevent vaults on offer. As befits a restaurant where wine is so important, chef Emile Cotte's menu concentrates on flavour: calamari topped with fine slices of chorizo and espelette pepper; roasted duckling and caramelised endives with gingerbread.

Alain Ducasse au Plaza Athénée

Hôtel Plaza Athénée, 25 av Montaigne, 8th (01.53.67.65.00, www.alain-ducasse. com). M° Alma Marceau. **Open** 7.45-10.15pm Mon-Wed; 12.45-2.15pm, 7.45-10.15pm Thur, Fri. Closed late July-late Aug & 1wk Dec. **€€€€**. **Haute cuisine**. Map p58 C4 ⑯

The sheer glamour would be enough to recommend this restaurant, Alain Ducasse's most lofty Paris undertaking. The ceiling drips with 10,000 crystals. An amuse-bouche of a single langoustine in a lemon cream with a touch of Iranian caviar starts the meal off beautifully. Cheese is delicious, as is the rum baba comme à Monte-Carlo.

Atao

86 rue Lemercier, 17th (01.46.27. 81.12). M° La Fourche. **Open** noon-2pm, 7-10pm Tue-Sun. **€€€**. **Seafood**. Map p59 F1 ⑰

Atao looks like a dream of a fisherman's cabin – marine blue on the outside, then wood, white and colourful touches inside, with an old mariner's portrait, an anchor and a black-and-white flag. At night, soft candlelight enhances the atmosphere even further. This pretty place is owned by the daughter of an oyster farmer from Morbihan, who serves up platters of fine oysters – flat native plates and huge Japanese creuses (alive and cooked). Main dishes – fish stew, dorado with basil, scallop carpaccio – are pricey but worth every cent.

Bar à Sushi Izimi

55 bd des Batignolles, 8th (01.45.22. 43.55, www.lebarasushi.com). M° Villiers. **Open** noon-2.30pm, 7.30-10pm Tue-Sat. **€€€**. **Sushi**. Map p59 E1 ⑱

Blink and you'll miss it, but this tiny sushi bar punches far above its size. It quickly made a name for itself when it opened in 2011, educating Paris diners about the delights of fatty tuna, eel and wagyu beef. The eel arrives still smoking, perfectly grilled, swiped with a delicious sweet sauce then arranged in a chirachi bowl with fish, omelette and prawns on a warm bed of rice and sesame. The wagyu beef, with its remarkable texture and nutty flavour, is served as tataki (a sort of half-cooked

Glory in glass

The Fondation Louis Vuitton is taking shape.

Like a butterfly emerging from its chrysalis, a daring glass structure has been slowly unfolding on the edge of the Bois de Boulogne. The **Fondation Louis Vuitton** (www.fondationlouisvuitton.fr), designed by star architect Frank Gehry, is described by LVMH chairman Bernard Arnault as 'an emblematic building of the 21st century', an ambitious statement project that proclaims the arrival of Louis Vuitton – previously active as a sponsor of exhibitions and heritage restoration – as an art-world force. The Fondation will open in autumn 2014, four years later than planned.

Gehry has described his inspiration behind the design: 'Within the Bois de Boulogne and the Jardin d'Acclimatation, the idea of a glass pavilion was the only way forward. It seemed inappropriate to create a solid object. I wanted to express a notion of transparency.'

This is not, of course, the first building by Gehry in the capital. Well before the Guggenheim Bilbao put him on the European art map, he designed what was originally the American Center (now the Cinémathèque Française) in 1994, giving the city a taste of his deconstructionist style. But the Fondation involves a new level of scale and complexity.

In a combination of extravagance and apparent weightlessness, a series of glass sails hover over the white concrete 'icebergs' of the galleries beneath. The building is intended to change with the light at different times of day and be integrated with the surrounding nature, right down to tree-lined terraces beneath the glass. The seemingly fluid sails are composed of thousands of panels of curved glass, developed with the help of a 3D modelling programme adapted from aerospace technology used by Dassault Aviation.

The appointment of Suzanne Pagé, long-time director of the Musée d'Art Moderne de la Ville de Paris, has given the project credibility within the Paris art world. As to what will actually be on show, that remains a mystery. The Fondation is keeping details of its first exhibition firmly under wraps. However, we can probably expect to see some of the artists who have created handbags for Louis Vuitton, such as Takashi Murakami and Richard Prince, along with Danish artist Olafur Eliasson, who designed the pitch-black lift leading to the rooftop gallery at Louis Vuitton's Champs-Elysées flagship. Then there are artists who Arnault is said to have purchased during the past 20 years – a panoply of big names including Jeff Koons, Gilbert & George, and Andreas Gursky.

carpaccio) or sushi. Have it with one of the sakes – fruity Tatenokawa, flavourful Muroka, intense Kenbishi, or a taster of all three.

Le Dada

*12 av des Ternes, 17th (01.43.80.60.12).
M° Ternes.* **Open** 6am-2am Mon-Sat;
7am-8pm Sun. **€€**. **Café**. **Map** p58 B1 ⑲
Perhaps the hippest café in this stuffy part of town, Le Dada is best known for its well-placed, sunny terrace. Inside, the wood-block carved tables and red walls provide a warm atmosphere for a crowd that tends towards the well-heeled, well-spoken and, well, loaded. That said, the atmosphere is friendly.

Granterroirs

*30 rue de Miromesnil, 8th (01.47.42.
18.18, www.granterroirs.com). M°
Miromesnil.* **Open** 9am-5.30pm Mon-Fri. Closed 2wks Aug. **€€**. **Bistro**.
Map p59 E2 ⑳
The walls of this *épicerie* heave with more than 600 enticing specialities originating from southern France, including Périgord foie gras, charcuterie from Aubrac and a fine selection of wines. They make great gifts – but why not try sampling some of the goodies by enjoying the midday *table d'hôte* feast? Come in early to ensure that you can choose from the five succulent *plats du jour*.

Le Hide

*10 rue du Général-Lanrezac, 17th (01.45.
74.15.81, www.lehide.fr). M° Charles de
Gaulle Etoile.* **Open** noon-2pm, 7-10pm
Mon-Fri; 7-10pm Sat. **€€**. **Bistro**.
Map p58 B1 ㉑
This bistro is packed with a happy crowd that appreciates Japanese-born chef Hide Kobayashi's superb cooking. Expect dishes such as duck foie gras terrine with pear-and-thyme compôte to start, followed by tender faux-filet steak in a light foie gras sauce. Desserts are excellent: perfect tarte tatin comes with crème fraîche from Normandy.

Ladurée

*75 av des Champs-Elysées, 8th (01.40.
75.08.75, www.laduree.fr). M° Franklin
D. Roosevelt or George V.* **Open** 7.30am-11pm Mon-Fri; 8.30am-midnight Sat;
8.30am-10pm Sun. **€€**. **Café**. **Map**
p58 C3 ㉒
Decadence permeates this elegant tearoom. While you bask in the glow of bygone wealth, indulge in tea, pastries and, above all, hot chocolate. It's a rich, velvety tar that will leave you in the requisite stupor for a lazy afternoon.

Lasserre

*17 av Franklin-Roosevelt, 8th (01.43.
59.02.13, www.restaurant-lasserre.
com). M° Franklin D Roosevelt.* **Open**
7-10pm Tue, Wed, Sat; noon-2pm,
7-10pm Thur, Fri. **€€€€**. **Haute
cuisine**. **Map** p59 D4 ㉓
Lasserre's rich history is definitely a part of the dining experience: Audrey Hepburn, André Malraux and Salvador Dali were regulars. But its illustrious past is nothing next to the food: chef Christophe Moret (ex-Plaza Athénée) and his pastry chef Claire Heitzler (ex-Ritz) create lip-smacking delicacies to die for. The upstairs dining room, accessed by a bellboy-operated lift, is a sumptuous affair in taupe and white, with solid silver table decorations and a retractable roof that opens just enough for you to see the stars at night.

Miss Kô

NEW *49 av George V, 8th (01.53.67.
84.60, www.miss-ko.com). M° George V.*
Open noon-2am daily. **€€€**. **Chinese**.
Map p58 B1 ㉔
Philippe Starck's latest venture is set up to look like a narrow Chinatown street, bustling and colourful at night with open kitchens at the end where chefs work away beneath an array of suspended woks and neon lights. There are a dozen dishes, of which the star is beef *tataki* at €29 – a sort of carpaccio with teriyaki sauce, shiitake mushrooms and purée perfumed with ginger. The 'black salmon & Kô' burger

at €19.50 is equally alluring, the bread coloured black with squid ink and garnished with avocado, mizuna, gravlax and tempura-fried green beans. For lighter meals, the creative sushi (gyoza with foie gras, perhaps) go perfectly with a cocktail or bubble tea. The bar and terrace are suitably hip.

Taillevent

15 rue Lamennais, 8th (01.44.95.15.01, www.taillevent.com). M° George V. **Open** 12.15-1.30pm, 7.15-9.30pm Mon-Fri. Closed Aug. €€€€. **Haute cuisine.** **Map** p58 C2 25

Rémoulade de coquilles St-Jacques is a technical feat, with slices of raw, marinated scallop wrapped in a tube shape around a diced apple filling, encircled by a *rémoulade* sauce. An earthier and lip-smacking dish is the trademark *épeautre* – an ancient wheat – cooked 'like a risotto' with bone marrow, black truffle, whipped cream and parmesan, and topped with sautéed frog's legs.

Shopping

Abercrombie & Fitch

23 av des Champs-Elysées, 8th (08.05.11.15.59, www.abercrombie. com). M° Franklin D Roosevelt. **Open** 10am-8pm Mon-Sat; 11am-7pm Sun. **Map** p59 D3 26

The US brand's flagship store has been causing a stir on the Champs since it opened in 2011, with banging tunes and topless male models standing in the doorway at all times. Worth a detour even if you're not a fan of preppy.

Alléosse

13 rue Poncelet, 17th (01.46.22.50.45, www.fromage-alleosse.com). M° Ternes. **Open** 9am-1pm, 4-7pm Tue-Thur; 9am-1pm, 3.30-7pm Fri, Sat; 9am-1pm Sun. **Map** p58 B1 27

People cross town for these cheeses – wonderful farmhouse camemberts, delicate st-marcellins, a choice of *chèvres* and several rarities.

Balenciaga

10 av George V, 8th (01.47.20.21.11, www.balenciaga.com). M° Alma Marceau or George V. **Open** 10am-7pm Mon-Sat. **Map** p58 C4 28

The Spanish fashion house is ahead of Japanese and Belgian designers in the hip stakes. Floating fabrics contrast with dramatic cuts, producing a sophisticated style that the fashion *haut monde* can't wait to slip into.

Balmain

44 rue François 1er, 8th (01.47. 20.57.58, www.balmain.com). M° George V. **Open** 10.30am-7pm Mon-Sat. **Map** p58 C3 29

A portrait of the late Pierre Balmain surveys the scene at his eponymous shop. What would he have made of the clothes around him? Long gone are the afternoon dresses with perfectly positioned waists, full skirts and trapezoidal necklines. The racks are these days lined with bondage trousers, studded jackets and animal print drainpipes.

Dior

26-30 av Montaigne, 8th (01.40.73. 73.73, www.dior.com). M° Franklin D. Roosevelt. **Open** 10am-7pm Mon-Sat. **Map** p59 D4 30

The Dior universe is here, from the main prêt-à-porter store and jewellery, menswear and eyewear to Baby Dior, where rich infants are coochy-cooed by drooling assistants.

Drugstore Publicis

133 av des Champs-Elysées, 8th (01.44.43.79.00, www.publicis drugstore.com). M° Charles de Gaulle Etoile. **Open** 8am-2am Mon-Fri; 10am-2am Sat, Sun. **Map** p58 B2 31

On the ground floor there's a newsagent, pharmacy, bookshop and upmarket deli. The basement is a macho take on Colette, keeping selected design items and lifestyle magazines, and replacing high fashion with wines and a cigar cellar.

La Pâtisserie des Rêves

French Touche

NEW *1 rue Jacquemont, 17th (01.42.
63.31.36, www.frenchtouche.com).
M° La Fourche.* **Open** *1-8pm Tue-Fri;
11am-8pm Sat.* **Map** p59 F1 ③②

Bags adorn the walls, trinkets sit atop
small wooden shelves, and lamps
are dotted around the room – French
Touche is a wonderful shop where one
could happily rummage for hours on
end. Dreamed up by the lovely Valérie,
it's teeming with all sorts of original creations, from retro knitted cat
badges to Beatles patches and micro-
notebook keychains.

Givenchy

*28 rue du Fbg-St-Honoré, 8th (01.42.
68.31.00, www.givenchy.com). M°
Madeleine.* **Open** *10.30am-7pm Mon-
Sat.* **Map** p59 F3 ③③

This flagship store for men's and
women's prêt-à-porter and accessories
incorporates surreal rooms within
rooms – cut-out boxes filled with white,
black or mahogany panelling – providing a contemporary art gallery setting.

LE66

*66 av des Champs-Elysées, 8th (01.53.
53.33.80, www.le66.fr). M° George V.*
Open *11am-8pm Mon-Fri; 11am-8.30pm
Sat; 1-8pm Sun.* **Map** p59 D3 ③④

This fashion concept store is youthful
and accessible. Assistants, who are
also the buyers and designers, make for
a motivated team. The store takes the
form of three transparent modules, the
first a bookstore run by Black Book of
the Palais de Tokyo, and the second two
devoted to fashion.

Louis Vuitton

*101 av des Champs-Elysées, 8th
(01.53.57.52.00, www.louisvuitton.fr).
M° George V.* **Open** *10am-8pm Mon-Sat;
11am-7pm Sun.* **Map** p58 C2 ③⑤

The 'Promenade' flagship sets the tone
for Vuitton's global image, from the
'bag bar', bookstore and new jewellery
department to the women's and men's
ready-to-wear.

La Pâtisserie des Rêves

NEW *11 rue de Longchamp, 16th (01.47.
04.00.24, www.lapatisseriedesreves.
com). M° Victor Hugo.* **Open** *Shop
10am-7pm Tue-Fri; 9am-7pm Sat,
Sun. Salon de thé noon-6.30pm Fri;
9am-6.30pm Sat, Sun.* **Map** p58 B4 ③⑥

Looking for your dream pâtisserie?
Look no further than cake-maker
extraordinaire Philippe Conticini's
contemporary boutique and tearoom
in the 16th. The Saint-Honoré (a circular puff-pastry delight filled with
whipped cream and caramelised
sugar) is rectangular so that you can
cut it into slices, and the famous Paris-
Brest (a praline cream éclair) comes
with a runny praline centre.

Prada

*10 av Montaigne, 8th (01.53.23.99.40,
www.prada.com). M° Alma Marceau.*
Open *10am-7pm Mon-Sat.* **Map** p58 C4 ③⑦

The high priestess of European
chic, Miuccia Prada's elegant stores
pull in fashion followers of all ages.
Handbags of choice are complemented
by the coveted ready-to-wear range.

Sephora

*70 av des Champs-Elysées, 8th (01.53.
93.22.50, www.sephora.fr). M° Franklin
D. Roosevelt.* **Open** *10am-8.30pm daily.*
Map p58 C3 ③⑧

The flagship of the cosmetic supermarket chain houses around 12,000
brands of scent and slap. Sephora
Blanc (14 cour St-Emilion, 12th, 01.40.
02.97.79) features beauty products in a
minimalist interior.

Nightlife

Le Baron

*6 av Marceau, 8th (01.47.20.04.01,
www.clublebaron.com). M° Alma
Marceau.* **Open** *11pm-6am daily.*
Map p58 C4 ③⑨

This small but supremely exclusive
hangout for the international jet set
only holds 150, most of whom are regulars you'll need to befriend in order to

My promenade in Paris...

SIGHTSEEING CRUISE, LUNCH CRUISE, DINNER CRUISE

Information and booking : +33(0)1 76 64 14 45

Boarding at the foot of the Eiffel Tower

Bateaux Parisiens, a **sodexo** company

Le Paris d'un grand voy...

get past the door. But if you manage to get in, you'll be rubbing shoulders with celebrities and super-glossy people.

Le Lido

116bis av des Champs-Elysées, 8th (01.40.76.56.10, www.lido.fr). M° *Franklin D. Roosevelt or George V.* **Dinner** 7pm. **Shows** 9.30pm, 11.30pm daily. **Map** p58 C2 ⓴
This is the largest cabaret of them all: high-tech touches optimise visibility, and chef Philippe Lacroix provides fabulous gourmet nosh. On stage, 60 Bluebell Girls slink around, shaking their boobs with panache.

Queen

102 av des Champs-Elysées, 8th (01.53. 89.08.90, www.queen.fr). M° George V. **Open** 11.30pm-6am Mon, Wed, Fri-Sun; midnight-6am Tue; 7pm-6am Thur. **Map** p58 C2 ⓛ
Once the city's most fêted gay club and the only venue that could hold a torch to the Rex, Queen's star faded in the early noughties. But it's now starting to shine more brightly again.

Le Régine

49 rue de Ponthieu, 8th (01.42.66. 22.78) M° St-Philippe-du-Roule. **Open** 7pm-5am Thur; midnight-6am Fri, Sat. **Map** p59 D2 ⓶
Régine was once a key figure on the Paris nightlife scene, and the club she created is experiencing a rejuvenation. Her portrait still sits by the entrance for a touch of '70s nostalgia, but the revamped venue has shifted from disco to sophisticated electro, inviting the cream of international DJs to the decks.

Showcase

Underneath Pont Alexandre III, 8th (01.45.61.25.43, www.showcase.fr). M° Champs-Elysées Clemenceau. **Open** 11.30pm-7am Fri, Sat. **Admission** free-€15. **Map** p59 E4 ⓸
This vast venue is where music-crazed insomniacs come on weekends to discover up-and-coming bands and dance

until daybreak. The club has lost some of its hype over the last couple of years, but high-profile guest DJs have been setting the bar higher lately.

Arts & leisure

Le Balzac

1 rue Balzac, 8th (01.45.61.10.60, www.cinemabalzac.com). M° George V. No credit cards. **Map** p58 C2 ⓸
Built in 1935 and boasting a mock ocean-liner foyer, the Balzac cinema scores highly for design and programming.

Salle Pleyel

252 rue du Fbg-St-Honoré, 8th (01.42.56.13.13, www.sallepleyel.fr). M° Ternes. **Box office** noon-7pm Mon-Sat; 2hrs before show Sun. *By phone* 11am-7pm Mon-Sat; 11am-5pm Sun & 1hr before performance. **Map** p59 E2 ⓸
Home to the Orchestre de Paris, this restored concert hall looks splendid. It's the capital's leading venue for large-scale symphonic concerts.

Théâtre des Champs-Elysées

15 av Montaigne, 8th (01.49.52.50.50, www.theatrechampselysees.fr). M° Alma Marceau. **Box office** noon-7pm Mon-Sat; 2hrs before show Sun. *By phone* 11am-6pm Mon-Fri; 2-6pm Sat. **Map** p58 C4 ⓸
This beautiful art nouveau theatre with bas-reliefs by Bourdelle celebrated its centenary in 2013, having hosted the première of Stravinsky's *Le Sacre du Printemps* in 1913.

Théâtre Marigny

Av de Marigny, 8th (08.92.22.23.33, www.theatremarigny.fr). M° Champs-Elysées Clemenceau or Franklin D. Roosevelt. **Box office** 11am-6.30pm Mon-Sat. **Map** p59 E3 ⓸
Théâtre Marigny boasts a location off the Champs-Elysées, a deluxe interior conceived by Charles Garnier, high-profile casts and an illustrious pedigree stretching back more than 150 years.

Musée du Louvre p74

Opéra to Les Halles

In centuries gone by, these two adjoining central districts – bounded by the Grands Boulevards to the north and the river to the south – were the city's commercial and provisioning powerhouses, home to most of the newspapers, banks and major mercantile institutions. Nowadays, although there is still a strong financial slant, thanks to the presence of the two stock exchanges and the Banque de France, the focus is on shopping: mass-market stuff in and around Les Halles, shading into more exclusive brands the further one moves west, in particular on and just off rue St-Honoré.

Les Halles itself was the city's wholesale food market until 1969, when the Second Empire iron-framed buildings that housed it were ripped out. The soulless shopping centre that filled the gap in the 1970s has been one of the city's least liked features, and is being uprooted itself, to be replaced by a 21st-century

glory of gardens, glass, open spaces and retail opportunities aplenty.

A short distance west of Les Halles is the Louvre, no longer the centre of French power though it still exerts considerable influence: first as a grandiose architectural ensemble, a palace within the city; and, second, as a symbol of the capital's cultural pre-eminence. Across rue de Rivoli from the Louvre stands the elegant Palais-Royal. After a stroll in its quiet gardens, it's hard to believe this was the starting point of the French Revolution.

Sights & museums

La Collection 1900

Maxim's, 3 rue Royale, 8th (01.42. 65.30.47, www.maxims-musee-art nouveau.com). M° Madeleine. **Open** *Guided tours* (reservations essential) 2pm Wed-Sun (English); 3.15pm, 4.30pm Wed-Sun (French). **Admission** €15. No credit cards. **Map** p72 A3 ❶

Couturier Pierre Cardin has owned belle époque restaurant Maxim's since 1981, and now he has added a museum of art nouveau, which he has been collecting since the age of 18. There are rooms and rooms of exhibits, arranged so as to evoke a 19th-century courtesan's boudoir. Read Zola's *Nana* before your visit to grasp the full effect of the dreamy lake maidens sculpted in glistening faience, pewter vanity sets in the shape of reclining nudes, and beds inlaid with opium flowers to promote sleep. Dinner settings on display include Gustave Eiffel's own chunky tureens, just crying out for turtle soup.

Eglise de la Madeleine

Pl de la Madeleine, 8th (01.44.51. 69.00, www.eglise-lamadeleine.com). M° Concorde or Madeleine. **Open** 9.30am-7pm daily. **Admission** free. **Map** p72 A2 ❷
The building of a church on this site began in 1764; in 1806 Napoleon sent instructions from Poland for Barthélémy Vignon to design a 'Temple of Glory' dedicated to his Grand Army. After the emperor's fall, construction slowed and the building, by now a church again, was finally consecrated in 1845. The exterior is ringed by fluted Corinthian columns, with a double row at the front, and a frieze of the Last Judgement above the portico. Inside are giant domes, an organ and pseudo-Grecian marble side altars.

Forum des Halles

1st. M° Les Halles/RER Châtelet Les Halles. **Map** p73 E4 ❸
The labyrinthine mall and transport interchange extends for three levels underground and includes the Ciné Cité multiplex and Forum des Images. All is changing with a new landscaping of the area due to be completed by 2016.

Jardin des Tuileries

Rue de Rivoli, 1st. M° Concorde or Tuileries. **Open** *Apr, May, Sept* 7am-9pm daily; *June-Aug* 7am-11pm

daily; *Oct-Mar* 7.30am-7.30pm daily. **Map** p72 B4 ❹
The gravelled alleyways of these gardens have been a chic promenade ever since they opened to the public in the 16th century. André Le Nôtre created the prototypical French garden with terraces and a central vista running down the Grande Axe past circular and hexagonal ponds. As part of Mitterrand's Grand Louvre project, sculptures such as Coysevox's winged horses were transferred to the Louvre and replaced by copies, and the Maillol sculptures were returned to the Jardins du Carrousel; a handful of modern sculptures have been added, including bronzes by Moore, Ernst, Giacometti, and Dubuffet's *Le Bel Costumé*.

Jeu de Paume

1 pl de la Concorde, 8th (01.47.03.12.50, www.jeudepaume.org). M° Concorde. **Open** 11am-9pm Tue; 11am-7pm Wed-Sun (last admission 30mins before closing). **Admission** €8.50; free-€5.50 reductions. **Map** p72 A3 ❺
The Centre National de la Photographie moved into this site in 2005. The building, which once served as a tennis court, has been divided into two white, almost hangar-like galleries. It is not an intimate space, but it works well for showcase retrospectives. A video art and cinema suite in the basement shows new digital installation work.

Musée des Arts Décoratifs

107 rue de Rivoli, 1st (01.44.55.57.50, www.lesartsdecoratifs.fr). M° Palais Royal Musée du Louvre or Pyramides. **Open** 11am-6pm Tue, Wed, Fri-Sun; 11am-9pm Thur (late opening during exhibitions only). **Admission** (with Musée de la Mode & Musée de la Publicité) €9.50; free-€8 reductions. **Map** p72 C4 ❻
Taken as a whole along with the Musée de la Mode et du Textile and Musée de la Publicité, this is one of the world's major collections of design and the decorative arts. The major focus here is French furniture and tableware,

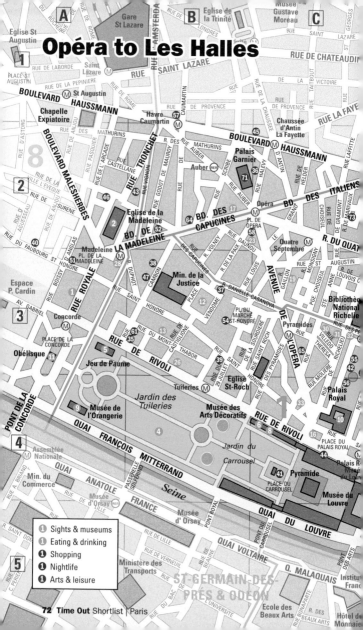

Opéra to Les Halles

from extravagant carpets to delicate crystal and porcelain. Of most obvious attraction to the layman are the reconstructed period rooms, ten in all, showing how the other half lived from the late 1400s to the early 20th century.

Musée du Louvre

Rue de Rivoli, 1st (01.40.20.50.50, www. louvre.fr). M° Palais Royal Musée du Louvre. **Open** 9am-6pm Mon, Thur, Sat, Sun; 9am-9.45pm Wed, Fri. **Admission** *Permanent collections* €12; free-€6 reductions. **Map** p72 C5 **7**

The world's largest museum is also its most visited, with a remarkable 9.7 million visitors in 2012. It is a city within the city, a vast, multi-level maze of galleries, passageways, staircases and escalators. It's famous for the artistic glories within, but the very fabric of the museum is a masterpiece in itself – or rather, a collection of masterpieces modified and added to from one century to another. And the additions and modifications continue into the present day, with the opening of a wonderful two-storey Islamic Arts department beneath the Cour Visconti in late 2012, and the franchising of the Louvre 'brand' via new outposts in Lens in northern France (www.louvre lens.fr) and Abu Dhabi.

Musée de la Mode et du Textile

107 rue de Rivoli, 1st (01.44.55.57.50, www.lesartsdecoratifs.fr). M° Palais Royal Musée du Louvre or Pyramides. **Open** 11am-6pm Tue, Wed, Fri-Sun; 11am-9pm Thur (late opening during exhibitions only). **Admission** (with Musée des Arts Décoratifs & Musée de la Publicité) €9.50; free-€8 reductions. **Map** p72 C4 **8**

This municipal fashion museum holds Elsa Schiaparelli's entire archive and hosts exciting themed exhibitions. Dramatic black-walled rooms make a fine background to the clothes, and video screens and a cinema space show how the clothes move, as well as interviews with the creators.

Musée de l'Orangerie

Jardin des Tuileries, 1st (01.44.77.80.07, www.musee-orangerie.fr). M° Concorde. **Open** 9am-6pm Mon, Wed-Sun. **Admission** €10; free-€7.50 reductions. **Map** p72 A4 **9**

The look of this Monet showcase is fuss-free, with the museum's eight, tapestry-sized *Nymphéas* (water lilies) paintings housed in two plain oval rooms. They provide a simple backdrop for the ethereal romanticism of Monet's works, which he painted late in his life. Downstairs, the Jean Walter and Paul Guillaume collection of Impressionism and the Ecole de Paris is a mixed bag of sweet-toothed Cézanne and Renoir portraits, with works by Modigliani, Rousseau, Matisse, Picasso and Derain.

Palais-Royal

Pl du Palais-Royal, 1st. M° Palais Royal Musée du Louvre. **Open** *Gardens* Apr, May 7am-10.15pm daily; June-Aug 7am-11pm daily; Sept 7am-9.30pm daily; Oct-Mar 7am-8.30pm daily. **Admission** free. **Map** p72 C4 **10**

Built for Cardinal Richelieu by Jacques Lemercier, the building was once known as Palais Cardinal. Richelieu left it to Louis XIII, whose widow Anne d'Autriche preferred it to the Louvre and rechristened it when she moved in with her son, the young Louis XIV. In the 1780s, the Duc d'Orléans enclosed the gardens in a three-storey peristyle and filled it with cafés, shops, theatres, sideshows and accommodation to raise money for rebuilding the burned-down opera. Daniel Buren's striped columns grace the main courtyard.

Place de la Concorde

1st/8th. M° Concorde. **Map** p72 A3 **11**

This is the city's largest square, its grand east–west perspectives stretching from the Louvre to the Arc de Triomphe, and north–south from the Madeleine to the Assemblée Nationale across the Seine. In 1792, the centre statue of Louis XV was replaced with the guillotine for Louis XVI, Marie-Antoinette and others.

Jeu de Paume p71

Place Vendôme

1st. M° Opéra or Tuileries. **Map** p72 B3 ⑫
Elegant place Vendôme got its name from a *hôtel particulier* built by the Duc de Vendôme that stood on the site. Opened in 1699, the eight-sided square was conceived by Hardouin-Mansart to show off an equestrian statue of the Sun King, torn down in 1792 and replaced in 1806 by the Colonne de la Grande Armée. During the 1871 Commune, this symbol of 'brute force and false glory' was pulled down; the present column is a replica. At no.12, you can visit the Grand Salon where Chopin died in 1849.

Eating & drinking

L'Ardoise

28 rue du Mont-Thabor, 1st (01.42.96. 28.18, www.lardoise-paris.com). M° Concorde or Tuileries. **Open** noon-3pm, 6.30-11pm Mon-Sat; 6.30-11pm Sun. €€. **Bistro**. **Map** p72 B3 ⑬
One of the city's finest modern bistros, L'Ardoise is regularly packed with gourmets eager to sample Pierre Jay's delicious cooking. A wise choice might be six oysters with warm chipolatas and pungent shallot dressing. Unusually, it's open on Sundays.

Blend

44 rue d'Argout, 2nd (01.40.26.84.57, www.blendhamburger.com). M° Bourse or Sentier. **Open** noon-11pm daily. €. **Burgers**. **Map** p73 D3 ⑭
Parisians have gone burger bonkers: after the Camion qui Fume (a mobile gourmet burger van) and Big Fernand (an über-trendy take-away burger joint in the 10th), Blend has opened its doors in the bobo quarters of Étienne Marcel. The secret is in the ingredients: made with hand-cut veal and beef mince, provided by star butcher Yves-Marie le Bourdonnec, burgers are succulent and flavoursome, and marry wonderfully with the fresh toppings (think bacon, bleu d'Auvergne cheese, spinach leaves, chorizo, mint and cheddar). The

bread and fries (both potato and sweet-potato) are also homemade, lending the whole affair a rather gourmet feel.

La Bourse ou la Vie

12 rue Vivienne, 2nd (01.42.60.08.83). M° Bourse. **Open** noon-10pm Mon-Fri. Closed 1wk Aug & 1wk Dec. €€. **Bistro**. **Map** p73 D3 ⑮
After a career as an architect, the owner of La Bourse ou la Vie has a new mission in life: to revive the dying art of the perfect steak-frites. The only decision you'll need to make is which cut of beef to order with your chips, unless you pick the cod. Choose between ultra-tender *coeur de filet* or a huge, tender bavette. Rich, creamy pepper sauce is the speciality here, but the real surprise is the chips, which gain a distinctly animal flavour from the suet in which they are cooked.

Café Marly

93 rue de Rivoli, cour Napoléon, 1st (01.49.26.06.60). M° Palais Royal Musée du Louvre. **Open** 8am-2am daily. €€. **Café**. **Map** p72 C4 ⑯
A class act, this, as you might expect of a Costes café whose lofty, arcaded terrace overlooks the Louvre's glass pyramid. It's reached through passage Richelieu (the entrance for advance Louvre ticket holders), and the prime location comes at a price: it's €6 for a Heineken – so you might as well splash out €12 on a chocolate martini or a Shark of vodka, lemonade and grenadine. Most wines are under €10 a glass, and everything is impeccably served by razor-sharp staff.

Café de la Paix

12 bd des Capucines, 9th (01.40.07. 36.36, www.cafedelapaix.fr). M° Opéra. **Open** 7am-midnight daily. €€. **Café**. **Map** p72 B2 ⑰
Lap up every detail – this is once-in-a-holiday stuff. Whether you're out on the historic terrace or looking up at the ornate stucco ceiling, you'll be sipping in the footsteps of the likes of

Oscar Wilde, Josephine Baker, Emile Zola, and Bartholdi and the Franco-American Union (as they sketched out the Statue of Liberty). Let the immaculate staff bring you a kir or, for an afternoon treat, the vanilla millefeuille – possibly the best in Paris.

Delaville Café

34 bd de Bonne-Nouvelle, 10th (01.48.24.48.09, www.delavillecafe.com). Mº Bonne Nouvelle. **Open** 8.30am-2am daily. **Bar**. Map p73 E2 ⑬

The Delaville Café is an unmissable stop on the Grands Boulevards, possessed as it is of a vast sunny terrace open from springtime onwards. The vibe is a little precious, but the decor of the huge venue is a delight, a lively mixture of ancient gilt rococo and post-industrial baroque (it used to be a *maison close*). DJs mix unobtrusive electro lounge sets at weekends.

Drouant

18 pl Gaillon, 2nd (01.42.65.15.16, www.drouant.com). Mº Pyramides or Quatre Septembre. **Open** noon-2.30pm, 7-11.30pm daily. **€€€. Brasserie**. Map p72 C3 ⑲

Star chef Antoine Westermann has whisked this landmark brasserie into the 21st century with bronze-coloured banquettes and butter-yellow fabrics. Westermann has dedicated this restaurant to the art of the hors d'oeuvre, in themed sets of four ranging from global (Thai beef salad with brightly coloured vegetables) to nostalgic (silky leeks in vinaigrette).

Frenchie

5 rue du Nil, 2nd (01.40.39.96.19, www.frenchie-restaurant.com). Mº Sentier. **Open** 7-11pm Mon-Fri. **€€. Bistro**. Map p73 E3 ⑳

Grégory Lemarchand honed his craft with Jamie Oliver in London before opening this loft-style bistro. It has been a huge hit, thanks to the bold flavours of dishes such as gazpacho with calamari, squash blossoms and plenty of herbs; braised lamb with roasted aubergine and spinach; and coconut tapioca with strawberry sorbet. It requires an almost superhuman effort to secure a table in the tiny dining room, but luckily there's Frenchie Bar à Vins across the street (see below).

Frenchie Bar à Vins

6 rue du Nil, 2nd (01.40.39.96.19, www.frenchie-restaurant.com). Mº Sentier. **Open** 7-11pm Mon-Fri. **Wine bar**. Map p73 E3 ㉑

See box p79.

Le Fumoir

6 rue de l'Amiral-de-Coligny, 1st (01.42.92.00.24, www.lefumoir.com). Mº Louvre Rivoli. **Open** 11am-2am daily. **Bar**. Map p73 D5 ㉒

This elegant bar facing the Louvre has become a local institution: neo-colonial fans whirr lazily and oil paintings adorn the walls. A sleek crowd sips martinis or reads papers at the mahogany bar (originally from a Chicago speakeasy), giving way to young professionals in the restaurant and pretty things in the library. Expertly mixed cocktails should take the edge off any evening.

Harry's New York Bar

5 rue Daunou, 2nd (01.42.61.71.14, www.harrys-bar.fr). Mº Opéra. **Open** noon-2am Mon-Thur, Sun; noon-3am Fri, Sat. **Bar**. Map p72 B2 ㉓

The city's most stylish American bar is beloved of expats, visitors and hard-drinking Parisians. The bartenders mix some of the most sophisticated cocktails in town, from the trademark bloody mary (invented here, so they say) to the Pétrifiant, an elixir of half a dozen spirits splashed into a beer mug. Gershwin composed *An American in Paris* in the piano bar here.

Kaï

18 rue du Louvre, 1st (01.40.15.01.99). Mº Louvre Rivoli. **Open** 12.30-2.15pm, 7.30-10.30pm Tue-Sat. Closed 1wk Apr & 3wks Aug. **€€€. Japanese**. Map p73 D4 ㉔

This restaurant has developed a following among fashionable diners. The 'Kaï-style' sushi is a zesty take on a classic: marinated and lightly grilled yellowtail is pressed on to a roll of shiso-scented rice. Not to be outdone, grilled aubergine with miso turns out to be a smoky, luscious experience. A main of breaded pork lacks the finesse of the starters, but is still satisfying.

Liza

14 rue de la Banque, 2nd (01.55.35. 00.66, www.restaurant-liza.com). M° Bourse. **Open** *noon-2.15pm, 8-10.30pm Mon-Thur; noon-2.15pm, 8-11pm Fri; 8-11pm Sat; noon-3.30pm Sun.* **€€**. **Lebanese**. Map p73 D3 ㉕

Liza Soughayar's eaterie showcases the style and superb food of Beirut. Lentil, fried onion and orange salad is delicious, as are the *kebbe* (minced seasoned raw lamb) and grilled halloumi cheese with home-made apricot preserve. Main courses such as minced lamb with coriander-spiced spinach and rice are light, flavoursome and well presented.

Le Meurice

Hôtel Meurice, 228 rue de Rivoli, 1st (01.44.58.10.55, www.lemeurice.com). M° Tuileries. **Open** *7-10.30am, 12.30-2pm, 7.30-10pm Mon-Fri; 7-11am Sat, Sun. Closed 2wks Feb & mid July-end Aug.* **€€€€**. **Haute cuisine**. Map p72 B3 ㉖

With the departure of Yannick Alléno in 2013, Alain Ducasse has now taken over the reins at Le Meurice's gorgeous dining room, launching a new menu that eschews excess and focuses instead on a simpler approach (to the food, not the prices). Head chef Christophe Saintagne turns out delightfully deconstructed dishes such as 'turbot, olives', 'mallard, grapes' and 'spicy lamb, artichokes'.

Ô Château

68 rue Jean-Jacques Rousseau, 1st (01.44.73.97.80, www.o-chateau.com). M° Les Halles. **Open** *4pm-midnight daily.* **Wine bar**. Map p73 D4 ㉗

The food is great and the vibe convivial, but a night here is all about the wine. There are no less than 500 by the bottle and 40 by the glass, including the chance to taste some very rare and expensive bottles in *soupçon*-sized quantities thanks to high-tech wine-saving devices. Tastings take place in the tasting rooms at 12.15pm daily.

Senderens

9 pl de la Madeleine, 8th (01.42.65. 22.90, www.senderens.fr). M° Madeleine. **Open** *noon-2.45pm, 7.30-11pm daily. Closed 1st 3wks Aug.* **€€€€**. **Haute cuisine**. Map p72 A3 ㉘

Alain Senderens reinvented his art nouveau institution a few years ago with a *Star Trek* interior and a mind-boggling fusion menu. You might find dishes such as roast duck foie gras with a warm salad of black figs and liquorice powder. Each dish comes with a suggested wine, whisky, sherry or punch.

Le Tambour

41 rue Montmartre, 2nd (01.42.33. 06.90). M° Sentier. **Open** *8.30am-5.30am daily.* **Bar**. Map p73 D3 ㉙

The Tambour is a classic nighthawk's bar decked with vintage public transport paraphernalia, its wooden banquettes and bus stop-sign bar stools occupied by chatty regulars who give the 24-hour clock their best shot. There's a long dining room memorable for its métro map from Stalingrad station.

Télescope Café

NEW *5 rue Villedo, 1st (01.42.61. 33.14, www.telescopecafe.com). M° Pyramides.* **Open** *8.30am-5pm Mon-Fri; 9.30am-6.30pm Sat.* **€€**. No credit cards. **Café**. Map p72 C3 ㉚

David Flynn is something of a coffee purist, and his newly opened Télescope Café has a stripped-down look to it; whitewashed walls, a pale blue wooden counter with a plate of cakes, Marzocco espresso machine and a strange water-heating device that he says is called

Top tipples

Frenchie's wine bar offshoot.

You'd be forgiven for suspecting that **Frenchie Bar à Vins** (see p77) was opened merely as a solution to the near impossible problem of getting a table – or even getting them to answer the phone – at the hugely successful Frenchie across the street. But it has quickly become a destination in its own right, drawing an agreeably eclectic mix of ages and nationalities to a part of Sentier otherwise deserted at night.

The look is similar to the sister restaurant – exposed stone walls and bare lightbulbs suspended from copper tubing – but here there are no reservations. You simply turn up (early or after 10pm is easiest) and grab one of the stools grouped around the high communal tables.

A similarly flexible approach applies to the food, with the choice of tucking into several courses or simply snacking on a starter or two. Plates are generally smaller and less complex than in the main restaurant, but the quality of dishes such as poached egg in frothy Jerusalem artichoke velouté, salsify with black mushrooms, and lamb shoulder with butternut squash helps you to understand why Frenchie has had such enormous acclaim since it opened.

Wines range in price from a simple €20 Loire to a Mouton Rothschild 1998 that'll set you back more than €1,000. 'Many are natural but not all, but we like to understand how the winemaker makes their wines,' says Canadian sommelier Laura Vidal, who chooses the wines with chef Gregory Marchand. 'The chef and I believe in having a very wide selection of wines and regions: a light red Beaujolais or a full-bodied Cahors to cater to different tastes and palates. His cuisine is often a twist on Italian and we serve a couple of pasta dishes, so we have a nice selection of Italian wines.' The list itself is curiously uninformative, simply arranged by colour and price, although on-the-spot sommelier Aurélien Massay can offer guidance.

an 'über-boiler'. Even the coffee menu looks pretty minimalist – no trendy flat whites here – but it turns out that Télescope also doubles as a coffee roaster, only keeping small stocks of beans to ensure freshness.

Thaïm

46 rue de Richelieu, 1st (01.42.96.54.67). M° Bourse or Palais Royal. **Open** noon-2.30pm, 7-11pm Mon-Fri; 7-11pm Sat. €€. **Thai. Map** p72 C3 ③1

Thaïm has an elegant decor of dark wood and plum fabrics. Particularly good value is the three-course lunch menu, which might bring crisp fried parcels filled with spiced vegetables, an aromatic green fish curry (there is a choice of fish, meat or poultry every day), and coconut-pumpkin soup. There is a vast choice of teas, including an iced ginger-coconut version.

Verjus

NEW *52 rue de Richelieu, 1st (01.42. 97.54.40, www.hkmenus.com). M° Pyramides.* **Open** 6-11pm Mon; 12.30-2pm, 6-11pm Tue-Fri. €€€. **Bistro. Map** p72 C3 ③2

Braden Perkins and Laura Adrian started out in Paris running a well-regarded supper club, 'Hidden Kitchen', so it's little surprise that Verjus – opened after rave reviews paved the way for a full-blown restaurant – hasn't quite lost its word-of-mouth feel. There's one eight-course tasting menu at dinner (plus an optional cheese board, and optional matched wines). At €60 a head without the extras, save it for a special occasion – but it will be special.

Zen

NEW *8 rue de l'Echelle, 1st (01.42.61. 93.99). M° Louvre Rivoli.* **Open** noon-2.30pm, 7-10.30pm Mon-Fri; noon-3pm, 7-10.30pm Sun. Closed Aug. €€. **Japanese. Map** p72 C4 ③3

There's no shortage of Japanese restaurants in this neighbourhood, but the recently opened Zen is refreshing in a couple of ways. First, there is no pale

wood in sight; the colour scheme here is sharp white, green and yellow. Second, the menu has a lot to choose from – bowls of ramen, sushi and *chirashi*, hearty dishes such as chicken with egg on rice or *tonkatsu* – yet no detail is neglected. A perfect choice if you're spending a day at the Louvre – you can be in and out in 30 minutes.

Shopping

Agnès b

2, 3, 4 & 6 rue du Jour, 1st (men 01.42. 33.04.13, women 01.45.08.56.56, www. agnesb.com). M° Les Halles. **Open** Oct-Apr 10am-7pm Mon-Sat; May-Sept 10.30am-7.30pm Mon-Sat. **Map** p73 D4 ③4

Agnès b rarely wavers from her design vision: pure lines in fine quality cotton, merino wool and silk. Best buys are shirts, pullovers and cardigans. Her mini-empire of men's, women's, children's, travel and sportswear shops is compact; see the website for details.

Alice Cadolle

4 rue Cambon, 1st (01.42.60.94.22, www.cadolle.com). M° Concorde or Madeleine. **Open** 10.30am-6.30pm Mon, Tue; 10am-7pm Wed-Sat. Closed Aug. **Map** p72 B3 ③5

Five generations of lingerie-makers are behind this boutique, founded by Hermine Cadolle, who claimed to be the inventor of the bra. Poupie Cadolle continues the tradition in a cosy space devoted to a luxury ready-to-wear line of bras, panties and corsets. For a treat, Cadolle Couture (255 rue St-Honoré, 1st, 01.42.60.94.94) will create bespoke lingerie (by appointment only).

Apple Store

12 rue Halévy, 9th (01.44.83.42.00, www.apple.com). M° Opéra. **Open** 9am-8pm Mon-Sat. **Map** p72 C2 ③6

Apple's second Paris store opened in 2010 in a stunning belle époque former bank facing the Opéra Garnier. To fit in with such hallowed surroundings, Apple strayed from its standard model, retaining the original carved wooden staircase, wrought-iron railings, marble columns and mosaic tile floor.

Boucheron

26 pl Vendôme, 1st (01.42.61.58.16, www.boucheron.com). Mº Opéra. **Open** 10.30am-7pm Mon-Sat. **Map** p72 B3 ③⑦
Boucheron was the first to set up shop on place Vendôme, attracting celebrity custom from the nearby Ritz hotel. Owned by Gucci, the grand jeweller produces stunning pieces, using traditional motifs with new accents: take, for example, its chocolate-coloured gold watch.

Chanel

31 rue Cambon, 1st (01.44.50.72.50, www.chanel.com). Mº Concorde or Madeleine. **Open** 10am-7pm Mon-Sat. **Map** p72 B3 ③⑧
Fashion legend Chanel has managed to stay relevant, thanks to Karl Lagerfeld. Coco opened her first boutique in this street, at no.21, in 1910, and the tradition continues in this elegant interior. Lagerfeld has been designing for Chanel since 1983, and keeps on revamping the classics – the little black dress and the Chanel suit – with great success.

Colette

213 rue St-Honoré, 1st (01.55.35. 33.90, www.colette.fr). Mº Pyramides or Tuileries. **Open** 11am-7pm Mon-Sat. **Map** p72 B3 ③⑨
The renowned one-stop concept and lifestyle store features a highly eclectic selection of accessories, fashion, books, media, gadgets, and hair and beauty brands, all in a swanky space.

Comme des Garçons

54 rue du Fbg-St-Honoré, 8th (01.53. 30.27.27, www.comme-des-garcons. com). Mº Concorde or Madeleine. **Open** 11am-7pm Mon-Sat. **Map** p72 A2 ④⓪
Rei Kawakubo's design ideas and revolutionary mix of materials have influenced fashions of the past two decades, and are showcased in this fibreglass store. Comme des Garçons Parfums

(23 pl du Marché-St-Honoré, 1st, 01.47. 03.15.03) provides a futuristic setting for the brand's fragrances.

Delfonics

NEW *Carrousel du Louvre, 99 rue de Rivoli, 1st (01.47.03.14.24, www. delfonics.fr). Mº Palais Royal Musée du Louvre.* **Open** 10am-8pm daily. **Map** p72 C4 ④①
Concentrating on minimalist designs using durable materials (linen, rayon, canvas, leather and resin), Delfonics is a haven for stationery addicts looking for Japanese and European notebooks, files, pens and much more. This flagship store offers nearly 55sq m of temptingly affordable things such as Post-it notes in cute designs, vinyl pencil cases and electronic letter-openers.

Didier Ludot

24 galerie de Montpensier, 1st (01.42. 96.06.56, www.didierludot.fr). Mº Palais Royal Musée du Louvre. **Open** 10.30am-7pm Mon-Sat. **Map** p72 C3 ④②
Didier Ludot's temples to vintage haute couture appear in Printemps, Harrods and New York's Barneys. The pieces are stunning: Dior, Molyneux, Balenciaga, Pucci, Féraud and Chanel, from the 1920s onwards. Ludot also curates exhibitions, using the Palais-Royal as a gallery. La Petite Robe Noire (125 galerie de Valois, 1st, 01.40.15.01.04) stocks Ludot's own line of little black dresses.

Erès

2 rue Tronchet, 8th (01.47.42.28.82, www.eres.fr). Mº Madeleine. **Open** 10am-7pm Mon-Sat. **Map** p72 B2 ④③
Erès's beautifully cut swimwear has embraced a sexy '60s look, with buttons on low-cut briefs. The top and bottom can be purchased in different sizes.

La Galerie du Carrousel du Louvre

99 rue de Rivoli, 1st (01.43.16.47.10, www.carrouseldulouvre.com). Mº Palais Royal Musée du Louvre. **Open** 10am-8pm daily. **Map** p72 C4 ④④

This massive underground centre – which is open every day of the year – is home to more than 35 shops, mostly big-name chains vying for your attention and cash. Options include an Apple Store, Swatch Store and L'Occitane en Provence.

Galeries Lafayette

40 bd Haussmann, 9th (01.42.82. 34.56, fashion shows 01.42.82.30.25, fashion advice 01.42.82.35.50, www. galerieslafayette.com). M° Chaussée d'Antin/RER Auber. **Open** 9.30am-8pm Mon-Wed, Fri, Sat; 9.30am-9pm Thur. **Map** p72 C2 ᴬⁱ⁵

Espace Luxe on the first floor features luxury prêt-à-porter and accessories and nine avant-garde designers, and a vast shoe department is home to some 150 brands. The men's fashion space on the third floor, Lafayette Homme, has natty designer corners and a 'Club' area with internet access. On the first floor, Lafayette Gourmet has exotic foods galore, and a wine cellar. Lafayette Maison over the road has five floors of home furnishings and design.

Hédiard

21 pl de la Madeleine, 8th (01.43.12. 88.88, www.hediard.fr). M° Madeleine. **Open** 9am-8pm Mon-Sat. **Map** p72 A2 ᴬⁱ⁶
Hédiard's charming shop dates back to 1880, when it was the first to introduce exotic foods to Paris, specialising in rare teas and coffees, spices, jams and candied fruits. Pop upstairs for a cuppa in the shop's posh tearoom.

Hervé Léger

24 rue Cambon, 1st (01.42.60.02.00, www.herveleger.com). M° Concorde. **Open** 10am-7pm Mon-Sat. **Map** p72 B3 ᴬⁱ⁷
A couple of decades ago, Hervé Léger's silhouette-cinching bandage dresses were as evocative of the era as super-models Linda, Christy, Naomi and Cindy. But somewhere in the mid-90s women lost their love of Lycra. In the past few seasons, however, updated reinterpretations of Léger's style, by

the likes of Christopher Kane and Marios Schwab, have been nothing short of a fashion phenomenon. Less modified versions, sold by the Léger label itself (now owned and designed by Max Azria of BCBG fame), have been less critically acclaimed.

Jean-Paul Gaultier

6 rue Vivienne, 2nd (01.42.86. 05.05, www.jeanpaulgaultier.com). M° Bourse. **Open** 9am-7pm daily. **Map** p73 D3 ᴬⁱ⁸
Having celebrated his 30th year in the fashion business, Gaultier is still going strong. His boudoir boutique stocks men's and women's ready-to-wear and the JPG Jeans lines. The haute couture department is by appointment only.

Kiliwatch

64 rue Tiquetonne, 2nd (01.42.21. 17.37, www.espacekiliwatch.fr). M° Etienne Marcel. **Open** 2-7pm Mon; 11am-7.30pm Tue-Sat. **Map** p73 E3 ᴬⁱ⁹
The trailblazer of the rue Etienne-Marcel revival is filled with hoodies, casual shirts and jeans. Brands include Gas, Edwin and Pepe Jeans.

Kokon To Zai

48 rue Tiquetonne, 2nd (01.42.36.92.41, www.kokontozai.co.uk). M° Etienne Marcel. **Open** 11.30am-7.30pm Mon-Sat. **Map** p73 E4 ᴬⁱ⁰
This tiny style emporium is sister to the Kokon To Zai in London. The neon-lit club feel of the mirrored interior matches the dark glamour of the designs. Unique pieces straight off the catwalk share space with creations by Marjan Peijoski, Noki, Raf Simons, Ziad Ghanem and new Norwegian designers.

Lanvin

22 rue du Fbg St-Honoré, 8th (01.44.71. 31.73, www.lanvin.com). M° Concorde or Madeleine. **Open** 10.30am-7pm daily. **Map** p72 A3 ᴬⁱ¹
The couture house that began in the 1920s with Jeanne Lanvin has been reinvented by the indefatigable Albert

Elbaz. In October 2007, he unveiled this revamped showroom that set new aesthetic standards for luxury fashion retailing. Lanvin has an exhibition room devoted to her in the Musée des Arts Décoratifs, and this apartment-boutique also incorporates original furniture from the Lanvin archive. All this would be nothing, of course, if the clothes themselves were not exquisite.

Lavinia

3 bd de la Madeleine, 1st (01.42.97.20.20, www.lavinia.fr). Mº Madeleine. **Open** 10am-8.30pm Mon-Sat. **Map** p72 B2 ♦
Lavinia stocks a broad selection of French and non-French wines; its *cave* has everything from a 1945 Mouton-Rothschild at €22,000 to trendy and 'fragile' wines for under €10. Have fun tasting wine with the *dégustation* machines on the ground floor, which allow customers to taste a sip of up to ten different wines each week for €10.

Legrand Filles et Fils

1 rue de la Banque, 2nd (01.42.60. 07.12, www.caves-legrand.com). Mº Bourse. **Open** 11am-7pm Mon; 10am-7.30pm Tue-Fri; 10am-7pm Sat. Closed Mon in Aug. **Map** p73 D3 ♦
Fine wines, teas and *bonbons*, and a showroom for regular wine tastings.

Marc by Marc Jacobs

19 pl du Marché-Saint-Honoré, 1st (01.40.20.11.30, www.marcjacobs.com). Mº Tuileries. **Open** 11am-7pm Mon-Sat. **Map** p72 B3 ♦
The store for Jacobs' casual, punky line has fashionistas clustering like bees round a honeypot, not least for the fabulously inexpensive accessories that add spice to a tired outfit. A skateboard table and giant pedalo in the form of a swan are the centrepieces of the store, which stocks men's and women's prêt-à-porter, shoes and special editions.

Marc Jacobs

34 galerie de Montpensier, 1st (01.55. 35.02.60, www.marcjacobs.com). Mº

Palais Royal Musée du Louvre. **Open** 11am-7pm Mon-Sat. **Map** p72 C3 ♦
Marc Jacobs brought new life and verve – and an influx of fashionistas – to these elegant cloisters. Stocking womenswear, menswear, accessories and shoes, the shop has become a place of pilgrimage for the designer's legion of admirers.

Martin Margiela

23 & 25bis rue de Montpensier, 1st (womenswear 01.40.15.07.55, menswear 01.40.15.06.44, www. maisonmartinmargiela.com). Mº Palais Royal Musée du Louvre. **Open** 11am-7pm Mon-Sat. **Map** p72 C4 ♦
This Paris outlet is a pristine, white, unlabelled space. Martin Margiela's collection for women (Line 1) has a blank label but is recognisable by external white stitching. You'll also find Line 6 (women's basics) and Line 10 (menswear), plus accessories for men and women and shoes.

Printemps

64 bd Haussmann, 9th (01.42.82. 50.00, www.printemps.com). Mº Havre Caumartin/RER Auber. **Open** 9.35am-8pm Mon-Wed, Fri, Sat; 9.35am-10pm Thur. **Map** p72 B1 ♦
Fashion is where Printemps excels; an entire floor is devoted to shoes, and the beauty department stocks more than 200 brands. In Printemps de la Mode, French designers sit alongside the big international designers. The Fashion Loft offers a younger take on current trends. Printemps de la Maison stocks everything from everyday tableware to design classics. For refuelling, there's a tearoom, sushi bar and Café Be, an Alain Ducasse bakery.

Repetto

22 rue de la Paix, 2nd (01.44.71.83.12, www.repetto.com). Mº Opéra. **Open** 9.30am-7.30pm Mon-Sat. **Map** p72 B2 ♦
This ballet shoe-maker struck gold when it decided to reissue its dance shoes with pavement soles several

years ago. The prowly *ballerines* and showbiz dance boots in black, metallic and spangly finishes are fun, timelessly stylish and exceptionally comfortable. The shoes are sold alongside the full range of real balletwear; what's more you can try out your *pointes* on a red carpet with a *barre*.

Salons du Palais-Royal Shiseido

142 galerie de Valois, Jardins du Palais-Royal, 1st (01.49.27.09.09, www.sergelutens.com). Mº Palais Royal Musée du Louvre. **Open** 10am-7pm Mon-Sat. **Map** p72 C3 ❺❾

Under the arcades of the Palais-Royal, Shiseido's perfumier Serge Lutens practises his aromatic arts. Lutens is a maestro of rare taste. Bottles of his concoctions – Tubéreuse Criminelle, Rahat Loukoum and Ambre Sultan – can be sampled by visitors. Look out for Fleurs d'Oranger, which the great man defines as the smell of happiness itself. Prices start at €69.

Stella McCartney

114-121 galerie de Valois, Jardins du Palais-Royal, 1st (01.47.03.03.80, www.stellamccartney.com). Mº Palais Royal Musée du Louvre. **Open** 10.30am-7pm Mon-Sat. **Map** p72 C3 ❻⓪

Thick carpets, maplewood and metal sculptures create a rarefied setting for women's prêt-à-porter, bags, shoes, sunglasses and McCartney's range of simple but stylish lingerie, as well as the perfume and skincare lines.

Yohji Yamamoto

4 rue Cambon, 1st (01.40.20.00.71, www.yohjiyamamoto.co.jp). Mº Concorde. **Open** 10.30am-7pm Mon-Sat. **Map** p72 B3 ❻❶

Yamamoto has achieved his dream of having a flagship store on rue Cambon. This temple to the creator is as impressive as those in New York and Antwerp, a pristine white gallery space. Behind an origami-screen window mannequins clothed in his

showpieces seem to float in the air. A grand staircase leads to womenswear on the first floor, while menswear is on the lower ground.

Nightlife

Au Duc des Lombards

42 rue des Lombards, 1st (01.42.33. 22.88, www.ducdeslombards.com). Mº Châtelet. **Open** Concerts 8pm, 10pm Mon-Sat. **Map** p73 E5 ❻❷

Some of the capital's venerated jazz spots have lost the fight for survival in recent years. But this one has endured and attracts a high class of performer.

Chacha Club

47 rue Berger, 1st (01.40.13.12.12, www.chachaclub.fr). Mº Châtelet. **Open** 8pm-6am Tue-Sat. **Map** p73 D4 ❻❸

Paris's fetishistic obsession with the cigarette has produced a new nightlife phenomenon: the *fumoir*. The Chacha Club was the first high-profile establishment to open one, and it forms just one of the sexy attributes of this hot haunt near Les Halles. It combines restaurant, bar and club in a suite of rooms with 1930s-inspired decor.

Olympia

28 bd des Capucines, 9th (08.92.68. 33.68, www.olympiahall.com). Mº Opéra. **Open** Box office noon-2pm, 6-9.30pm Mon-Fri; 5-9.30pm Sat, Sun & 2hrs before shows. By phone 10am-6pm Mon-Fri; 2-6pm Sat, Sun. Concerts times vary. **Map** p72 B2 ❻❹

The Beatles, Frank Sinatra, Jimi Hendrix and Edith Piaf all performed here over the years. Now it's mostly home to nostalgia and *variété*.

Le Paris Paris Club

5 av de l'Opéra, 8th (01.42.60.64.45, www. parisparisclub.com). Mº Pyramides. **Open** 11pm-6am Tue, Thur-Sat; 10pm-6am Wed. Concerts 8.30pm. **Map** p72 C3 ❻❺

This small club is all about electro-rock, with black-painted walls and live acts taking to the stage at weekends.

Rex

5 bd Poissonnière, 2nd (01.42.36.10.96, www.rexclub.com). M° Bonne Nouvelle. **Open** 11.30pm-7am Thur-Sat. **Map** p73 E2 ⑥⑥

The Rex's sound system puts over 40 different sound configurations at the DJ's fingertips. Once associated with techno pioneer Laurent Garnier, the Rex still occupies an unassailable position as the city's serious club music venue.

Silencio

142 rue de Montmartre, 2nd (www. silencio-club.com). M° Bourse or Grands Boulevards. **Open** 6pm-4am Tue-Thur; 6pm-6am Fri, Sat. **Map** p73 D3 ⑥⑦

David Lynch's first Paris joint, named after the cult setting in his 2001 movie *Mulholland Drive*, is mainly for private members. If you're not up for full-blown membership, access is after midnight.

Théâtre du Châtelet

1 pl du Châtelet, 1st (01.40.28.28.40, www.chatelet-theatre.com). M° Châtelet. **Open** times vary. **Map** p73 E5 ⑥⑧

This venerable theatre and classic music hall has another life as a jazz and *chanson* venue, with performances by top-notch international musicians.

Arts & leisure

Châtelet – Théâtre Musical de Paris

1 pl du Châtelet, 1st (01.40.28.28.40, www.chatelet-theatre.com). M° Châtelet. **Box office** 11am-7pm Mon-Sat; 1hr before performance Sun. **Map** p73 E5 ⑥⑨

The Châtelet is fast becoming Paris's main venue for musicals hailing from Broadway and the West End – such as *West Side Story* and *Carousel*.

Forum des Images

2 rue du Cinéma, Forum des Halles, 1st (01.44.76.63.00, www.forumdesimages. net). M° Les Halles. **Map** p73 E4 ⑦⓪

The Forum was conceived partly as a screening venue for old and little-known movies, and partly as an archive

centre for every kind of moving picture featuring Paris; today, the collection numbers over 6,500 documentaries, adverts, newsreels and films.

Opéra National de Paris, Palais Garnier

Pl de l'Opéra, 9th (08.92.89.90.90, www. operadeparis.fr). M° Opéra. **Box office** 11.30am-6.30pm Mon-Sat & 1hr before performance. *By phone* 9am-6pm Mon-Fri; 9am-1pm Sat. **Map** p72 B2 ⑦①

The Palais Garnier is the jewel in the crown of Paris music-making. The Opéra National often favours the high-tech Bastille for new productions, but the matchless acoustics of the Palais Garnier are superior to the new house.

Spa Nuxe

32 rue Montorgueil, 1st (01.42.36.65.65, www.nuxe.com). M° Les Halles. **Open** 10am-9pm Mon-Fri; 9.30am-7.30pm Sat. **Map** p73 E4 ⑦②

This luxurious day spa housed in stone vaults with wooden cabins and safari-style tents offers massages and skin treatments using Nuxe's gentle, plant-based products. The facials begin with a short foot, tummy and neck massage.

Théâtre National de l'Opéra Comique

Pl Boieldieu, 2nd (01.42.44.45.40, www.opera-comique.com). M° Richelieu Drouot. **Box office** 11am-7pm Mon-Sat; 11am-5pm Sun. **Map** p72 C2 ⑦③

Its promotion to national theatre status has brought this jewel box of a theatre back to life, exploring a French repertoire often ignored by larger houses.

Théâtre de la Ville

2 pl du Châtelet, 4th (01.42.74.22.77, www.theatredelaville-paris.com). M° Châtelet. **Box office** 11am-7pm Mon; 11am-8pm Tue-Sat. *By phone* 11am-7pm Mon-Sat. **Map** p73 E5 ⑦④

Features hip chamber music outfits such as the Kronos and Takács Quartets, Early Music pioneer Fabio Biondi, and pianist Aleksandar Madzar.

Sacré-Coeur p88

Montmartre & Pigalle

Perched up on a hill (or *butte*), Montmartre is the highest point in Paris, its tightly packed houses spiralling round the mound below the dome of Sacré-Coeur. Despite the many tourists (chiefly around place du Tertre), it's surprisingly easy to fall under the spell of this romantic district. Climb stairways, peer down alleys and into ivy-covered houses and quiet squares, and explore streets such as rue des Abbesses, rue des Trois-Frères and rue des Martyrs, with their cafés, boutiques and bohemian residents.

At the bottom of the hill, in once-notorious Pigalle, the seediness of yesteryear's sex clubs and brothels is steadily being replaced by hip music venues and clubs.

Sights & museums

Cimetière de Montmartre

20 av Rachel, access by staircase from rue Caulaincourt, 18th (01.53.42.36.30).
Mº Blanche or Place de Clichy. **Open** *6 Nov-15 Mar* 8am-5.30pm Mon-Fri; 8.30am-5.30pm Sat; 9am-5.30pm Sun, public hols. *16 Mar-5 Nov* 8am-6pm Mon-Fri; 8.30am-6pm Sat; 9am-6pm Sun, public hols. **Admission** free. **Map** p89 A1 ❶
Truffaut, Nijinsky, Berlioz, Degas, Offenbach and German poet Heine are all buried here. So, too, are La Goulue, the first great cancan star, and consumptive heroine Alphonsine Plessis, inspiration for *La Traviata*. Flowers are still left on the grave of diva Dalida.

Musée d'Art Halle St-Pierre

2 rue Ronsard, 18th (01.42.58.72.89, www.hallesaintpierre.org). Mº Anvers. **Open** *Jan-July, Sept-Dec* 10am-6pm Mon-Fri; 10am-7pm Sat; 11am-6pm Sun. *Aug* noon-6pm Mon-Fri. **Admission** prices vary. **Map** p89 C2 ❷
The former market in the shadow of Sacré-Coeur specialises in *art brut*, *art outsider* and *art singulier* from its own and other collections.

Musée de l'Erotisme

72 bd de Clichy, 18th (01.42.58.28.73, www.musee-erotisme.com). M° Blanche. **Open** 10am-2am daily. **Admission** €10; €8 reductions. **Map** p89 A2 ❸

Seven floors of erotic art and artefacts. The first three run from first-century Peruvian phallic pottery through Etruscan fertility symbols to Yoni sculptures from Nepal; the fourth gives a history of Paris brothels; the top floors host exhibitions of erotic art.

Musée de Montmartre

12 rue Cortot, 18th (01.49.25.89.37, www.museedemontmartre.fr). M° Lamarck-Caulaincourt. **Open** 10am-6pm daily. **Admission** €9; free-€7 reductions. **Map** p89 B1 ❹

This 17th-century manor house displays the history of the hilltop, with rooms devoted to composer Gustave Charpentier and a tribute to the Lapin Agile cabaret. There are paintings by Suzanne Valadon, who had a studio above the entrance pavilion. The studio is undergoing restoration and will open to the public in late 2014. The museum's three gardens have recently been renovated and make a delightful place for a stroll away from the tourist bustle.

Musée National Gustave Moreau

14 rue de la Rochefoucauld, 9th (01.48. 74.38.50, www.musee-moreau.fr). M° Trinité. **Open** 10am-12.45pm, 2-5.15pm Mon, Wed, Thur; 10am-5.15pm Fri-Sun. **Admission** €5; free-€3 reductions. **Map** p89 A4 ❺

This wonderful museum combines the private apartment of Symbolist painter Gustave Moreau (1825-98) with the vast gallery he built to display his work. Don't miss the trippy *Jupiter et Sémélé* on the second floor.

Musée de la Vie Romantique

Hôtel Scheffer-Renan, 16 rue Chaptal, 9th (01.55.31.95.67, www.vie-romantique.paris.fr). M° Blanche or St-Georges. **Open** 10am-6pm Tue-Sun. **Admission** free. *Exhibitions* prices vary. **Map** p89 A3 ❻

When Dutch artist Ary Scheffer lived in this small villa, the area teemed with composers, writers and artists. Aurore Dupin, Baronne Dudevant (George Sand) was a guest at Scheffer's soirées and the museum is devoted to Sand, although the watercolours, jewels and plastercast of her right arm that she left behind show little of her ideas or affairs.

Sacré-Coeur

35 rue du Chevalier-de-la-Barre, 18th (01.53.41.89.00, www.sacre-coeur-montmartre.com). M° Abbesses or Anvers. **Open** *Basilica* 6am-11pm daily. *Crypt & dome* Winter 10am-5.45pm daily. Summer 9am-6.45pm daily. **Admission** free. *Crypt & dome* €8. **Map** p89 C2 ❼

Work on this enormous mock Romano-Byzantine edifice began in 1877. It was commissioned after the nation's defeat by Prussia in 1870, voted for by the Assemblée Nationale and built from public subscription. Finally completed in 1914, it was consecrated in 1919. The interior boasts lavish mosaics.

Eating & drinking

Big Fernand

55 rue du Faubourg Poissonnière, 9th (01.73.70.51.52, www.bigfernand.com). M° Cadet or Poissonnière. **Open** noon-2.30pm, 7.30-10.30pm Mon-Sat. €€. **Burgers.** **Map** p89 C4 ❽

This trendy takeaway burger joint has been dubbed '*l'atelier du hamburger*' – 'the hamburger workshop'. The concept is for customers to build their own burgers, selecting a combination of meat (beef, chicken, lamb or veal), cheese (goat's cheese, saint nectaire, tomme de savoie), grilled vegetables, spices and an array of sauces.

Buvette Gastrothèque

NEW *28 rue Henry Monnier, 9th (01.44.63.41.71, www.ilovebuvette. com). M° Pigalle or Saint-Georges.*

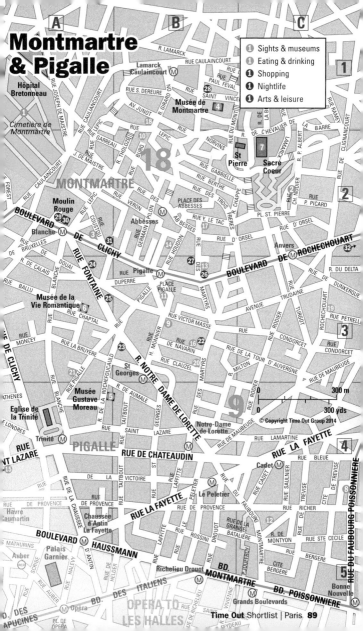

Montmartre & Pigalle

A   **B**   **C**

Sights & museums
Eating & drinking
Shopping
Nightlife
Arts & leisure

1
2
3
4
5

Hôpital
Bretonneau

Cimetière de
Montmartre

R. LAMARCK
RUE CAULAINCOURT
Lamarck
Caulaincourt
RUE
PAUL FEVAL
SAINT VINCENT
Musée de
Montmartre
AV. JUNOT
RUE S. DEREURE
RUE CAULAINCOURT
RUE JOSEPH DE MAISTRE

18
MONTMARTRE
RUE CAULAINCOURT
RUE LEPIC
RUE THOLOZE
BIRD
RUE GARREAU
J. DE MAISTRE
RUE TOURLAQUE

NORVINS
St
Pierre
Sacré
Coeur
R. DE LA BARRE
R. DE CHEVALIER DE LA BARRE
CLIGNANCOURT
R. P. ALBERT
R. DU MONT CENIS

RUE GABRIELLE
RUE DES
RUE BERTHE
RUE DES TROIS FRERES
PLACE DES
ABBESSES
RUE CHAPPE
R. C. NODIER
RUE CH. PICARD
PL. ST. PIERRE

Moulin
Rouge
BOULEVARD
Blanche
DE CLICHY
Abbesses
RUE VERON
RUE DES ABBESSES
RUE Y. LE TAC
RUE D'ORSEL
RUE D'ORSEL
Anvers
BOULEVARD DE ROCHECHOUART

RUE FONTAINE
Pigalle
PLACE PIGALLE
DUPERRE
RUE DUNKERQUE
R. DU DELTA
RUE DE MAUBEUGE

Musée de la
Vie Romantique
RUE CHAPTAL
AVENUE
TRUDAINE
RUE CONDORCET
RUE PETRELL
ROCHECHOUART

RUE MONCEY
RUE LA BRUYERE
RUE VICTOR MASSE
RUE DE NAVARIN
RUE CONDORCET
RUE DE LA TOUR D'AUVERGNE
RUE MILTON
RUE CLAUZEL
RUE DES MARTYRS
RUE RODIER

St
Georges
Musée
Gustave
Moreau
R. NOTRE DAME DE LORETTE
R. DE AUMALE

9

Notre-Dame
de Lorette
RUE DE MAUBEUGE
RUE LAMARTINE
RUE LA FAYETTE

Eglise de
la Trinité
Trinité
PIGALLE
RUE DE CHATEAUDIN
RUE LA FAYETTE
RUE BLEUE
Cadet
RUE SAULNIER
CITE DE TREVISE

RUE LAZARE
RUE DE PROVENCE
Le Peletier
RUE RICHER
RUE STE CECILE

Havre
Caumartin
Chaussée
d'Antin
La Fayette
RUE LAFFITTE
RUE DU FAUBOURG
RUE ROSSINI
R. DE
MONTYON
CITE
BERGERE
RUE DE LA GRANGE BATALIERE
BERGERE

BOULEVARD HAUSSMANN
Palais
Garnier
Auber
Opéra
Richelieu Drouot
BD. MONTMARTRE
BD. POISSONNIERE
Bonne
Nouvelle

OPÉRA TO
LES HALLES
Grands Boulevards

© Copyright Time Out Group 2014

300 m
300 yds

Buvette Gastrothèque p88

Open 10am-midnight Tue-Sun. €.
Bistro. **Map** p89 B3 ❾

Jody Williams, a purebred New Yorker, has brought a bit of Greenwich Village to Pigalle. There's nothing ostentatious about the interior, all rough brick walls and wooden tables that sit well around the huge marble bar. The menu is a selection of small plates and fresh sandwiches, with an interesting wine list arranged by region.

Le Coq Rico

98 rue Lepic, 18th (01.42.59.82.89, www.lecoqrico.com). M° Abbesses or Lamarck-Caulincourt. **Open** noon-2.30pm, 7.30-11pm daily. €€€. **Bistro**. **Map** p89 B1 ❿

Antoine Westermann's new venture is a classy 'bistrotisserie' where comfort food is transformed into gourmet treats – gooey boiled egg comes with crunchy soldiers and truffle-infused butter. There's a list of poultry suppliers at the bottom of the menu, a transparency that appeals to health-conscious locals.

Dirty Dick

NEW *10 rue Frochot, 9th (no phone). M° Pigalle.* **Open** 7pm-2am daily.
Bar. **Map** p89 B3 ⓫

SoPi (South Pigalle) welcomes another hip venue. A former hostess bar (they've kept the name, evidently), the only phallic elements now are Polynesian totems scattered throughout the bar, which has a kitsch, exotic 'tiki' vibe and lots of free-flowing rum. The flower-shirted barmen cater to the crowds with a list of 20 or so cocktails served in giant shells or miniature volcanoes.

Les Fils à Maman

7 bis Rue Geoffroy-Marie, 9th (01.48.24. 59.39, www.lesfilsamaman.com). M° Grands Boulevards. **Open** 11.30am-2.30pm, 7-11pm Mon-Fri; 7-11pm Sat. €€. **Bistro**. **Map** p89 C5 ⓬

In the area near the Folies Bergère a band of five 'mothers' boys' has created a restaurant evoking their mums' home cooking. Even the mums get into the kitchen on the first Tuesday of the month to turn out *blanquette de veau*, chicken cordon bleu and Nutella-flavoured puddings.

La Fourmi

74 rue des Martyrs, 18th (01.42.64. 70.35). M° Pigalle. **Open** 8am-2am Mon-Thur; 8am-4am Fri, Sat; 10am-2am Sun. **Bar**. **Map** p89 B3 ⓭

La Fourmi is an old bistro that has been converted for today's tastes, with picture windows lighting the spacious interior. The classic zinc bar counter is crowned by industrial lights, and an excellent music policy and cool clientele ensure a pile of flyers.

Le Kremlin

NEW *6 rue André Antoine, 18th (no phone). M° Abbesses or Pigalle.* **Open** 6pm-2am daily. **Bar**. **Map** p89 B3 ⓮

This new Russian outpost has been heaving from the word go – it's difficult to navigate a path to the bar to order one of the fantastic imported vodkas or original cocktails. Once you've finally got hold of your drink, pass an eye over the sumptuous communist red decor, punctuated with propaganda posters and Soviet-style furniture.

Lazare Brasserie

NEW *Parvis de la Gare St Lazare, 8th (01.44.90.80.80, www.lazare-paris.fr). M° St Lazare.* **Open** 7.30am-midnight daily. €€€. **Brasserie**. **Map** p89 A4 ⓯

See box p93.

La Maison Mère

4 rue de Navarin, 9th (01.42.81.11.00, www.lamaisonmere.fr). M° Pigalle or Saint-Georges. **Open** noon-2.30pm, 7.30-11pm Mon-Thur; noon-2.30pm, 7.30-11.30pm Fri; noon-4pm, 7.30-11.30pm Sat; noon-4pm Sun. €€. **Bistro**. **Map** p89 B3 ⓰

Forget any ideas of a traditional French kitchen: this place is more Mom than Mère. Embrace, instead, the New York-style decor and menu, with crab cake, Brooklyn platters, Long Island platters and so on. The five burgers will delight enthusiasts. The house fries could be better and the whole doesn't come cheap, but nobody's perfect. Friendly service, a good wine selection and top cheesecake all go a long way towards sweetening the bill.

Le Miroir

94 rue des Martyrs, 18th (01.46.06. 50.73). Mº Abbesses. **Open** noon-2pm, 7.30-10.30pm Tue-Sat. €€. **Bistro**. Map p89 B2 ⑰

This friendly bistro is a welcome addition to the neighbourhood. Big mirrors, red banquettes and a glass ceiling at the back give it character, while the professional food and service reflect the owners' haute cuisine training.

Le Moulin de la Galette

83 rue Lepic, 18th (01.46.06.84.77, www.lemoulindelagalette.eu). Mº Notre-Dame-de-Lorette. **Open** noon-11pm daily. €€. **Bistro**. Map p89 B1 ⑱

The Butte Montmartre was once dotted with windmills, and this survivor houses a chic restaurant. It's hard to imagine a more picturesque setting in Montmartre. The kitchen makes an effort with dishes such as foie gras with melting beetroot or suckling pig.

Pétrelle

34 rue Pétrelle, 9th (01.42.82.11.02, www.petrelle.fr). Mº Anvers. **Open** 8-10pm Tue-Sat. Closed 4wks July/Aug & 1wk Dec. €€. **Bistro**. Map p89 C3 ⑲

Jean-Luc André is as inspired a decorator as he is a cook, and the quirky charm of his dining room has made it popular with fashion designers and film stars. The no-choice menu is huge value (marinated sardines with tomato relish, rabbit with roasted vegetables, deep purple poached figs).

Rose Bakery

46 rue des Martyrs, 9th (01.42.82. 12.80). Mº Notre-Dame-de-Lorette. **Open** 9am-6pm Tue-Sun. €. **Café**. Map p89 B3 ⑳

This English-themed café stands out for the quality of its ingredients, as well as the too-good-to-be-true puddings.

Rouge Passion

14 rue Jean-Baptiste Pigalle, 9th (01.42. 85.07.62, www.rouge-passion.fr). Mº Pigalle or St Georges. **Open** noon-3pm Mon; noon-3pm, 7pm-midnight Tue-Fri; 7pm-midnight Sat; 11.30am-4pm Sun. Closed 3wks Aug. **Wine bar**. Map p89 A3 ㉑

Two bright upstarts are behind this venture. Offering a long list of wines, a small but mouthwatering selection of hot dishes, salads, cheese and saucisson platters and decor that's satisfyingly vintage, the formula is spot on.

Shopping

Arnaud Delmontel

39 rue des Martyrs, 9th (01.48.78. 29.33, www.arnaud-delmontel.com). Mº St-Georges. **Open** 7am-8.30pm Mon, Wed-Sun. Map p89 B3 ㉒

Delmontel's Renaissance bread is one of the finest in Paris. He puts the same skill into his almond croissants and *tarte au citron à l'ancienne*.

Causses

55 rue Notre-Dame de Lorette, 9th (01.53.16.10.10, www.causses.org). Mº Pigalle or Saint Georges. **Open** 10am-9pm Mon-Sat. Map p89 B3 ㉓

SoPi's (South Pigalle) new *alimentation générale extraordinaire* feels like an urban farm shop, offering a winning formula of quality seasonal produce, gourmet preserves, breads, salads and sandwiches, plus British treats.

La Fausse Boutique

32 rue Pierre Fontaine, 9th (09.52. 43.25.71, www.lafausseboutique. com). Mº Blanche or Pigalle. **Open** 2-8pm Mon; 11am-8pm Tue-Sat. Map p89 A3 ㉔

The False Boutique is an unusual spot – it's half-office, half-retail store. You might find offbeat tourist guides

First class food

Lazare is no ordinary station brasserie.

The biggest buzz on the Paris food scene in 2013 wasn't caused by an haute cuisine restaurant or a primped-up bistro, but by a railway brasserie. **Lazare** (see p91), in the eponymous station, is run by star chef Eric Frechon, who won the Hôtel Bristol's restaurant its third Michelin star and opened the Mini Palais in 2010. Gare St Lazare was the station that originally brought Frechon to Paris from his native Normandy, and he calls the restaurant a '*retour aux sources*' – a return to the roots of country cooking from all over France.

Entering from the recently revamped station, the centrepiece is a magnificent copper bar. A blackboard above the bar lists different 'arrivals' – tea with girlfriends, afterwork drinks, dinner with friends – in the style of a timetable, each claiming to be '*à l'heure*'. To the left are floor-to-ceiling shelves piled high with

plates and jugs, while clusters of globe lights make for a modern take on traditional brasserie decor. A glance around the tables shows a real cross-section of Paris life – not just foodies but families, first-daters and after-workers.

As befits a station brasserie, food arrives swiftly – a starter of salmon 'marinated like a herring' on warm potatoes, perhaps, or a whole cold mackerel in white wine gelée with horseradish sauce; bread is plonked on the table in its paper bag with artful nonchalance.

Then the main courses arrive, and you see what all the fuss is about as you tuck into the likes of grilled pork belly on a bed of turnip choucroute. Prices are no station buffet bargain, but daily specials are €19 (think *pot-au-feu* or beef *bourgignon*). Cheeses from Claire Griffon include stunning rocamadour and comté, perfect with a bottle of Morgon.

such as *Paris à Gratter* (modelled on a scratchcard, where you scratch to reveal monuments) and satirical board games such as Méditations Foireuses (half-assed meditations), produced by a collective of designers.

Nightlife

Le Bus Palladium

6 rue Pierre Fontaine, 9th (01.45.26. 80.35, www.lebuspalladium.com). M° St-Georges, Pigalle or Blanche. **Open** Concerts 9pm-12.30am. *Club* 12.30-5am Thur-Sat. **Map** p89 A3 ㉕
This legendary rock venue is back on the map with a vintage house vibe somewhere between retro rockabilly and punk psychedelia.

La Cigale/La Boule Noire

120 bd de Rochechouart, 18th (01.49.25.81.75, www.lacigale.fr). M° Anvers or Pigalle. **Open** times vary. **Map** p89 B3 ㉖
One of Paris's finest venues, the horseshoe-shaped theatre La Cigale is linked to more cosy venue La Boule Noire, which is good for catching cultish visiting acts.

Le Divan du Monde

75 rue des Martyrs, 18th (01.40.05. 06.99, www.divandumonde.com). M° Abbesses or Pigalle. **Open** times vary. **Map** p89 B3 ㉗
After a drink in the Fourmi opposite, pop over to the Divan for one-off parties and events. Upstairs specialises in VJ events, and downstairs holds dub, reggae, funk and world club nights.

Au Lapin Agile

22 rue des Saules, 18th (01.46.06.85.87, www.au-lapin-agile.com). M° Lamarck Caulaincourt. **Shows** 9pm-1am Tue-Sun. No credit cards. **Map** p89 B1 ㉘
The prices have gone up, tourists outnumber the locals and they sell their own compilation CDs these days, but that's all that seems to have changed since this bar first opened in 1860.

La Machine du Moulin Rouge

90 bd de Clichy, 18th (01.53.41.88.89, www.lamachinedumoulinrouge.com). M° Blanche. **Open** times vary. **Map** p89 A2 ㉙
This three-floor bar/club/live venue has had a makeover and is now reborn with a dash of decadence. The main dancefloor, La Chaufferie, used to be the Moulin Rouge's boiler room.

Moulin Rouge

82 bd de Clichy, 18th (01.53.09.82.82, www.moulin-rouge.com). M° Blanche. **Dinner** 7pm. **Shows** 9pm, 11pm daily. **Map** p89 A2 ㉚
Toulouse-Lautrec posters, plus glittery lamp-posts and fake trees lend tacky charm to this revue, while 60 Doriss dancers cavort with faultless synchronisation. Costumes are flamboyant and the *entr'acte* acts funny.

Les Trois Baudets

64 bd de Clichy, 18th (01.42.62.33.33, www.lestroisbaudets.com). M° Pigalle. **Open** times vary. **Map** p89 A2 ㉛
With a 250-seater theatre, an enviable sound system, two bars and a restaurant, this new concert hall encourages *chanson française* and other musical genres (rock, electro, folk and slam).

Arts & leisure

Le Louxor

NEW *170 bd Magenta, 10th (01.44. 63.96.96, www.cinemalouxor.fr). M° Barbès Rochechouart.* **Open** times vary. No credit cards. **Map** p89 C2 ㉜
Opened in 1921 and once a temple of silent cinema, the art deco Louxor fell on hard times after World War II and became a drug den, 1980s club and gay disco before being abandoned for 25 years. It reopened triumphantly as a cinema in April 2013, with a new brief to promote cultural, artistic and educational projects. You can admire the fabulous architecture from the handsome third-floor bar.

Parc des Buttes-Chaumont p96

North-east Paris

The Canal St-Martin's iron footbridges and tree-shaded quays formed the backdrop for some of *Amélie*'s most atmospheric scenes, and nowadays this 19th-century waterway draws a hipster crowd to its shabby-chic bars and bistros. Heading north along the canal, the must-visit den of artistic creation is Point Ephemère. From here the canal widens into the Bassin de la Villette and Canal de l'Ourcq, famed for its twin MK2 cinemas, retro-futurist 1970s tower blocks and watersports during Paris-Plages.

Once you've crossed the quirky 1885 hydraulic lift bridge, Pont de Crimée, you're in Parc de la Villette territory. Futuristic and cutting-edge, this is where you can visit major science and music museums, picnic on the lawns, and take in concerts at major venues such as the Cité de la Musique, Cabaret Sauvage, Trabendo and Zénith (and Jean Nouvel's Philharmonie come 2015).

Sights & museums

Canauxrama

13 quai de la Loire, 19th (01.42.39. 15.00, www.canauxrama.fr). **Tickets** €16; free-€12 reductions. **Map** p97 C1 **1**
Take an alternative trip up the city's second waterway, the Canal St-Martin. The tree-lined canal is a pretty sight, and the cruise even goes underground, where the tunnel walls are enlivened by a light show.

Gare du Nord

Rue de Dunkerque, 10th. Mº Gare du Nord. **Map** p97 A2 **2**
The grandest of the great 19th-century train stations (and Eurostar terminal since 1994) was designed by Jacques Hittorff between 1861 and 1864. The conventional stone façade, with Ionic capitals and statues representing the towns served by the station, hides a vast iron-and-glass vault. The Gare du Nord is one of the busiest stations in Europe.

Musée de la Musique

Cité de la Musique, 221 av Jean-Jaurès, 19th (01.44.84.44.84, www.cite-musique. fr). M° Porte de Pantin. **Open** noon-6pm Tue-Sat; 10am-6pm Sun. **Admission** €7; free-€5.60 reductions. **Map** p97 E1 **3**

This innovative museum houses a collection of instruments from the old Conservatoire, interactive computers and scale models of opera houses and concert halls. Visitors are supplied with an audio guide in a choice of languages, and the musical commentary is a joy, playing the appropriate instrument as you approach each exhibit.

Parc des Buttes-Chaumont

Rue Botzaris, rue Manin, rue de Crimée, 19th. M° Buttes Chaumont. **Open** Oct-Apr 7am-8pm daily. May-Sept 7am-10pm daily. **Map** p97 E2 **4**

Set high up in Belleville and often missed by weekenders keen not to stray too far from the tourist loop, this is one of the city's most magical spots. The park, with its meandering paths, waterfalls, temples and vertical cliffs, was designed by Adolphe Alphand for Haussmann, and was opened as part of the celebrations for the Universal Exhibition in 1867. It was created on the site of a former gypsum quarry. After lounging with the locals, head for the park's Rosa Bonheur *guinguette* (www.rosabonheur.fr). Open till midnight, it makes the perfect place to sip an *apéro* and take in the stunning views of the city below. The park is undergoing renovations until 2015, but will remain open throughout.

Eating & drinking

Le 9b

68 bd de la Villette, 19th (01.40.18. 08.10, www.le9b.com). M° Colonel Fabien. **Open** 10am-2am daily. **Bar**. **Map** p97 C3 **5**

Does the name remind you of anything? It's old favourite Le 9 Billards. This bar – which preceded Les Disquaires on rue Jean-Pierre Timbaud – has been

reborn on boulevard de la Villette. It's full to bursting each night with a blend of electro, hip hop, funk and rock on the crammed dancefloor, and cocktails and couscous on the menu.

Bar Ourcq

68 quai de la Loire, 19th (01.42.40. 12.26). M° Laumière. **Open** *Summer* 3pm-midnight Wed, Thur; 3pm-2am Fri, Sat; 3-10pm Sun. *Winter* 3pm-2am Sat; 3-10pm Sun. No credit cards. **Bar**. **Map** p97 D1 **6**

This was one of the first hip joints to pitch up on the Canal de l'Ourcq, with an embankment broad enough to accommodate *pétanque* games (ask at the bar) and a cluster of deckchairs. The cabin-like interior is pretty cosy, and drinks are listed in a hit parade of prices, starting with €2.50 for a *demi*.

Chez Jeanette

47 rue du Fbg-St Denis, 10th (01.47. 70.30.89, www.chezjeanette.com). M° Château d'Eau or Strasbourg St-Denis. **Open** 9am-1.45am daily. €. **Café**. **Map** p97 A3 **7**

When she sold her café a few years ago, Jeanette handed over to the young team from Chez Justine. Now the awful 1940s lights, the tobacco-stained wallpaper depicting the Moulin Rouge and the PVC-covered banquettes have been rewarded with a Fooding prize for decor, and the café is one of Paris's hippest spots for an aperitif.

Chez Prune

36 rue Beaurepaire, 10th (01.42.41. 30.47). M° Jacques Bonsergent. **Open** 8am-2am Mon-Sat; 10am-2am Sun. **Bar**. **Map** p97 B3 **8**

This supremely hip retro café, with high ceilings and low lighting, sticks to a blissfully simple formula: groups of friends crowd around the banquettes, picking at cheese or meat platters. Mostly, though, they come for a few leisurely drinks or an *apéro* before heading to one of the late-night venues in the area.

North-east Paris

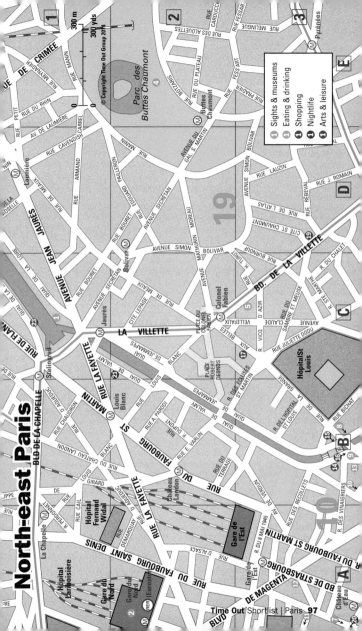

1 | **2** | **3**

E

D

C

B

A

Parc des Buttes Chaumont

Buttes Chaumont

19

Colonel Fabien

LA VILLETTE

Louis Blanc

Hôpital St Louis

Stalingrad

Jaurès

Hôpital Fernand Widal

Château Landon

Gare de l'Est

Gare du Nord

Gare de l'Est

La Chapelle

Hôpital Lariboisière

Eurostar

Sights & museums
Eating & drinking
Shopping
Nightlife
Arts & leisure

300 m
300 yds

© Copyright Time Out Group 2014

Le Cinquante

50 rue de Lancry, 10th (01.42.02.36.83).
Mº Jacques Bonsergent. **Open** 5.30pm-
2am daily. Closed Aug. **Wine bar.**
Map p97 B3 ⑨

The bare brick, Formica and framed
'50s ads of this funky venue attract an
inner circle of regulars. These days, it's
established enough to produce its own
T-shirts and customised bar stools.
Reasonable prices – half-litre pitchers
of sauvignon, Brouilly and Chablis in
the €10 range – attract a mixed bag of
tastes and generations. The two rooms
behind the main bar are set aside for
dining (affordable classics) and music
(generally acoustic).

Le Coq

NEW *12 rue du Château d'Eau, 10th*
(01.42.40.85.68, www.barlecoq.com).
Mº Jacques Bonsergent. **Open** 6pm-2am
Tue-Sat. **Bar. Map** p97 B3 ⑩

Here's a cocktail bar that gives its
cutting-edge neighbours a run for
their money. Tony Conigliaro, joint
owner with Thierry Daniel and Eric
Fossard, knows what he's doing: he
also opened 69 Colebrook Row and
Zetter Townhouse in London. There
are 12 mixes on the menu, at €11 a
throw. The walls host exhibitions of
work by 1970s-influenced artists, coupled with a soundtrack ranging from
Serge Gainsbourg to Grace Jones via
Fela Kuti. The shelves behind the bar,
stocked with bottles of chartreuse, ver-
mouth, cognac and other rare liquors,
enhance the speakeasy vibe.

Le Fantôme

NEW *36 rue de Paradis, 10th (09.66.*
87.11.20, www.lefanto.me). Mº
Poissonnière or Château d'Eau. **Open**
11am-2am Mon-Fri; 6pm-2am Sat.
Bar. Map p97 A3 ⑪

Le Fantôme is the new venue from the
crew behind Le Baron. The enormous
space is a fantasy venue for fans of
retrogaming: as well as a huge bar,
the Fantôme offers a fistful of arcade
games, a Pacman table and table
football. Drinks-wise, the mixologist
is an inspired Californian called David
West who has produced a list of five
inventive cocktails to go with the menu
of hefty pizzas.

La Fidélité

12 rue de la Fidélité, 10th (01.47.
70.19.34, www.lafidelite.com). Mº
Gare de L'Est. **Open** 8pm-1am Mon-Sat.
€€. Brasserie. Map p97 A3 ⑫

There was a huge buzz when La Clique
took this place over, and so far the
brasserie is setting a decent standard
with its elegant styling and good, well-
priced food – the lunchtime prix fixe is
a bargain and the *joue de boeuf* is sublime. On Thursdays and Fridays, the
basement morphs into a jukebox bar.

Le Verre Volé

67 rue de Lancry, 10th (01.48.03.
17.34). Mº Jacques Bonsergent. **Open**
9.30am-1am daily. Closed Aug. **€€.**
Bistro. Map p97 B3 ⑬

This organic-only *cave à vins* doubles
up as a minuscule wine bar and
restaurant. Although wine is the focus,
you're obliged to eat; a hearty sausage
and mash will set you back around
€15. Purists who would prefer a simple
snack with their *bon vin* should opt for
a plate of charcuterie and cheese. For
lunch on the hoof, head for the Verre
Volé's deli offshoot (54 rue de la Folie-
Méricourt), which serves gourmet
sandwiches such as calf's head pâté,
gribiche sauce and watercress.

Shopping

Antoine et Lili

95 quai de Valmy, 10th (01.40.37.41.55,
www.antoineetlili.com). Mº Jacques
Bonsergent. **Open** 11am-7pm Mon, Sun;
11am-8pm Tue-Sat. **Map** p97 B3 ⑭

Antoine et Lili's cutesy fuchsia-pink,
custard-yellow and apple-green shop-
fronts are a new raver's dream. The
Canal St-Martin 'village' comprises
womenswear, a kitsch home decoration boutique and childrenswear.

Culture(s)

46 rue de Lancry, 10th (01.48.03.58.71).
Mº Jacques Bonsergent or République.
Open 11am-2pm, 3-7pm Tue-Sat.
Map p97 B3 ⑮
Located in an airy loft-style studio, this unusual, quirky florist combines exotic flowers, trees and garden-themed items, such as floral printed rain hats. Truly original.

Du Pain et des Idées

*34 rue Yves Toudic, 10th (01.42.
40.44.52, www.dupainetdesidees.
com). Mº Jacques Bonsergent.*
Open 6.45am-8pm Mon-Fri.
Map p97 B3 ⑯
Christophe Vasseur is a former winner of the Gault-Millau prize for Best Bakery. Among his specialities are Le Pagnol aux Pommes, bread studded with apple (skin on), raisins and orange flower water.

Viveka Bergström

*23 rue de la Grange aux Belles, 10th
(01.40.03.04.92, www.viveka-bergstrom.
com). Mº Colonel Fabien.* **Open** noon-7pm Tue-Sat. **Map** p97 B3 ⑰
The daughter of Saab's aeroplane designer during the 1950s, Viveka Bergström turns out a wonderful selection of slinky tassel necklaces, oversized beaten gold rings and brooches, as well as conversation starters such as the angel-wing bracelet and a necklace featuring a map of Paris.

Nightlife

Le Cabaret Sauvage

*59 Bd Macdonald, 19th (01.42.09.
03.09, www.cabaretsauvage.com).
Mº Porte de la Villette.* **Open** 9pm-dawn, days vary. **Map** p97 E1 ⑱
A stylish venue that's taken over by outside promoters for occasional club nights. There often used to be a world music element, but this has recently been superseded by electronic and drum 'n' bass nights. Check the website for full details.

Café Chéri(e)

*44 bd de la Villette, 19th (01.42.02.
02.05). Mº Belleville.* **Open** noon-2am daily. **Map** p97 D3 ⑲
A popular DJ bar, especially in summer when people flock to enjoy the terrace. Expect anything from DJ Jet Boy's electro punk to rock, funk, hip hop, rare groove, indie, jazz and '80s classics.

New Morning

*7-9 rue des Petites-Ecuries, 10th (01.45.
23.51.41, www.newmorning.com).*
Map p97 A3 ⑳
One of the best places for the latest cutting-edge jazz exponents, with a policy that also embraces *chanson*, blues, world and sophisticated pop.

Point Ephémère

*200 quai de Valmy, 10th (01.40.34.
02.48, www.pointephemere.org).
Mº Jaurès or Louis Blanc.* **Open** noon-2am Mon-Sat; noon-9pm Sun.
Map p97 C2 ㉑
This is a classy affair, bringing together local rock, jazz and world gigs with a decent restaurant, dance and recording studios and exhibitions.

Arts & leisure

Hammam Med Centre

*43-45 rue Petit, 19th (01.42.02.31.05,
www.hammammed.com). Mº Ourcq.*
Open *Women* 11am-10pm Mon-Fri;
9am-7pm Sun. *Mixed (swimwear
required)* 10am-9pm Sat. **Map** p97 E1 ㉒
This hammam is hard to beat – spotless mosaic-tiled surroundings, flowered sarongs and a relaxing pool.

MK2 Bibliothèque

*14 quai de la Seine, 19th (08.92.69.
84.84, www.mk2.fr). Mº Stalingrad.*
Open times vary. **Map** p97 C1 ㉓
MK2's mini multiplex on the quai de la Loire was seen as a key factor in the social rise of this part of town. Now the chain has opened a multiplex across the water, with a boat shuttling from one to the other.

PARIS BY AREA

Centre Pompidou

The Marais & Eastern Paris

Ww hereas historic *quartiers* like Montmartre and St-Germain-des-Prés are well past their heyday, the Marais has been luckier, and for the last two decades has been one of the hippest parts of the city, stuffed with modish hotels, boutiques and restaurants – in no small part due to its popularity with the gay crowd. It's also prime territory for arts-lovers, thanks to its generous quotient of museums. The Marais' neighbour to the west is Beaubourg, whose focal point is the iconic Centre Pompidou, with the city's Hôtel de Ville to the south. Further east is Oberkampf, a nightlife hub for the last decade.

Sights & museums

Atelier Brancusi

Piazza Beaubourg, 4th (01.44.78.12.33, www.centrepompidou.fr). Mº Hôtel de Ville or Rambuteau. **Open** 2-6pm Mon, Wed-Sun. **Admission** free. **Map** p102 A2 ❶

When Constantin Brancusi died in 1957, he left his studio and its contents to the state, and it was later rebuilt by the Centre Pompidou. His fragile works in wood and plaster, the endless columns and streamlined bird forms show how he revolutionised sculpture.

Centre Pompidou (Musée National d'Art Moderne)

Rue St-Martin, 4th (01.44.78.12.33, www.centrepompidou.fr). Mº Hôtel de Ville or Rambuteau. **Open** 11am-10pm (last entry 8pm) Mon, Wed-Sun (until 11pm some exhibitions). **Admission** *Museum & exhibitions* €11-€13; free-€10 reductions. **Map** p102 A2 ❷

The Centre Pompidou (or 'Beaubourg') holds the largest collection of modern art in Europe. For the main collection, buy tickets on the ground floor and take the escalators to level four for post-1960s art. Level five spans 1905 to 1960. Masterful ensembles let you see the span of Matisse's career on canvas and in bronze, the variety of Picasso's invention, and the development of cubic orphism by Sonia and Robert Delaunay. Others on the hits list include Braque, Duchamp, Mondrian, Malevich, Kandinsky, Dali, Giacometti, Ernst, Miró, Calder, Magritte, Rothko and Pollock. Video art and installations by the likes of Mathieu Mercier and Dominique Gonzalez-Foerster are in a room given over to *nouvelle création*.

Cimetière du Père-Lachaise

Bd de Ménilmontant, 20th (01.55.25. 82.10). M° Père-Lachaise. **Open** *6 Nov- 15 Mar* 8am-5.30pm Mon-Fri; 8.30am- 5.30pm Sat; 9am-5.30pm Sun. *16 Mar-5 Nov* 8am-6pm Mon-Fri; 8.30am-6pm Sat; 9am-6pm Sun & hols. **Map** p103 F2 ❸
Père-Lachaise is the celebrity cemetery – it has the mortal remains of almost anyone French, talented and dead that you care to mention. Not even French, for that matter. Creed and nationality have never prevented entry: you just had to have lived or died in Paris or have an allotted space in a family tomb. Highlights include Chopin's medallion portrait and the muse of Music, Jim Morrison's grave, plus neighbours La Fontaine and Molière, who knew each other in real life and now share the same fenced-off plot.

Hôtel de Ville

29 rue de Rivoli, 4th (01.42.76.40.40, www.paris.fr). M° Hôtel de Ville. **Open** 10am-7pm Mon-Sat. *Tours* by appointment only. **Map** p102 A3 ❹
The palatial, multi-purpose Hôtel de Ville is the heart of the city administration. Free exhibitions are held in the Salon d'Accueil (10am-6pm Mon-Fri). The rest of the building is accessible by weekly tours (book in advance).

Maison Européenne de la Photographie

5-7 rue de Fourcy, 4th (01.44.78.75.00, www.mep-fr.org). M° St-Paul. **Open** 11am-8pm Wed-Sun. **Admission** €8; free-€4.50 reductions. **Map** p102 B4 ❺

Probably the capital's best photography exhibition space, hosting retrospectives by Larry Clark and Martine Barrat, along with work by emerging photographers. The building, an airy mansion with a modern extension, contains a huge permanent collection.

Maison de Victor Hugo

Hôtel de Rohan-Guéménée, 6 pl des Vosges, 4th (01.42.72.10.16, www. musee-hugo.paris.fr). M° Bastille or St-Paul. **Open** 10am-6pm Tue-Sun. **Admission** free. *Exhibitions* prices vary. **Map** p102 C4 ❻
Victor Hugo lived here from 1833 to 1848, and today the house is a museum devoted to the great man. On display are his first editions, nearly 500 drawings and Hugo's home-made furniture.

Le Mémorial de la Shoah

17 rue Geoffroy-l'Asnier, 4th (01.42. 77.44.72, www.memorialdelashoah.org). M° Pont Marie or St-Paul. **Open** 10am- 6pm Mon-Wed, Fri, Sun; 10am-10pm Thur. *Research centre* 10am-5.30pm Mon-Wed, Fri, Sun; 10am-7.30pm Thur. **Admission** free. **Map** p102 A4 ❼
Airport-style security checks mean queues are likely, but don't let that put you off: the Mémorial de la Shoah is an impressively presented and moving memorial to the Holocaust. Enter via the Wall of Names, where limestone slabs are engraved with the first and last names of each of the 76,000 Jews deported from France from 1942 to 1944 with, as an inscription reminds the visitor, the say-so of the Vichy government. The basement-level exhibition documents the plight of French and European Jews.

Musée d'Art et d'Histoire du Judaïsme

Hôtel de St-Aignan, 71 rue du Temple, 3rd (01.53.01.86.60, www.mahj.org). M° Rambuteau. **Open** 11am-6pm Mon- Fri; 10am-6pm Sun. Closed Jewish hols. **Admission** €6.80; free-€4.50 reductions. **Map** p102 A2 ❽

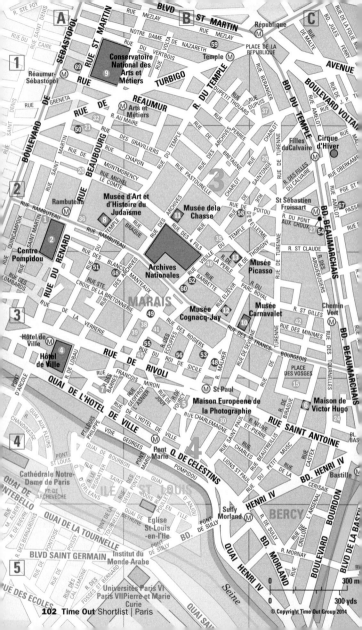

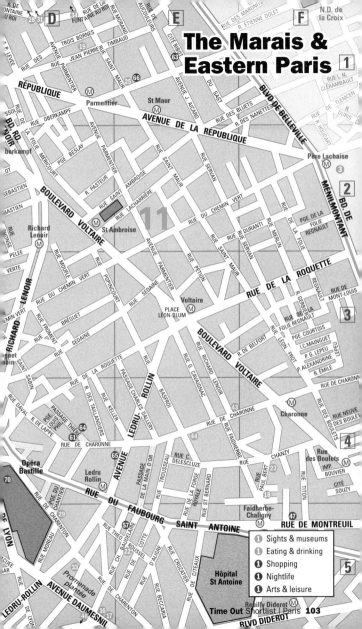

The Marais & Eastern Paris

Sights & museums
Eating & drinking
Shopping
Nightlife
Arts & leisure

This museum sprang from the collection of a private association formed in 1948 to safeguard Jewish heritage after the Holocaust. Displays illustrate ceremonies, rites and learning, and show how styles were adapted around the globe through examples of Jewish decorative arts. Photographic portraits of modern French Jews, with audio soundtrack, bring a contemporary edge. The Holocaust is marked by Boris Taslitzky's stark sketches from Buchenwald and Christian Boltanski's courtyard memorial to the Jews who lived in the building in 1939, 13 of whom died in the camps.

Musée des Arts et Métiers

60 rue Réaumur, 3rd (01.53.01.82.00, www.arts-et-metiers.net). M° Arts et Métiers. **Open** 10am-6pm Tue, Wed, Fri-Sun; 10am-9.30pm Thur. **Admission** €6.50; free-€4.50 reductions. **Map** p102 A1 ⑨

Europe's oldest science museum is a fascinating, well laid out and vast collection of treasures. Here are beautiful astrolabes, celestial spheres, barometers, clocks, some of Pascal's calculating devices, the Lumière brothers' cinematograph, an enormous 1938 TV set, and still larger exhibits like Cugnot's 1770 'Fardier' (the first powered vehicle) and Clément Ader's steam-powered Avion 3. The visit concludes in the chapel, which contains old cars, a scale model of the Statue of Liberty and the monoplane in which Blériot crossed the Channel in 1909.

Musée Carnavalet

23 rue de Sévigné, 3rd (01.44.59.58.58, www.carnavalet.paris.fr). M° St-Paul. **Open** 10am-6pm Tue-Sun. **Admission** free. *Exhibitions* prices vary. **Map** p102 B3 ⑩

Here, 140 rooms show the history of Paris, from pre-Roman Gaul to the 20th century. Original 16th-century rooms house Renaissance collections, with portraits by Clouet and furniture and pictures relating to the Wars of Religion. The first floor covers the period up to 1789 and neighbouring Hôtel Le Peletier de St-Fargeau covers the period from 1789 onwards. Displays relating to 1789 detail that year's convoluted politics and bloodshed, with prints and memorabilia, including a chunk of the Bastille. There are items belonging to Napoleon, a cradle given by the city to Napoleon III, and a reconstruction of Proust's bedroom.

Musée de la Chasse et de la Nature

Hôtel Guénégaud, 62 rue des Archives, 3rd (01.53.01.92.40, www.chassenature. org). M° Rambuteau. **Open** 11am-6pm Tue, Thur-Sun; 11am-9.30pm Wed. **Admission** €6; free-€4.50 reductions. **Map** p102 B2 ⑪

The history of hunting and man's larger relationship with the natural world are examined in such things as a series of wooden cabinets devoted to the owl, wolf, boar and stag, each equipped with a bleached skull, small drawers you can open to reveal droppings and footprint casts, and a binocular eyepiece you can peer into for footage of the animal in the wild.

Musée Cognacq-Jay

Hôtel Donon, 8 rue Elzévir, 3rd (01.40.27.07.21, www.cognacq-jay. paris.fr). M° St-Paul. **Open** 10am-6pm Tue-Sun. **Admission** free. **Map** p102 B3 ⑫

This museum houses a collection put together in the early 1900s by La Samaritaine founder Ernest Cognacq and his wife Marie-Louise Jay. They stuck mainly to 18th-century French works (Watteau, Fragonard, Boucher, Greuze and pastellist Quentin de la Tour), though some English artists (Reynolds, Romney, Lawrence) and Dutch and Flemish names (an early Rembrandt, Ruysdael, Rubens), plus Canalettos and Guardis, have managed to slip in. Pictures are displayed in panelled rooms with furniture, porcelain, tapestries and sculpture of the period.

Pablo's back

The Musée Picasso reopens after a lengthy revamp.

After being closed for five years, the **Musée Picasso** (see p106) is finally reopening in late 2014, tripled in size and with more works on show, yet keeping the domestic scale that has always made the museum so attractive and which, says head curator Anne Baldessari, is essential to appreciating Picasso's work.

For the first time, visitors will be able to roam the whole of the magnificent Hôtel Salé, built in 1659 for Pierre Aubert de Fontenay, collector of the *gabelle* or salt tax. Like many Marais mansions, the Hôtel Salé has had a chequered history, serving as an embassy and technical school before becoming a museum.

Architect Jean-François Bodin, working in collaboration with Monuments Historiques head architect Stéphane Thouin, was keen to respect not only the original 17th-century *hôtel particulier* but also the modern style of the prize-winning 1985 conversion by Roland Simounet, who intended 'to give it the atmosphere of a grand residence'.

The newly enlarged museum will still be centred on the grand Baroque stairway, but has now also colonised the two upper storeys previously occupied by offices and archives. A new entrance lobby and ticket desk have been created in the former stable wing lining the Cour d'Honneur, with technical services and educational facilities moved to garages in the garden.

While the old display seemed remarkably comprehensive, spanning the artist's prolific career from early Spanish paintings and his Blue period to bawdy late artist-and-model works, it was always short of space; only a fraction of the museum's vast holding of some 5,000 works has ever been on show. The new display will present around 550 works (rather than 450 in the past) in a less convoluted route, along with a series of temporary exhibitions deemed essential for getting locals to make return visits alongside the tourists.

The revamp has had its difficulties, finishing more than a year late, with a budget said to have more than doubled from the original estimate of €25 million amid tales of union discontent. But with the rehung display opening in autumn 2014 and the first temporary exhibitions scheduled for 2015, the revamped space should hopefully be worth the wait.

Musée National Picasso

Hôtel Salé, 5 rue de Thorigny, 3rd (01.42.71.25.21, www.musee-picasso.fr). M° Chemin Vert or St-Paul. **Map** p102 B3 ⑬
See box p105.

Place de la Bastille

4th/11th/12th. M° Bastille. **Map** p102 C4 ⑭
Nothing remains of the prison that, on 14 July 1789, was stormed by revolutionary forces. Parts of the foundations can be seen in the métro. The Colonne de Juillet, topped by a gilded *génie* of Liberty, is a monument to Parisians who fell during the revolutions of July 1830 and 1848.

Place des Vosges

4th. M° St-Paul. **Map** p102 C4 ⑮
Paris's first planned square was commissioned in 1605 by Henri IV and inaugurated by his son Louis XIII in 1612. With harmonious red-brick and stone arcaded façades and pitched slate roofs, it differs from the later pomp of the Bourbons. Mme de Sévigné, salon hostess and letter-writer, was born at no.1bis in 1626. At that time the garden hosted duels and trysts.

La Promenade Plantée

Av Daumesnil, 12th. M° Gare de Lyon or Ledru-Rollin. **Map** p103 D5 ⑯
The railway tracks atop the Viaduc des Arts were replaced in the late 1980s by a promenade planted with roses, shrubs and rosemary. It continues at ground level through the Jardin de Reuilly and the Jardin Charles Péguy on to the Bois de Vincennes.

Le Viaduc des Arts

15-121 av Daumesnil, 12th (www.viaducdesarts.fr). M° Gare de Lyon or Ledru-Rollin. **Map** p103 D5 ⑰
Glass-fronted workshops in the arches beneath the Promenade Plantée provide showrooms for furniture and fashion designers, picture-frame gilders, tapestry restorers, porcelain decorators, and chandelier, violin and flute makers.

Eating & drinking

Le 6 Paul Bert

NEW *6 rue Paul Bert, 11th (01.43.79.14.32). M° Charonne or Faidherbe Chaligny.* **Open** 7.30-11pm Mon; noon-2.30pm, 7.30-11pm Tue-Fri. **€€**. **Bistro**. **Map** p103 F4 ⑱
Bertrand Auboyneau (Bistrot Paul Bert, Ecailler du Bistrot) opened Le 6 Paul Bert in 2013. The menu revisits bistro jazz standards (tartare, herring, seasonal vegetables), but they're adapted according to the produce available in the market and the whims of the chef. You might enjoy roasted scallops with parsley and lemon, or a little quail with beetroot purée and a bouquet of pickled carrots. In the best bistro tradition, a short but well-chosen wine list offers bottles from all over France.

L'Alimentation Générale

64 rue Jean-Pierre-Timbaud, 11th (01.43.55.42.50, www.alimentation-generale.net). M° Parmentier. **Open** 7pm-2am Wed, Sun; 7pm-4am Thur-Sat. **Bar**. **Map** p103 D1 ⑲
The 'Grocery Store' is rue Jean-Pierre-Timbaud's answer to La Mercerie: it, too, is a big old space filled with junk. Cupboards of kitsch china and lampshades made from kitchen sponges are an inspired touch. The beer is equally well chosen – Flag, Sagres, Picon and Orval – and the house cocktail involves basil and figs.

L'Ambassade d'Auvergne

22 rue du Grenier-St-Lazare, 3rd (01.42.72.31.22, www.ambassade-auvergne.com). M° Arts et Métiers. **Open** noon-2pm, 7.30-10pm daily. **€€**. **Bistro**. **Map** p102 A2 ⑳
This rustic auberge is a fitting embassy for the hearty fare of central France. An order of cured ham comes as two hefty, plate-filling slices, and the salad bowl is chock-full of green lentils cooked in goose fat, studded with bacon and shallots. The *rôti d'agneau* arrives as a pot of melting chunks of

lamb in a rich sauce with a helping of tender white beans. Dishes arrive with the flagship *aligot*, the creamy, elastic mash-and-cheese concoction.

Andy Whaloo

69 rue des Gravilliers, 3rd (01.42.71. 20.38). M° Arts et Métiers. **Open** 7pm-2am Tue-Sat. **Bar**. Map p102 A2 ㉑
Andy Whaloo, created by the people behind its neighbour 404 and London's Momo and Sketch, is Arabic for 'I have nothing'. Bijou? This place brings new meaning to the word. The formidably fashionable crowd fights for coveted 'seats' on upturned paint cans; it's a beautifully designed venue, crammed with Moroccan artefacts and a spice rack of colours. It's quiet early on, with a surge around 9pm.

Le Baron Rouge

1 rue Théophile-Roussel, 12th (01.43. 43.14.32). M° Ledru-Rollin. **Open** 10am-2pm, 5-10pm Tue-Fri; 10am-10pm Sat; 10am-4pm Sun. **Bar**. Map p103 E5 ㉒
It sells wine, certainly – great barrels of the stuff are piled high and sold by the glass at very reasonable prices. But the Red Baron is not just a wine bar – more a local chat room, where regulars congregate to yak over their *vin*, along with a few draught beers and perhaps a snack of sausages or oysters. Despite its lack of seating (there are only four tables), it's a popular pre-dinner spot.

Le Bistrot Paul Bert

18 rue Paul-Bert, 11th (01.43.72.24.01). M° Charonne or Faidherbe Chaligny. **Open** noon-2pm, 7.30-11pm Tue-Sat. Closed Aug. €€. **Bistro**. Map p103 F4 ㉓
This heart-warming bistro gets it right almost down to the last crumb. A starter salad of *ris de veau* illustrates the point, with lightly browned veal sweetbreads perched on a bed of green beans and baby carrots with a sauce of sherry vinegar and deglazed cooking juices. A roast shoulder of suckling pig and a thick steak with a raft of golden, thick-cut *frites* look inviting indeed.

Desserts are superb too, including what may well be the best *île flottante* in Paris. If you happen to be in the area at lunchtime, bear in mind that the prix fixe menu is remarkable value.

Bofinger

5-7 rue de la Bastille, 4th (01.42.72.87.82, www.bofingerparis.com). M° Bastille. **Open** noon-3pm, 6.30pm-midnight Mon-Sat; noon-3pm, 6.30-11.30pm Sun. €€. **Brasserie**. Map p102 C4 ㉔
Bofinger draws big crowds for its art nouveau setting and brasserie atmosphere. Downstairs is the prettiest place in which to eat, but the upstairs room is air-conditioned. An à la carte selection might start with garlicky snails or a well-made langoustine terrine, followed by an intensely seasoned salmon tartare, a generous (if unremarkable) cod steak, or calf's liver accompanied by cooked melon. Alternatively, you could have the foolproof brasserie meal of oysters and fillet steak, washed down by the fine Gigondas.

Café Charbon

109 rue Oberkampf, 11th (01.43.57. 55.13). M° Ménilmontant or Parmentier. **Open** 9am-2am Mon-Wed, Sun; 9am-4am Thur-Sat. **Bar**. Map p103 E1 ㉕
The bar in this restored belle époque building sparked the Oberkampf nightlife boom. Its booths, mirrors and adventurous music policy put trendy locals at ease, capturing the essence of café culture spanning each end of the 20th century. After more than 15 years, the formula still works.

Candelaria

52 rue de Saintonge, 3rd (01.42.74. 41.28, www.candelariaparis.com). M° Filles du Calvaire or République. **Open** 12.30-11pm Mon-Wed, Sun; noon-midnight Thur-Sat. **Bar**. Map p102 C2 ㉖
Has Paris woken up to the temptations of the taco? Apparently so, thanks to this taqueria, where local hipsters come to sip margaritas or house specials such as the *guêpe verte* (tequila,

lime, pepper, cucumber, spices and agave syrup). On the food front, you have the choice between tacos and *tostadas* (€3 for one, €5.50 for two).

Cantine Merci

111 bd Beaumarchais, 3rd (01.42.77. 78.92). M° St-Sébastien Froissart. **Open** noon-3.30pm Mon-Sat (until 6pm for tea). **€**. **Café**. **Map** p102 C2 ㉗
Concept store Merci is all about feeling virtuous even as you indulge, and its basement canteen is a perfect example. Salads, soup and risotto of the day, an organic salmon plate, and the *assiette merci* (perhaps chicken kefta with two salads) make up the brief menu, complete with invigorating teas and juices.

Le Chateaubriand

129 av Parmentier, 11th (01.43.57. 45.95, www.lechateaubriand.net). M° Goncourt. **Open** 7.30-11pm Tue-Sat. Closed 2wks Dec. **€€€**. **Bistro**. **Map** p103 D1 ㉘
Basque chef Iñaki Aizpitarte runs this stylish bistro. Dishes have been deconstructed down to their essence and put back together again. You'll understand if you try starters such as steak tartare garnished with a quail's egg or asparagus with tahini foam and little splinters of sesame-seed brittle. The cooking's not always so cerebral – goat's cheese with stewed apple jam is brilliant.

China

50 rue de Charenton, 12th (01.43.46. 08.09, www.lechina.eu). M° Bastille or Ledru Rollin. **Open** 10am-2am Mon-Thur, Sun; 10am-4am Fri, Sat. Closed Aug. **Bar**. **Map** p103 D5 ㉙
This sexy take on a 1930s Shanghai gentleman's club, with red walls, leather chesterfields and the longest bar in Paris, serves some of the finest cocktails in town (including its signature singapore sling). The Cantonese cuisine is pricey, so skip dinner and head upstairs to the cigar bar or downstairs to the cellar for weekly jazz, pop and world music concerts.

Cru

7 rue Charlemagne, 4th (01.40.27.81.84, www.restaurantcru.fr). M° St-Paul. **Open** 12.30-2.30pm, 7-11pm Tue-Sat; 12.30-3pm Sun. **€€**. **Bistro**. **Map** p102 B4 ㉚
Opening a raw-food restaurant is a gamble, so the owners of Cru cheat here and there, offering root vegetable 'chips' and a few *plancha* dishes. Still, the menu has plenty for the crudivore, such as some unusual carpaccios (the veal with preserved lemon is particularly good) and intriguing 'red' and 'green' plates, variations on the tomato and cucumber.

Le Dauphin

131 av Parmentier, 11th (01.55.28. 78.88, www.restaurantledauphin.net). M° Goncourt. **Open** noon-1.30pm, 7-11pm Tue-Fri; 7-11pm Sat. **€**. **Wine bar**. **Map** p103 D1 ㉛
Iñaki Aizpitarte's Le Dauphin, a Rem Koolhaus-designed tapas-style place a few doors from Le Chateaubriand, offers dishes such as *magret séché, tempura de gambas* and *tarte au citron meringuée*. As at Le Chateaubriand, sourcing is all-important.

Derrière

69 rue des Gravilliers, 3rd (01.44.61. 91.95, www.derriere-resto.com). M° Arts et Métiers. **Open** noon-2.30pm, 8-11.30pm Mon-Sat; noon-4pm, 8-11.30pm Sun. **€€**. **Bistro**. **Map** p102 A1 ㉜
Mourad Mazouz, the man behind Momo and Sketch in London, hit on another winning formula with this apartment-restaurant in the same street as his restaurant 404 and bar Andy Wahloo. The cluttered-chic look mixes contemporary fixtures and antique furniture. It attracts a young, hip crowd that appreciates the comfort food, such as roast chicken with buttery mash.

L'Encrier

55 rue Traversière, 12th (01.44.68. 08.16). M° Gare de Lyon or Ledru-Rollin. **Open** noon-2.30pm, 7.30-11pm Mon-Sat. Closed Aug. **€**. **Bistro**. **Map** p103 D5 ㉝

Candelaria p107

Through the door and past the velvet curtain, you find yourself face to face with the kitchen – and a crowd of locals, many of whom seem to know the charming boss personally. Start with fried rabbit kidneys on a bed of salad dressed with raspberry vinegar, an original and wholly successful combination, and follow with goose *magret* with honey served with sautéed potatoes. To end, share a chocolate cake or try the popular profiteroles.

Le Floréal

73 rue du Fbg-du-Temple, 10th (01.40.18.46.79). Mº Goncourt. **Open** 8am-1.30am Mon-Sat; 9.30am-1.30am Sun. €. **Diner**. **Map** p103 D1 ㉞

The proprietors of Chez Jeanette and Chez Justine chose a prime site opposite Le Chateaubriand and Le Dauphin for their latest venture, Le Floréal – an American-style diner serving hamburgers and cupcakes.

Glou

NEW *101 rue Vieille du Temple, 3rd (01.42.74.44.32, www.glou-resto.com). Mº St-Sébastien Froissart.* **Open** 12.30-2.30pm, 8-11pm Mon-Fri; noon-5pm, 8-11.30pm Sat; noon-3pm, 8-10.30pm Sun. €€. **Bistro**. **Map** p102 B2 ㉟

For a restaurant founded by a man the *New York Times* dubbed the 'wizard of offal', it's initially disappointing that Glou keeps its tongue (and heart, testicles and other offcuts) in cheek and off the menu. Instead this charming bistro plays things straight with Spanish meat boards, subtle pasta dishes and bold French desserts. Glou is a 'food with friends' affair, with friendly staff and a communal table that reverberates with the laughter of Marais hipsters.

Le Hangar

12 impasse Berthaud, 3rd (01.42.74. 55.44). Mº Rambuteau. **Open** noon-2.30pm, 7.30-11pm Tue-Sat. Closed Aug. €. No credit cards. **Bistro**. **Map** p102 A2 ㊱

It's worth making the effort to find this bistro by the Centre Pompidou, with its terrace tucked away in a hidden alley and its excellent cooking. A bowl of tapenade and toast are supplied to keep you going while choosing from the comprehensive *carte*. It yields, for starters, tasty and grease-free *rillettes de lapereau* (rabbit) alongside perfectly balanced pumpkin and chestnut soup. Main courses include pan-fried foie gras on a smooth potato purée.

L'Ilot

4 rue de la Corderie, 3rd (06.95.12. 86.61). Mº Filles du Calvaire, République or Temple. **Open** 7-10pm Tue; noon-3pm, 7-10pm Wed-Sat. €€. **Seafood**. **Map** p103 D5 ㊲

At l'Ilot, you don't have to pay Paris prices for the best catch of the day. The venue is tiny but beautiful, with big slate menus, earthenware pots and white parquet, a bay window, a few photos on the walls and a terrace for nice days – it all has a solid charm. Perch yourself on a stool and order a glass of white wine, then browse the menu: €5 for a serving of tuna or salmon rillettes, €4.50 to €9.50 for grey or pink Madagascan prawns, €6.50 for whelks and €8 for a half crab (€14 for the whole). There are also beautiful oysters, while the fish is smoked or marinated. The value of the set menu is unbeatable, at €12.50 for a starter, main and glass of wine. A delight.

Jaja

3 rue Sainte-Croix-de-la-Bretonnerie, 4th (01.42.74.71.52, www.jaja-resto.com). Mº Hôtel de Ville. **Open** noon-2.30pm, 8-11pm Mon-Fri; noon-3pm, 8-10.30pm Sat, Sun. €€. **Bistro**. **Map** p102 B3 ㊳

Natural wines figure heavily on the list at Jaja. Founded by former wine journalist Julien Fouin in a small *hôtel particulier*, the look is stylish with wood floors and 1950s chairs. Much of the menu is organic – Poujauran bread, Aubrac beef – and most of the wines are organic or even biodynamic. You'll find some classy Bordeaux grands crus, plus a few interesting foreign wines, on a list arranged not by appellation but by mood.

Lizard Lounge

18 rue du Bourg-Tibourg, 4th (01.42. 72.81.34, www.cheapblonde.com). M°Hôtel de Ville. **Open** noon-2am daily. **Bar. Map** p102 B3 ❸❾

An anglophone favourite deep in the Marais, this loud and lively joint provides lager in pints, plus cocktails and a viewing platform for beer-goggled oglers. Bargain boozing kicks off at 5pm; from 8pm to 10pm there's another happy hour in the cellar bar; on Mondays, it lasts all day.

La Perle

78 rue Vieille-du-Temple, 3rd (01.42.72.69.93). M°Chemin Vert or St-Paul. **Open** 6.30am-2am Mon-Fri; 8am-2am Sat, Sun. **Bar. Map** p102 B3 ❹⓿

The Pearl achieves a rare balance between all-day and late-night venue, and has a good hetero/homo mix. It feels like a neighbourhood bar; labourers and screenwriters rub elbows with young dandies, keeping an eye on the mirror and an ear on the electro-rock.

Le Petit Fer à Cheval

30 rue Vieille-du-Temple, 4th (01.42. 72.47.47, www.cafeine.com). M°St-Paul. **Open** 9am-2am daily. **Bar. Map** p102 B3 ❹❶

Even a miniature Shetland pony would be pushed to squeeze his hoof into this *fer à cheval* (horseshoe) – this adorable little café has one of France's smallest bars. Tucked in behind the glassy façade is a friendly dining room lined with reclaimed métro benches; if you want scenery, the tables out front overlook the bustle of rue Vieille-du-Temple. The café enjoyed a retro make-over by Xavier Denamur in the 1990s.

Le Petit Marché

9 rue de Béarn, 3rd (01.42.72.06.67). M°Chemin Vert. **Open** noon-4pm, 7.30pm-midnight daily. **€€. Bistro. Map** p102 C3 ❹❷

Petit Marché's menu is short and modern with Asian touches. Raw tuna is flash-fried in sesame seeds and served with a Thai sauce, making for a refreshing starter; crispy-coated deep-fried king prawns have a similar oriental lightness. The main vegetarian risotto is rich in basil, coriander, cream and green beans. Pan-fried scallops with lime are precision-cooked and accompanied by a good purée and more beans. There's a short wine list.

La Pulpéria

1 rue Richard Lenoir, 11th (01.40.09. 03.70). M°Charonne or Voltaire. **Open** 8-11pm Mon, Sat; noon-2.30pm, 8-11pm Tue-Fri. **€€. South American. Map** p102 C3 ❹❸

The meat at La Pulpéria comes with a capital M, served in a noisy, welcoming little dining room. The menu changes daily, but dishes might include a pretty cod ceviche surrounded with fine slices of sweet potato, avocado purée and a splash of lemon juice, or a bloody, magnificent *churrasco* cut of beef served with rissole potatoes and garlicky *chimichurri* sauce.

Septime

NEW *80 rue de Charonne, 11th (01.43.67.38.29, www. septime-charonne.fr). M°Charonne, Faidherbe-Chaligny or Ledru-Rollin.* **Open** 7.30-10pm Mon; 12.15-2pm, 7.30-10pm Tue-Sat. **€€€. Bistro. Map** p103 E4 ❹❹

Bertrand Grébaut's latest restaurant is decked out with huge mirrors, industrial installations, antique flooring and furniture, reinforced concrete and bare wood. The cooking is direct, pure and serious: raw horse mackerel with yoghurt and red cabbage is superb; Iberico ham and pumpkin is tender and delicious. Service is charming.

Stolly's

16 rue Cloche-Perce, 4th (01.42.76.06.76, www.cheapblonde.com). M°Hôtel de Ville or St-Paul. **Open** 4pm-2am daily. **Bar. Map** p102 B3 ❹❺

This seen-it-all drinking den has been serving a mainly anglophone crowd for nights immemorial. The staff make the place what it is, and a summer terrace eases libation, as do the long happy hours; but don't expect anyone at Stolly's to faff about with food.

Le Train Bleu

Gare de Lyon, pl Louis-Armand, 12th (01.43.43.09.06, www.le-train-bleu.com). Mº Gare de Lyon. **Open** 11.30am-2.45pm, 7-10.45pm daily. **€€€. Brasserie.** Map p103 D5 ❹⑥

This listed dining room exudes a pleasant air of anticipation. Don't expect cutting-edge food, but rather fine renderings of French classics. Lobster served on walnut oil-dressed salad leaves is a beautifully prepared starter. Mains of veal chop topped with a cap of cheese, and *sandre* (pike-perch) coupled with a 'risotto' of *crozettes* are also pleasant. A few reasonably priced wines would be a welcome addition.

Shopping

L'Autre Boulange

43 rue de Montreuil, 11th (01.43.72.86.04). Mº Faidherbe Chaligny or Nation. **Open** 7.30am-1.30pm, 3-7.30pm Mon-Fri; 7.30am-1pm Sat. Closed Aug. Map p103 F5 ❹⑦

Michel Cousin bakes up to 23 different types of organic loaf in his wood-fired oven – varieties include the *flutiot* (rye bread with raisins, walnuts and hazelnuts), the *sarment de Bourgogne* (sourdough and a little rye) and a spiced cornmeal bread.

L'Eclaireur

40 rue de Sévigné, 4th (01.48.87.10.22, www.leclaireur.com). Mº St-Paul. **Open** 11am-7pm Mon-Sat; 2-7pm Sun. Map p102 B3 ❹⑧

Sophisticated, avant-garde L'Eclaireur stocks designs by Comme des Garçons, Martin Margiela and Dries van Noten. Among its finds, check out smocks by Finnish designer Jasmin Santanen.

Free 'P' Star

8 rue Ste-Croix-de-la-Bretonnerie, 4th (01.42.76.03.72, www.freepstar.com). Mº St-Paul. **Open** 11am-9pm Mon-Sat; noon-9pm Sun. Map p102 B3 ❹⑨

Late-night shopping is fun at this Aladdin's cave of retro glitz, ex-army wear and glad rags that has provided fancy dress for many a Paris party.

Galerie Fatiha Selam

58 rue Chapon, 3rd (09.83.33.65.69, www.fatihaselam.com). Mº Arts et Métiers or Rambuteau. **Open** 11am-7pm Tue-Sat. Map p102 A2 ❺⓪

This new addition to a burgeoning gallery street opened in late 2012 with an exhibition of US artist Stephen Schultz's dreamlike canvases. Fatiha Selam brings a fresh eye to the NoMa art scene and promises to explore figurative and abstract contemporary artists both known and emerging.

I Love My Blender

36 rue du Temple, 3rd (01.42.77.50.32, www.ilovemyblender.fr). Mº Hôtel de Ville. **Open** 10am-7pm Tue-Sat; 10am-5pm Sun. Map p102 A3 ❺①

Christophe Persouyre left a career in advertising to share his passion for English and American literature: all the books he stocks were penned in English, and here you can find their mother-tongue and translated versions.

Jimmy Fairly

NEW *64 rue Vieille du Temple, 4th (01.79.72.60.20, www.jimmyfairly.com). Mº St-Paul.* **Open** 11am-7pm daily. Map p102 B3 ❺②

Probably the city's largest supplier of eyewear to bearded hipsters, Jimmy Fairly launched as a website before opening a store in late 2012. There are around 30 retro-style designs: pick up a Monroe, Hamilton or Watson for just €95, lenses included (if you don't need a prescription or to have them fitted with anti-reflective glass). What's more, the 'Buy one give one' model means that for every pair of glasses sold,

Jimmy Fairly gives a brand new pair to someone in need.

K Jacques

16 rue Pavée, 4th (01.40.27.03.57, www.kjacques.fr). M° St-Paul. **Open** 10am-7.15pm Mon-Sat; 1-7.15pm Sun. **Map** p102 B3 ❸

Set up in Saint-Tropez in 1933 by Jacques Keklikian and his wife, the K Jacques workshop started life stitching together basic leather sandals for visitors to the Med resort. The Homère (or Homer) was, and still is, the signature piece – Picasso loved them, and over the years they've counted Colette and Brigitte Bardot among their fans.

Merci

111 bd Beaumarchais, 3rd (01.42. 77.00.33, www.merci-merci.com). M° St-Sébastien Froissart. **Open** 10am-7pm Mon-Sat. **Map** p102 C2 ❸

Concept store Merci is housed in an elaborately reconfigured 19th-century fabric factory. Inside, three loft-like floors heave with furniture, jewellery, stationery, fashion, household products, kidswear and a haberdashery.

Nodus

22 rue Vieille-du-Temple, 4th (01.42. 77.07.96, www.nodus.fr). M° Hôtel de Ville or St-Paul. **Open** 10.45am-2pm, 3-7.30pm Mon-Sat; 1-7.30pm Sun. **Map** p102 B3 ❸

Under the wooden beams of this cosy men's shirt specialist are rows of striped, checked and plain dress shirts, stylish silk ties with subtle designs, and silver-plated crystal cufflinks.

Noir Kennedy

22 rue du Roi de Sicile, 4th (01.44.61. 79.71, www.noirkennedyparis.com). M° Saint-Paul. **Open** 1-8pm Mon; 11am-8pm Tue-Sat; 2-8pm Sun. **Map** p102 B3 ❸

This vintage clothes store maintains a strong sense of style. Classic pieces by Cheap Monday mingle with British rockabilly-style items, and traditional red phone booths serve as changing rooms. With not a sequinned top in sight, Noir Kennedy is totally and deliciously rock 'n' roll.

Première Pression Provence

3 rue Antoine Vollon, 12th (01.53. 33.03.59, www.premiere-pression-provence.com). M° Ledru Rollin. **Open** 10.30am-3.30pm Wed, Sat; 10.30am-3.30pm, 7-9.30pm Thur, Fri. **Map** p103 E5 ❺❼

This is L'Occitane creator Olivier Baussan's latest project, where you are encouraged to taste spoonfuls of single-producer olive oil to educate your palate about the nuances of *vert*, *mûr* and *noir* (known as the '*fruités*') before buying.

Shine

15 rue de Poitou, 3rd (01.48.05.80.10). M° Filles du Calvaire. **Open** 11am-7.30pm Mon-Sat; 1-7pm Sun. **Map** p102 B2 ❺❽

See by Chloé, Marc by Marc Jacobs and Acne Jeans are among the goodies in this glossy showcase.

WAIT

9 rue Notre-Dame de Nazareth, 3rd (09.82.52.84.34, www.wait-paris-com). M° République. **Open** 11am-7pm Mon-Sat. **Map** p102 B1 ❺❾

Imagine a man's ultimate fantasy living room and you have WAIT, a shop filled with everything from retro video game consoles, surfboards, skateboards and shades to a reconditioned racing bike, vintage furniture, cool shirts, T-shirts and baseball caps. Plus the crucial accessory for the modern man – scented candles.

Zadig & Voltaire

42 rue des Francs-Bourgeois, 3rd (01.44.54.00.60, www.zadig-et-voltaire. com). M° Hôtel de Ville or St-Paul. **Open** 10.30am-7.30pm Mon-Sat; noon-7.30pm Sun. **Map** p102 B3 ❻⓿

Zadig & Voltaire's relaxed collection is a winner. Popular separates include cotton tops, shirts and faded jeans.

Gaîté Lyrique

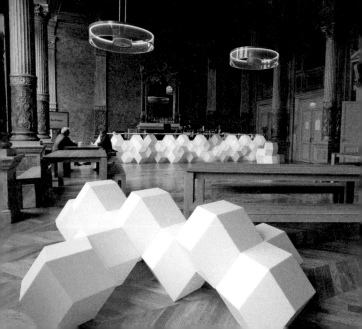

Nightlife

Ateliers de Charonne

21 rue de Charonne, 11th (01.40.21. 83.35, www.ateliercharonne.com). Mº Charonne or Ledru-Rollin. **Open** 8pm-1am daily. *Concerts* 9pm Mon-Sat; 7pm Sun. **Map** p103 D4 ⑥
This club is the place to see the rising stars of gypsy jazz (*jazz manouche*). If you want a spot near the front of the stage, reserve for dinner and the show.

Le Bataclan

50 bd Voltaire, 11th (01.43.14.00.30, www.le-bataclan.com). Mº Oberkampf. **Open** times vary. **Map** p103 D2 ⑥
Established in 1864, this highly distinctive venue remains admirably discerning in its booking of rock, world, jazz and hip hop acts.

L'International

5-7 rue Moret, 11th (01.49.29.76.45, www.linternational.fr). Mº Ménilmontant. **Open** 6pm-2am daily. **Map** p103 E1 ⑥
This concert-bar is a breath of fresh air, with free entry and a string of on-the-up bands playing to hip indie crowds every night of the week.

La Mécanique Ondulatoire

8 passage Thière, 11th (01.43.55.69.14). Mº Bastille or Ledru Rollin. **Open** 6pm-2am Mon-Sat. *Concerts* times vary. **Map** p103 D4 ⑥
Cementing Bastille's status as Paris's prime hangout for rockers, this exciting venue has three levels and alternates eclectic DJs with live acts in the cellar, plus there's jazz on Tuesday nights.

Le Motel

8 passage Josset, 11th (01.58.30.88.52, www.myspace.com/lemotel). Mº Ledru Rollin. **Open** 6pm-1.45am Tue-Sun. **Map** p103 E4 ⑥
This most Anglophile of Paris bars, with Stone Roses and Smiths posters adorning the walls, manages to fit plenty of bands, including some of the best local talent, on to its tiny stage.

Nouveau Casino

109 rue Oberkampf, 11th (01.43.57. 57.40, www.nouveaucasino.net). Mº Parmentier. **Open** *Concerts* times vary. **Map** p103 E1 ⑥
Nouveau Casino is a gig venue that hosts some of the city's liveliest club nights.

Panic Room

101 rue Amelot, 11th (01.58.30.93.43, www.panicroomparis.com). Mº St-Sébastien Froissart. **Open** 6.30pm-2am Mon-Sat. **Map** p102 C2 ⑥
The excellent Goldrush collective has live acts and DJs blasting the sound system in the basement, while upstairs friendly barmen serve affordable cocktails.

Arts & leisure

Les Bains du Marais

31-33 rue des Blancs-Manteaux, 4th (01.44.61.02.02, www.lesbainsdumarais. com). Mº St-Paul. **Open** times vary. **Map** p102 A3 ⑥
This hammam and spa mixes the modern and traditional (lounging beds and mint tea). Facials, waxing and oil massages (€70) are also available.

Gaîté Lyrique

3bis rue Papin, 3rd (01.53.01.51.51, www.gaite-lyrique.net). Mº Réaumur Sébastopol. **Box office** 2-8pm Tue-Sat; 2-6pm Sun. **Map** p102 A1 ⑥
This multidisciplinary concert hall-cum-gallery thrusts visitors deep into the realms of digital art, music, graphics, film, fashion, design and video games.

Opéra National de Paris, Bastille

Pl de la Bastille, 12th (08.92.89.90.90, www.operadeparis.fr). Mº Bastille. **Box office** 2.30-6.30pm Mon-Sat & 1hr before performance. *By phone* 9am-6pm Mon-Fri; 9am-1pm Sat. **Map** p103 D4 ⑦
The Bastille is never going to be a beautiful building. But the standard of performance is what matters, and the 2013 season brought to the stage great classics such as *Falstaff* and *Carmen*.

Cathédrale Notre-Dame
de Paris p118

The Seine & Islands

The Seine

It's perhaps surprising that it took
so long for the Seine to become a
tourist magnet. For much of the
19th and 20th centuries, the Seine
was barely given a second thought
by anyone who wasn't working
on it or driving along its quayside
roads. But in 1994, UNESCO added
12 kilometres (7.5 miles) of Paris
riverbank to its World Heritage
register. Floating venues such as
Batofar became super-trendy; and in
the last couple of decades, it's been
one new attraction after another.

It's at its absolute best in summer.
Port de Javel and Jardin Tino-Rossi
become open-air dancehalls; and
there's the jamboree of Paris-Plages,
the hugely successful city beach that
brings sand, palm trees, loungers
and free entertainment to both sides
of the Seine. And, of course, there's
a wealth of boat tours on offer if you
want to get out on the water.

In 2013, Bertrand Delanoë's
ambitious redesign plans for the
traffic-choked *berges* saw a stretch
of Left Bank road running from
Pont de l'Alma to Pont Royal – from
just east of Musée du Quai Branly
up to and including the Musée
d'Orsay – converted into a wonderful
pedestrian promenade dotted with
gardens, play areas, cafés and bars
galore. Forget the Côte d'Azur next
August – and head for the banks of
the Seine instead.

Sights & museums

Vedettes du Pont-Neuf
*Square du Vert-Galant, 1st (01.46.33.
98.38, www.vedettesdupontneuf.com).
Mº Pont Neuf.* **Tickets** €13; free-€7
reductions. **Map** p117 B1 ❶
The hour-long cruise takes in all the
major sights, from the Eiffel Tower to
Notre-Dame. You can sit inside just a
foot or two above water level or outside
on the top deck.

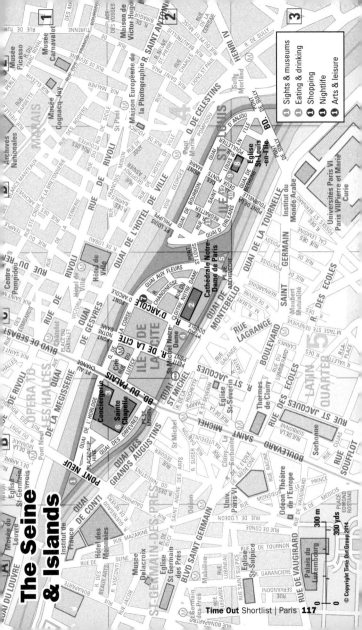

The Seine & Islands

Key

- ① Sights & museums
- ② Eating & drinking
- ③ Shopping
- ④ Nightlife
- ⑤ Arts & leisure

© Copyright Time Out Group 2014.

The bridges

From the honeyed arches of the oldest, the Pont Neuf (1607), to the swooping lines of the newest, the Passerelle Simone-de-Beauvoir (2006), the 37 bridges are among the best-known landmarks in the city, and enjoy some of its best views.

Over the years, the city's *ponts* have been bombed, bashed by buses and boats, weather-beaten and even trampled to destruction: in 1634, the Pont St-Louis collapsed under the weight of a religious procession.

The 19th century was boom time for bridge-building: 21 of them were built in all, including the city's first steel, iron and suspension bridges. The Pont de la Concorde used up what was left of the Bastille after the storming of 1789; the romantic Pont des Arts was the capital's first solely pedestrian crossing (built in 1803 and rebuilt in the 1980s). The most glitteringly exuberant bridge is the Pont Alexandre III, with its bronze and glass, garlanding and gilded embellishments.

More practical is the Pont de l'Alma, with its Zouave statue that has long been a flood monitor: when the statue's toes get wet, the state raises the flood alert and starts to close the quayside roads; when he's up to his ankles in Seine, it's no longer possible to navigate the river by boat. This offers some indication of just how devastating the famous 1910 flood was, when the plucky Zouave disappeared up to his neck – as did parts of central Paris.

The 20th century brought some spectacular additions. Pont Charles-de-Gaulle, for example, stretches like the wing of a huge aeroplane, and iron Viaduc d'Austerlitz (1905) is striking yet elegant as it cradles métro line 5. The city's newest crossing, the Passerelle Simone-de-Beauvoir, links the Bibliothèque Nationale to the Parc de Bercy.

Ile de la Cité

The Ile de la Cité is where Paris was born around 250 BC, when the Parisii, a tribe of Celtic Gauls, founded a settlement on this convenient bridging point of the Seine. Romans, Merovingians and Capetians followed, in what became a centre of political and religious power right into the Middle Ages: royal authority at one end, around the Capetian palace; the Church at the other, by Notre-Dame.

Every Sunday, the Ile de la Cité's flower market comes alive with a cacophony of squawking and chirping birds as the Marché aux Fleurs is joined by the Marché aux Oiseaux. Kids will love the line-up of parrots, chickens and canaries. Other animals such as ferrets and mice are on sale, too, plus ridiculously cute dwarf bunnies for some intense petting. It's a great way to spend time after braving the queues at nearby Notre-Dame.

Perhaps the most charming spot on the island is the western tip, where Pont Neuf spans the Seine. Despite its name, it is the oldest bridge in Paris. Its arches are lined with grimacing faces, said to be modelled on some of the courtiers of Henri III. Down the steps is leafy square du Vert-Galant. In the centre of the bridge is an equestrian statue of Henri IV; the original went up in 1635, was melted down to make cannons during the Revolution, and replaced in 1818.

Sights & museums

Cathédrale Notre-Dame de Paris

Pl du Parvis-Notre-Dame, 4th (01.42. 34.56.10, www.cathedraledeparis.com). M° Cité/RER St-Michel Notre-Dame. **Open** 8am-6.45pm Mon-Fri; 8am-7.15pm Sat, Sun. *Towers* Apr-Sept 10am-6.30pm daily (June-Aug until

From top: **Pont des Arts**;
Pont Neuf; **Passerelle
Simone-de-Beauvoir**

11pm Sat, Sun). Oct-Mar 10am-5.30pm daily. **Admission** free. *Towers €8.50; free-€5.50 reductions.* **Map** p117 C2 ❷

Notre-Dame was constructed between 1163 and 1334, and the amount of time and money spent on it reflected the city's growing prestige. The west front remains a high point of Gothic art for the balanced proportions of its twin towers and rose window, and the three doorways with their rows of saints and sculpted tympanums: the *Last Judgement* (centre), *Life of the Virgin* (left) and *Life of St Anne* (right). Inside, take a moment to admire the long nave with its solid foliate capitals and high altar with a marble *Pietà* by Coustou.

Climb up the towers to appreciate the masonry. The route runs up the north tower and down the south. Between the two you get a close-up view of the gallery of chimeras – the fantastic birds and hybrid beasts designed by Viollet-le-Duc along the balustrade. After a detour to see the massive bell, a staircase leads to the top of the south tower. In February 2013, Notre-Dame received eight new bells, forged to try to reproduce the sound of pre-Revolutionary Paris as part of the cathedral's 850th anniversary year.

La Conciergerie

2 bd du Palais, 1st (01.53.40.60.80). Mº Cité/RER St-Michel Notre-Dame. **Open** 9.30am-6pm daily. **Admission** €8.50; free-€5.50 reductions. *With Sainte-Chapelle €12.50; €8.50 reductions.* **Map** p117 B1 ❸

The Conciergerie looks every inch like a medieval fortress. However, much of the façade was added in the 1850s. The visit takes you through the Salle des Gardes, the medieval kitchens with their four huge chimneys, and the Salle des Gens d'Armes, a vaulted Gothic hall built between 1301 and 1315. After the royals moved to the Louvre, the fortress became a prison under the watch of the Concierge. The wealthy had private cells with their own furniture, which they paid

for; others had to make do with straw beds. A list of Revolutionary prisoners, including a hairdresser, shows that not all the victims were nobles. In Marie-Antoinette's cell, the Chapelle des Girondins, are her crucifix, some portraits and a guillotine blade.

La Crypte Archéologique

Pl Jean-Paul II, 4th (01.55.42.50.10, www.crypte.paris.fr). Mº Cité/RER St-Michel Notre-Dame. **Open** 10am-6pm Tue-Sun. **Admission** €5; free-€3.50 reductions. **Map** p117 C2 ❹

Hidden under the forecourt in front of the cathedral is a large void containing pieces of Roman quaysides, ramparts and hypocausts, medieval cellars, shops and pavements, the foundations of the Eglise Ste-Geneviève-des-Ardens, an 18th-century foundling hospital and a 19th-century sewer. You get a vivid sense of the layers of history piled one atop another during 16 centuries.

Mémorial des Martyrs de la Déportation

Sq de l'Ile de France, 4th (01.46.33. 87.56). Mº Cité/RER St-Michel Notre-Dame. **Open** Oct-Mar 10am-5pm Tue-Sun. *Apr-Sept* 10am-7pm Tue-Sun. **Admission** free. **Map** p117 C2 ❺

This moving tribute to the 200,000 Jews, Communists, homosexuals and *résistants* who were deported to concentration camps from France in World War II stands on the eastern tip of the island. A blind staircase descends to river level, where the chambers are lined with tiny lights and the walls are inscribed with verse. A barred window looks on to the Seine.

Sainte-Chapelle

4 bd du Palais, 1st (01.53.40.60.80). Mº Cité/RER St-Michel Notre-Dame. **Open** *Mar-Oct* 9.30am-6pm daily. *Nov-Feb* 9am-5pm daily. **Admission** €8.50; free-€5.50 reductions. *With Conciergerie €12.50; €8.50 reductions.* **Map** p117 B2 ❻

Devout King Louis IX (St Louis, 1226-70) had a hobby of accumulating holy relics (and children: he fathered 11). In the 1240s, he bought what was advertised as the Crown of Thorns, and ordered Pierre de Montreuil to design a shrine. The result was the exquisite Flamboyant Gothic Sainte-Chapelle. With 15m (49ft) windows, the upper level, intended for the royal family and the canons, appears to consist almost entirely of stained glass. The windows depict hundreds of scenes from the Old and New Testaments, culminating with the Apocalypse in the rose window.

Shopping

L'Occitane en Provence

1 rue d'Arcole, 4th (01.55.42.06.11, www.loccitane.com). M° Cité. **Open** 10.30am-7.30pm daily. **Map** p117 C2 ❼
The many branches of this popular Provençal chain offer natural beauty products in neat packaging.

Ile St-Louis

The Ile St-Louis is one of the most exclusive residential addresses in the city. Delightfully unspoiled, it has fine architecture, narrow streets and pretty views from the tree-lined quays, and still retains the air of a tranquil backwater. At the western end there are great views of the buttresses of Notre-Dame from the Brasserie de l'Ile St-Louis.

Sights & museums

Eglise St-Louis-en-l'Ile

19bis rue St-Louis-en-l'Ile, 4th (01.46.34. 11.60, www.saintlouisenlile.catholique. fr). M° Pont Marie. **Open** 9.30am-1pm, 2-7.30pm Mon-Sat; 9am-1pm, 2-7pm Sun. **Admission** free. **Map** p117 D3 ❽
The island's church was built between 1664 and 1765, following plans by Louis Le Vau and later completed by Gabriel Le Duc. The interior boasts Corinthian columns and a sunburst over the altar, and the church hosts occasional classical music concerts.

Eating & drinking

Berthillon

29-31 rue St-Louis en l'Ile, 4th (01.43.54.31.61, www.berthillon.fr). M° Pont Marie. **Open** 10am-8pm Wed-Sun. **€€. Ice-cream. Map** p117 D2 ❾
The flavours here change throughout the season, but if it's available don't miss the bitter chocolate sorbet.

Isami

NEW *4 quai d'Orléans, 4th (01.40.46. 06.97). M° Pont Marie.* **Open** noon-2pm, 7-10pm Tue-Sat. **€€€. Japanese. Map** p117 D3 ❿
This is one of the best sushi restaurants in Paris. The dining room is simply decorated with rows of Japanese earthenware stacked behind the bar, and in front of them the *itamae* (master sushi chef) works away in a frenzy.

Mon Vieil Ami

69 rue St-Louis-en-l'Ile, 4th (01.40.46. 01.35, www.mon-vieil-ami.com). M° Pont Marie. **Open** noon-2.30pm, 6.30-11pm Wed-Sun. Closed 3wks Jan & 1st 3wks Aug. **€€. Bistro. Map** p117 D2 ⓫
Antoine Westermann has created a true foodie destination here. Starters such as tartare of diced raw vegetables with sautéed baby squid arranged on top impress with deft seasoning. Typical of the main courses is a casserole of roast duck with caramelised turnips and couscous.

Le Sergent Recruteur

41 rue St-Louis-en-l'Ile, 4th (01.43. 54.75.42, www.lesergentrecruteur.fr). M° Pont Marie or Sully-Morland. **Open** noon-2pm, 7-10pm Tue-Sat. **€€€. Haute cuisine. Map** p117 D2 ⓬
Avant-garde designer Jaime Hayón and chef Antonin Bonnet have turned this former pub into a handsome restaurant. The 'carte blanche' menus, where you're led by the whims of the chef, offer daring versions of classic French dishes: foie gras with rhubarb confit, wild duck with spelt, mango and herb ice cream.

Eiffel Tower

The 7th & Western Paris

The seventh arrondissement is dotted with the machinery of state and diplomacy: it's home to France's parliament, a gaggle of foreign embassies and the HQ of UNESCO. Thankfully, though, three of its greatest attractions – an A-shaped assembly of 19th-century iron lattice, a gallery in an old Beaux Arts train station and the river itself – have embraced the future with thoroughly modern makeovers. The Eiffel Tower is installing a dramatic glass floor and the Musée d'Orsay is gleaming after a stunning renovation, and the riverbanks are blissfully car-free after Bertrand Delanoë came good on his plans to pedestrianise parts of the *berges*.

Sights & museums

Les Egouts de Paris

Opposite 93 quai d'Orsay, by Pont de l'Alma, 7th (01.53.68.27.81).

M° Alma Marceau/RER Pont de l'Alma. **Open** 11am-4pm (until 5pm May-Sept) Mon-Wed, Sat, Sun. Closed 2wks Jan. **Admission** €4.30; free-€3.50 reductions. No credit cards. **Map** p123 B1 ❶

For centuries, the main source of drinking water in Paris was the Seine, which was also the main sewer. Construction of an underground sewerage system began at the time of Napoleon. Today, the Égouts de Paris constitutes a smelly museum; each sewer in the 2,100km (1,305-mile) system is marked with a replica of the street sign above.

Eiffel Tower

Champ de Mars, 7th (08.92.70.12.39, www.tour-eiffel.fr). M° Bir-Hakeim/RER Champ de Mars Tour Eiffel. **Open** *By lift* Mid June-Aug 9am-12.45am daily (last ascent 11pm). Sept-mid June 9.30am-11.45pm daily (last ascent 10.30pm). *By stairs* (1st & 2nd levels) Mid June-Aug 9am-12.45am daily (last ascent midnight). Sept-mid June 9.30am-6.30pm

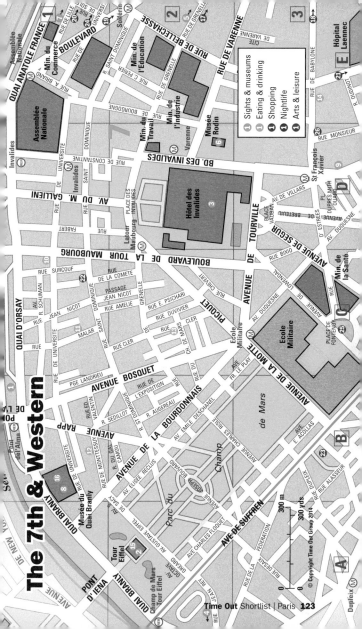

The 7th & Western

	Sights & museums	
	Eating & drinking	
	Shopping	
	Nightlife	
	Arts & leisure	

© Copyright Time Out Group 2014

daily (last ascent 6pm). **Admission** *By stairs* €5; free-€3.50 reductions. *By lift* (1st & 2nd levels) €8.50; free-€7 reductions; (3rd level) €14.50; free-€13 reductions. Map p123 A2 **2**

Maupassant claimed he left Paris because of it, William Morris visited daily to avoid having to see it from afar – and it was originally meant to be a temporary structure. Construction took just over two years and used some 2,500,000 rivets. And not much has changed since – until now. The Eiffel Tower is undergoing its third facelift since opening more than 120 years ago: the €25m revamp is radical, to say the least, with the first-floor central void being filled in with a solid glass floor surrounded by inclined safety barriers, so visitors with a head for heights will be able to eyeball the queues 57m below.

Les Invalides & Musée de l'Armée

Esplanade des Invalides, 7th (08.10. 11.33.99, www.invalides.org). M° La Tour-Maubourg or Les Invalides. **Open** *Apr-Oct* 10am-6pm Mon, Wed-Sun (Dôme until 7pm July, Aug); 10am-9pm Tue. *Nov-Mar* 10am-5pm daily. Closed 1st Mon of mth. **Admission** *Musée de l'Armée & Eglise du Dôme* €9.50; free-€7.50 reductions. Map p123 D2 **3**

Topped by its gilded dome, the Hôtel des Invalides was (and in part still is) a hospital. Commissioned by Louis XIV for wounded soldiers, it once housed up to 6,000 invalids. The complex contains two churches – the Eglise St-Louis was for the soldiers, the Eglise du Dôme for the king.

The Invalides complex also houses the enormous Musée de l'Armée. The Antique Armour wing is packed full of armour and weapons that look as good as new. The Plans-Reliefs section is a collection of 18th- and 19th-century scale models of French cities, used for military strategy. The World War I rooms are moving, with the conflict brought into focus by uniforms, paintings, a scale model of a trench on the western front and, most sobering of all, white plastercasts of the hideously mutilated faces of two soldiers. The World War II wing takes in not just the Resistance, but also the Battle of Britain and the war in the Pacific (there's a replica of Little Boy, the bomb dropped on Hiroshima). Included in the entry price is the Historial Charles de Gaulle.

Maison de la Culture du Japon

101bis quai Branly, 15th (01.44.37. 95.01, www.mcjp.asso.fr). M° Bir-Hakeim/RER Champ de Mars Tour Eiffel. **Open** noon-7pm Tue, Wed, Fri, Sat; noon-8pm Thur. Closed Aug. **Admission** free. Map p123 A2 **4**

This glass-fronted Japanese cultural centre screens films and puts on exhibitions and plays. It also contains a library, an authentic tea pavilion on the roof and a well-stocked shop.

Musée Maillol

59-61 rue de Grenelle, 7th (01.42.22. 59.58, www.museemaillol.com). M° Rue du Bac. **Open** 10.30am-7pm (last admission 6.15pm) Mon-Thur, Sat, Sun; 10.30am-9.30pm (last admission 8.45pm) Fri. **Admission** €11; free-€9 reductions. Map p123 E2 **5**

Dina Vierny was 15 when she met Aristide Maillol (1861-1944) and became his principal model for the next decade, idealised in such sculptures as *Spring, Air* and *Harmony*. In 1995, she opened this museum, exhibiting Maillol's drawings, engravings, pastels, tapestry panels, ceramics and early Nabis-related paintings, as well as sculptures and terracottas that epitomise his calm classicism. The venue has works by Picasso, Rodin, Gauguin, Degas and Cézanne, a room of Matisse drawings, rare Surrealist documents and works by naïve artists. Vierny has also championed Kandinsky and Ilya Kabakov, whose *Communal Kitchen* installation recreates the atmosphere of Soviet domesticity.

Musée National Rodin

Hôtel Biron, 79 rue de Varenne, 7th (01.44.18.61.10, www.musee-rodin.fr). Mº Varenne. **Open** 10am-5.45pm Tue, Thur-Sun; 10am-8.45pm Wed. **Admission** €9; free-€5 reductions. *Gardens* free-€1. **Map** p123 D2 ⑥

The Rodin museum occupies the *hôtel particulier* where the sculptor lived in the final years of his life. The *Kiss*, the *Cathedral*, the *Walking Man*, portrait busts and early terracottas are exhibited indoors. Rodin's works are accompanied by pieces from his mistress and pupil, Camille Claudel. The walls are hung with paintings by Van Gogh, Monet, Renoir, Carrière and Rodin himself. Most visitors have greatest affection for the gardens: look out for the *Burghers of Calais*, the elaborate *Gates of Hell*, and the *Thinker*.

Musée d'Orsay

1 rue de la Légion-d'Honneur, 7th (01.40.49.48.14, www.musee-orsay.fr). Mº Solférino/RER Musée d'Orsay. **Open** 9.30am-6pm Tue, Wed, Fri-Sun; 9.30am-9.45pm Thur. **Admission** €9; free-€6.50 reductions. **Map** p123 E1 ⑦

The Musée d'Orsay's famed upper galleries recently underwent a serious brush-up, reopening to gasps of admiration. The museum, originally a train station designed by Victor Laloux in 1900, houses a huge collection spanning the period between 1848 and 1914, and is home to a profusion of works by Delacroix, Manet, Renoir, Pissarro, Gauguin, Monet, Cézanne, Van Gogh, and others. The results of the renovations are a better display of artworks, more spacious exhibition areas, fine Solux lighting, and Tokujin Yoshioka-designed chairs.

Musée du Quai Branly

37 quai Branly, 7th (01.56.61.70.00, www.quaibranly.fr). RER Pont de l'Alma. **Open** 11am-7pm Tue, Wed, Sun; 11am-9pm Thur-Sat. **Admission** €8.50; free-€6 reductions. **Map** p123 B1 ⑧

Surrounded by trees on the banks of the Seine, this museum is a showcase for non-European cultures. Treasures include a tenth-century anthropomorphic Dogon statue from Mali, Aztec statues, Gabonese masks, Vietnamese costumes and Peruvian feather tunics.

Musée Valentin Haüy

5 rue Duroc, 7th (01.44.49.27.27, www.avh.asso.fr). Mº Duroc. **Open** 2.30-5pm Tue, Wed. Closed July-mid Sept. **Admission** free. **Map** p123 D3 ⑨

This tiny museum is devoted to the history of braille. You can explore on your own with the aid of French, English or braille explanatory texts, or allow the curator, Noële Roy, to show you round. She will give a tour in English if preferred. The first exhibit is a shocking print, depicting the fairground freak show that inspired Valentin Haüy to devote his life to educating not only the blind, but also the public who came to laugh at the likes of this blind orchestra forced to perform in dunce's hats.

Eating & drinking

Le 144 Petrossian

144 rue de l'Université, 7th (01.44.11.32.32, www.petrossian.fr). Mº La Tour Maubourg. **Open** 12.15-2.30pm, 7.30-10.30pm Tue-Sat. €€€. **Russian**. **Map** p123 C1 ⑩

At this famed caviar house you'll find Russian specialities such as blinis, salmon and caviar (at €44 an ounce) from the Petrossian boutique downstairs, plus preparations and spices from all over the world. You might start with a divine risotto made with carnaroli rice, codfish caviar and parmesan. In similar Med-meets-Russia vein are main courses such as roast sea bream with a lemon-vodka sauce.

L'Ami Jean

27 rue Malar, 7th (01.47.05.86.89, www.amijean.eu). Mº Ecole Militaire. **Open** noon-2pm, 7-10pm Tue-Sat. Closed Aug. €€. **Bistro**. **Map** p123 C1 ⑪

This long-running Basque address is an ongoing hit thanks to chef Stéphane Jégo. Veal shank comes de-boned with a side of baby onions and broad beans with tiny cubes of ham, and house-salted cod is soaked, sautéed and doused with an elegant vinaigrette.

Au Bon Accueil

14 rue de Monttessuy, 7th (01.47.05. 46.11, www.aubonaccueilparis.com). Mº Alma Marceau. **Open** noon-2.30pm, 7-10.30pm Mon-Fri. Closed 3wks Aug. **€€€. Bistro. Map** p123 B1 ⑫

Jacques Lacipière runs Au Bon Accueil, and Keita Kitamura turns out the beautiful food. Perhaps most impressive is the restaurant's use of little-known fish such as grey mullet and meagre (*maigre*), rather than the usual endangered species. The lunch menu might highlight such ingredients as *suprême de poulet noir du Cros de la Géline*, free-range chicken from a farm run by two former cabaret singers.

Le Café du Marché

38 rue Cler, 7th (01.47.05.51.27). Mº Ecole Militaire. **Open** 7am-midnight Mon-Sat; 7am-8pm Sun. **€. Café. Map** p123 C2 ⑬

This address is frequented by trendy locals, shoppers hunting down a particular type of cheese and tourists who've managed to make it this far from the Eiffel Tower. Its *pichets* of decent house plonk go down a treat, and mention must be made of the food – such as the house salad with lashings of foie gras.

Le Coutume Café

NEW *47 rue de Babylone, 7th (01.45.51.50.47, www.coutumecafe. com). Mº Saint-François-Xavier or Sèvres-Babylone.* **Open** 8am-7pm Tue-Fri; 10am-7pm Sat, Sun. **€. Café. Map** p123 E3 ⑭

Owned by two stalwarts of the Paris coffee revolution – Antoine Netien and his Australian partner, Tom Clarke – Coutume is part café, part *torréfacteur*, supplying roasted beans to more than 60 bars, restaurants and hotels across the city. It's also one of the rare coffee bars to sell artisan beers.

Jules Verne

Pilier Sud, Eiffel Tower, 7th (01.45.55. 61.44, www.lejulesverne-paris.com). Mº Bir Hakeim or RER Champ de Mars Tour Eiffel. **Open** 12.15-1.30pm, 7-9.30pm daily. **€€€€. Haute cuisine. Map** p123 A2 ⑮

You have to have courage to take on an icon like the Eiffel Tower, but Alain Ducasse has done just that. Ducasse protégé Pascal Féraud updates French classics, combining all the grand ingredients you'd expect with light, modern textures. Try dishes such as sea bass steamed with seaweed, chicken and crayfish fricassée. Book ahead.

Les Ombres

27 quai Branly, 7th (01.47.53.68.00, www.lesombres-restaurant.com). Mº Alma-Marceau. **Open** noon-2.30pm, 7-11pm daily. **€€€. Bistro. Map** p123 B1 ⑯

The view of the Eiffel Tower at night would be reason enough to come to this restaurant on the top floor of the Musée du Quai Branly, but Auvergne-born chef Cyril Lenoir's food also demands you take notice. In summer, you can book a table on the terrace.

Shopping

L'Artisan Parfumeur

24 bd Raspail, 7th (01.42.22.23.32, www.artisanparfumeur.com). Mº Rue du Bac. **Open** 10.30am-7.30pm Mon-Sat. **Map** p123 E2 ⑰

Among the scented candles, potpourri and charms, you'll find the best vanilla perfume that Paris can offer – Mûres et Musc, a bestseller for two decades.

Le Bon Marché

24 rue de Sèvres, 7th (01.44.39.80.00, www.bonmarche.fr). Mº Sèvres Babylone. **Open** 10am-8pm Mon-Wed, Sat; 10am-9pm Thur, Fri. **Map** p123 E3 ⑱

Luxury boutiques take pride of place on the ground floor; escalators designed by Andrée Putman take you up to the fashion floor, which has an excellent selection of designer labels. Designer names also abound in Balthazar, the men's section. For top-notch nibbles, try the new Rose Bakery Tea Room.

Deyrolle

46 rue du Bac, 7th (01.42.22.30.07, www.deyrolle.com). M° Rue du Bac. **Open** 10am-1pm, 2-7pm Mon; 10am-7pm Tue-Sat. **Map** p123 E2 ⑲

Famous taxidermy shop Deyrolle has a bizarre menagerie of lions, giraffes, polar bears, butterflies and bugs of all shapes and sizes. It remains a great place to buy a tiger for the living room, purchase creepy crawlies to scare friends and family or fire your children's imagination.

Epicerie Générale

43 rue de Verneuil, 7th (01.42.60.51.78, www.epiceriegenerale.fr). M° Solférino or Rue du Bac. **Open** 11am-7.30pm Mon-Fri; 10.30am-7.30pm Sat. **Map** p123 E1 ⑳

Maud, Claude and Lucio opened Epicerie Générale in 2011. Here, gourmands can pick up cheese, charcuterie, fruit and vegetables, along with products such as Miel Béton ('concrete honey'), made on the roofs of Saint-Denis. L'Epicerie Générale is also developing its own range of branded products, such as La Strix, the first organic French vodka.

Fromagerie Quatrehomme

62 rue de Sèvres, 7th (01.47.34.33.45). M° Duroc or Vaneau. **Open** 9am-7.45pm Tue-Sat. **Map** p123 E3 ㉑

Marie Quatrehomme runs this *fromagerie*. Famous for her comté fruité, beaufort and st-marcellin, she also sells treats such as goat's cheese with pesto.

Gâteaux Thoumieux

NEW *58 rue St-Dominique, 7th (www. thoumieux.fr). M° Latour Maubourg.* **Open** 9am-7pm Mon, Wed-Sat; 8.30am-2pm Sun. **Map** p123 C1 ㉒

Chef Jean-François Piège's stunning new pastry shop is a den of delectable naughties. Tuck into the likes of *kouign amann* (a buttery, sugary Breton cake). Resistance is futile.

Marie-Anne Cantin

12 rue du Champ-de-Mars, 7th (01.45. 50.43.94, www.cantin.fr). M° Ecole Militaire or La Tour Maubourg. **Open** 2-7.30pm Mon; 8.30am-7.30pm Tue-Sat; 8.30am-1pm Sun. **Map** p123 B3 ㉓

Cantin, supplier to posh Paris restaurants, offers aged *chèvres* and amazing morbier, mont d'or and comté.

Ryst Dupeyron

79 rue du Bac, 7th (01.45.48.80.93, www.vintageandco.com). M° Rue du Bac. **Open** 12.30-7.30pm Mon; 10.30am-7.30pm Tue-Sat. Closed 2wks Aug. **Map** p123 E2 ㉔

The Dupeyrons have been selling armagnac for four generations, and still have bottles in stock from 1868. Treasures here include more than 200 fine Bordeaux wines and an extensive range of vintage port.

Saxe-Breteuil

Av de Saxe, 7th. M° Ségur. **Open** 7am-2.30pm Thur; 7am-3pm Sat. **Map** p123 C3 ㉕

This market has an unrivalled setting facing the Eiffel Tower, as well as a selection of the city's most chic produce. Look out for farmer's goat's cheese, abundant oysters and a handful of small producers.

Arts & leisure

La Pagode

57bis rue de Babylone, 7th (01.45.55. 48.48, www.etoile-cinemas.com). M° St-François-Xavier. No credit cards. **Map** p123 D3 ㉖

This glorious edifice is a 19th-century replica of a pagoda. It's one of the loveliest cinemas in the world.

Église St-Sulpice p130

St-Germain-des-Prés & Odéon

St-Germain-des-Prés may be rather more Louis Vuitton than Boris Vian these days, but there are still enough small galleries and bookshops to ensure that it retains a whiff of its bohemian past. In the middle third of the 20th century, the area was prime arts and *intello* territory, a place known as much for its high jinks as for its lofty thinking: the haunt of Picasso, Giacometti, Camus, Prévert and, *bien sûr*, the Bonnie and Clyde of French philosophy, Jean-Paul Sartre and Simone de Beauvoir; the hotspot of the Paris jazz boom after World War II; and the heart of the Paris book trade. This is where the cliché of café terrace intellectualising was coined, but nowadays couturiers have largely replaced publishers. Never mind: it's a very smart and attractive part of the city to wander around in, and also has some very good restaurants.

St-Germain-des-Prés grew up around the medieval abbey, the oldest church in Paris and site of an annual fair that drew merchants from across Europe. There are still traces of its cloister and part of the abbot's palace behind the church on rue de l'Abbaye. Constructed in 1586 in red brick with stone facing, the palace prefigured the architecture of place des Vosges. Charming place de Furstemberg (once the palace stables) is home to the house and studio where the elderly Delacroix lived when painting the murals in St-Sulpice; it now houses the Musée National Delacroix. Wagner, Ingres and Colette all lived on nearby rue Jacob; its elegant 17th-century *hôtels particuliers* now contain specialist book, design and antiques shops and a few pleasant hotel options. Further east, rue de Buci hosts a market and upmarket food shops.

Ecole Nationale Supérieure des Beaux-Arts (Ensb-a)

14 rue Bonaparte, 6th (01.47.03.50.00, www.ensba.fr). M° St-Germain-des-Prés.
Open 1-7pm Tue-Sun. **Admission** €4; €2 reductions. *Exhibitions* prices vary.
Map p131 C1 ❶

The city's most prestigious fine arts school resides in what remains of the 17th-century Couvent des Petits-Augustins, the 18th-century Hôtel de Chimay, some 19th-century additions and chunks of various French châteaux moved here after the Revolution (when the buildings briefly served as a museum of French monuments).

Eglise St-Germain-des-Prés

3 pl St-Germain-des-Prés, 6th (01.55. 42.81.10, www.eglise-sgp.org). M° St-Germain-des-Prés. **Open** 8am-7.45pm Mon-Sat; 9am-8pm Sun.
Admission free. **Map** p131 C2 ❷

The oldest church in Paris. On the advice of Germain (later Bishop of Paris), Childebert, son of Clovis, had a basilica and monastery built here around 543. It was first dedicated to St Vincent, and came to be known as St-Germain-le-Doré because of its copper roof, then later as St-Germain-des-Prés ('of the fields'). During the Revolution the abbey was burned and a saltpetre refinery installed; the spire was added in a 19th-century restoration. Still, most of the present structure is 12th century, and ornate carved capitals and the tower remain from the 11th. Tombs include those of Jean-Casimir, deposed King of Poland who became Abbot of St-Germain in 1669, and Scots nobleman William Douglas.

Eglise St-Sulpice

Pl St-Sulpice, 6th (01.42.34.59.98, www.paroisse-saint-sulpice-paris.org). M° St-Sulpice. **Open** 7.30am-7.30pm daily. **Admission** free. **Map** p131 C3 ❸

It took 120 years (starting in 1646) and six architects to finish St-Sulpice. The grandiose Italianate façade, with its two-tier colonnade, was designed by Jean-Baptiste Servandoni. He died in 1766 before the second tower was finished, leaving one tower five metres shorter than the other. The trio of murals by Delacroix in the first chapel – *Jacob's Fight with the Angel, Heliodorus Chased from the Temple* and *St Michael Killing the Dragon* – create a suitably sombre atmosphere.

Jardin & Palais du Luxembourg

Pl André Honorat, pl Edmond-Rostand or rue de Vaugirard, 6th (01.44.54. 19.49, www.senat.fr/visite). M° Odéon/ RER Luxembourg. **Open** *Jardin* summer 7.30am-dusk daily; winter 8am-dusk daily. **Map** p131 C4 ❹

The palace itself was built in the 1620s for Marie de Médicis, widow of Henri IV, by Salomon de Brosse on the site of the former mansion of the Duke of Luxembourg. Its Italianate style was intended to remind her of the Pitti Palace in her native Florence. The palace now houses the French parliament's upper house, the Sénat.

The mansion next door (Le Petit Luxembourg) is the residence of the Sénat's president. The gardens, though, are the real draw: part formal (terraces and gravel paths), part 'English garden' (lawns and mature trees), they are the quintessential Paris park. The garden is crowded with sculptures: a looming Cyclops, queens of France, a miniature Statue of Liberty, wild animals, busts of Flaubert and Baudelaire, and a monument to Delacroix. There are orchards and an apiary. The Musée du Luxembourg hosts prestigious exhibitions. Most interesting, though, are the people: the park attracts an international mix of *flâneurs* and *dragueurs*, chess players and martial-arts practitioners, as well as children on ponies, in sandpits and playing with sailing boats on the pond.

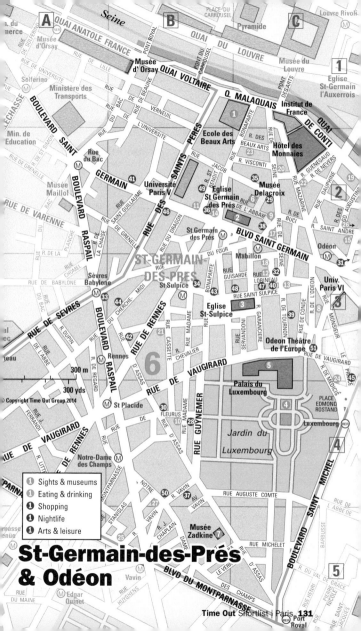

St-Germain-des-Prés
& Odéon

Musée du Luxembourg

*19 rue de Vaugirard, 6th (01.40.13.
62.00, www.museeduluxembourg.fr).
M° Cluny La Sorbonne or Odéon/RER
Luxembourg.* **Open** 10am-10pm Mon,
Fri; 10am-7.30pm Tue-Thur, Sat, Sun.
Admission Prices vary. **Map** p131 C3 **⑤**
When it opened in 1750, this small
museum was the first public gallery
in France. Its current stewardship by
the national museums and the French
Senate has brought imaginative touches
and some impressive coups, from
Matisse collages to Arcimboldo portraits, Cranach and Cézanne, passing
by Titian and Veronese. Book ahead to
avoid the queues.

Musée National Delacroix

*6 rue de Furstenberg, 6th (01.44.41.
86.50, www.musee-delacroix.fr). M°
St-Germain-des-Prés.* **Open** 9.30am-
5pm Mon, Wed-Sun. **Admission** €5;
free reductions. **Map** p131 C2 **⑥**
Eugène Delacroix moved to this apartment and studio in 1857 to be near the
Eglise St-Sulpice, where he was painting murals. This collection includes
small oil paintings, free pastel studies
of skies, sketches and lithographs.

Musée Zadkine

NEW *100bis rue d'Assas, 6th (01.55.
42.77.20, www.zadkine.paris.fr). M°
Notre-Dame-des-Champs/RER Port-
Royal.* **Open** 10am-6pm Tue-Sun.
Admission free. *Exhibitions* €4;
free-€3 reductions. **Map** p131 B5 **⑦**
See box p133.

Eating & drinking

Le Bar Dix

*10 rue de l'Odéon, 6th (01.43.26.
66.83, www.lebar10.com). M° Odéon.*
Open 6pm-2am daily. No credit cards.
Bar. **Map** p131 C3 **⑧**
Generations of students have glugged
back jugs of the celebrated home-made
sangria (just €3 a glass in happy hour)
while squeezed into the cramped upper

bar, tattily authentic with its Jacques
Brel record sleeves, Yves Montand
handbills and pre-war light fittings.
Spelunkers and hopeless romantics
negotiate the hazardous stone staircase
to drink in the cellar bar, with its candlelight and old advertising murals.
Can someone please come and slap a
preservation order on the place?

Le Bar du Marché

*75 rue de Seine, 6th (01.43.26.55.15).
M° Mabillon or Odéon.* **Open** 8am-2am
daily. **Bar**. **Map** p131 C2 **⑨**
The market in question is the Cours
des Halles, the bar a hugely convivial
corner café opening on to the pleasing
bustle of St-Germain-des-Prés. Simple
dishes such as a ham omelette or
a plate of herring in the €7 range,
and Brouilly or muscadet at €4-€5 a
glass, are proffered by beret-topped
waiters. Locals easily outnumber the
tourists, confirming Rod Stewart's
astute observation that Paris gives the
impression that no one is ever working.

Bread & Roses

*7 rue de Fleurus, 6th (01.42.22.06.06,
www.breadandroses.fr). M° St-Placide.*
Open 8am-8pm Mon-Sat. **€€**. **Café**.
Map p131 B4 **⑩**
Giant wedges of cheesecake sit alongside French pastries, and huge savoury
puff-pastry tarts are perched on the
counter. Attention to detail shows even
in the taramasalata, which is matched
with buckwheat-and-seaweed bread.
Prices reflect the quality of the often
organic ingredients.

Café de Flore

*172 bd St-Germain, 6th (01.45.48.55.26,
www.cafedeflore.fr). M° St-Germain-des-
Prés.* **Open** 7am-2am daily. **€€**. **Café**.
Map p131 B2 **⑪**
Bourgeois locals crowd the terrace
tables at lunch, eating club sandwiches
with knives and forks as anxious waiters frown at couples with pushchairs
or single diners occupying tables for
four. This historic café, former HQ

of the Lost Generation intelligentsia, attracts tourists, and celebrities from time to time. But a *café crème* is €4.60, and the omelettes and croques are best eschewed in favour of the better dishes on the menu. There are play readings on Mondays and philosophy debates on the first Wednesday of the month.

La Compagnie des Vins Surnaturels

NEW *7 rue Lobineau, 6th (09.54.90. 20.20, www.compagniedesvins surnaturels.com). Mº Mabillon or Odéon.* **Open** 6pm-2am daily. €€€. **Wine bar**. **Map** p131 C3 ⑫

Forget cheap plonk – both the drinks and food here are nothing but the best. The wine list features more than 3,000 bottles, and to go with the booze there are some first-class treats such as *burrata*, *prosciutto al tartufo*, truffles and fine cheeses. The menu performs leaps and bounds from €20 to €4,000 a bottle. But even if you don't have four months' rent to spare, the lower end of the selection is worth a look.

Le Comptoir

Hôtel Le Relais Saint-Germain, 9 carrefour de l'Odéon, 6th (01.43.29. 12.05). Mº Odéon. **Open** noon-6pm, 8.30-11pm (last orders 9pm) Mon-Fri; noon-11pm Sat, Sun. €€. **Brasserie**. **Map** p131 C3 ⑬

Yves Camdeborde runs the bijou 17th-century Hôtel Le Relais Saint-Germain, whose art deco dining room, modestly dubbed Le Comptoir, serves brasserie fare from noon to 6pm and on weekend nights, and a five-course prix fixe feast on weekday evenings. The single dinner sitting lets the chef take real pleasure in his work. On the daily menu, you might find dishes like rolled saddle of lamb with vegetable-stuffed 'Basque ravioli'. The catch? Dinner can be booked up six months in advance.

Les Deux Magots

6 pl St-Germain-des-Prés, 6th (01.45. 48.55.25, www.lesdeuxmagots.com).

Well hung

The Musée Zadkine is gleaming after a revamp.

The **Musée Zadkine** (see p132), which reopened in autumn 2012 after a major renovation, is one of the most intimate museums in the French capital, a rare peaceful, almost secret corner where you can also get a good dose of modern art. The former studio of Russian-born Cubist sculptor Ossip Zadkine was converted into a museum in 1932, and has always had a particular charm, conserving the spirit of the place where the sculptor and his wife, painter Valentine Prax, lived for more than 40 years.

The reception area features a traditional samovar that provides tea for visitors, and beyond this is a procession of small, light-filled rooms displaying sculptures in wood, stone, plaster and clay. *Rebecca*, a large sculpture of a water-carrier, looks wonderful bathed in natural light. There's barely a wink to Valentine Prax, though, just a solitary canvas at the head of a staircase.

Zadkine is the master of this place, which is dominated by his angular portraits and women's bodies carved out of tree trunks in African-inspired elliptical forms. Don't miss the garden planted with stylised bronze statues (including the famous *Monument à la Ville Détruite de Rotterdam*), to extend your experience of avant-garde St-Germain which, in Zadkine's time, was the haunt of Amedeo Modigliani, Blaise Cendrars and Arthur Miller.

Mᵒ St-Germain-des-Prés. **Open** 7.30am-1am daily. €€. **Café. Map** p131 B2 ⑭
If you stand outside Les Deux Magots, you have to be prepared to photograph tourists wanting solid proof of their encounter with French philosophy. The former haunt of Sartre and de Beauvoir now draws a less pensive crowd that can be all too *m'as-tu vu*, particularly at weekends. The hot chocolate is still good, though. Visit on a weekday afternoon when the editors return, manuscripts in hand, to the inside tables, leaving enough elbow room to engage in some serious discussion.

L'Epigramme
9 rue de l'Eperon (01.44.41.00.09). Mᵒ Odéon. **Open** noon-2.30pm, 7-10.30pm Tue-Sat. €€. **Bistro. Map** p131 C2 ⑮
L'Epigramme is a pleasantly bourgeois dining room with terracotta floor tiles, wood beams, a glassed-in kitchen and comfortable chairs. Like the decor, the food doesn't aim to innovate but sticks to tried and true classics with the occasional twist. Marinated mackerel in a mustardy dressing on toasted country bread gets things off to a promising start, but the chef's skill really comes through in main courses such as perfectly seared lamb with glazed root vegetables and intense *jus*. It's rare to find such a high standard of cooking at this price. Be sure to book.

La Ferrandaise
8 rue de Vaugirard, 6th (01.43.26.36.36, www.laferrandaise.com). Mᵒ Odéon/RER Luxembourg. **Open** 7-10.30pm Mon, Sat; noon-2.30pm, 7-10.30pm Tue-Fri. €€. **Bistro. Map** p131 A4 ⑯
A platter of excellent ham, sausage and terrine arrives as you study the blackboard menu, and the bread is crisp-crusted, thickly sliced sourdough. Two specialities are the potato stuffed with *escargots* in a camembert sauce, and a wonderfully flavoured, slightly rosé slice of veal. Desserts might include intense chocolate with rum-soaked bananas.

Germain
25-27 rue de Buci, 6th (01.43.26.02.93, www.beaumarly.com). Mᵒ Mabillon or Odéon. **Open** 9am-2am daily. €€.
Brasserie. Map p131 C2 ⑰
Quaint rue de Buci has been shaken up by the sheer extravagance of Germain, a versatile brasserie that sits halfway between *Alice in Wonderland* and London's Sketch. The heated terrace is great for people watching, and the main ground-floor room, which features the lower part of a vast yellow statue piercing through the ceiling above, is perfect for a quick lunch. There's also a cosy salon for cocktails, a more conservative dining room at the back, and a private room on the first floor with a snooker table and the top half of the yellow statue. The food is almost childishly classic, but always with a twist (ham and butter macaroni with truffle, perhaps).

J'Go
Rue Clément, 6th (01.43.26.19.02, www.lejgo.com). Mᵒ Mabillon or Odéon. **Open** 11am-midnight daily. €€.
Wine bar. Map p131 C3 ⑱
As its name suggests, J'Go (pronounced *gigot*) is all about lamb – well, meat of various kinds, actually: a buzzing wine bar by day, it becomes a *rôtisserie* at meal times, serving its speciality spit-roasted lamb from Quercy, black pig from Bigorre, and whole roasted chickens. The set menu is well worth it, offering perhaps a whole jar of pâté, a giant salad, and lamb with creamy stewed *haricots blancs*. If you'd rather just stick to wine and tapas, sidle up to one of the wooden barrels, choose your poison and share a plate of charcuterie or foie gras *tartines*.

Lapérouse
51 quai des Grands-Augustins, 6th (01.43.26.68.04, www.laperouse.com). Mᵒ St-Michel. **Open** noon-2.30pm, 7.30-11pm Mon-Fri; 7.30-11pm Sat. €€€€. **Brasserie. Map** p143 A2 ⑲

PARIS BY AREA

Lapérouse was formerly a clandestine rendezvous for French politicians and their mistresses; the tiny private dining rooms upstairs used to lock from the inside. Chef Alain Hacquard does a reasonable take on classic French cooking: his beef fillet is smoked for a more complex flavour; a tender saddle of rabbit is cooked in a clay crust, flavoured with lavender and rosemary and served with ravioli of onions. The only snag is the cost, especially of the wine – a half-bottle of Pouilly-Fuissé will set you back around €35.

La Palette

43 rue de Seine, 6th (01.43.26.68.15). M° *Odéon.* **Open** 7am-2am Mon-Sat; 10am-2pm Sun. **€€. Café.** Map p131 C2 ⑳
La Palette is the café-bar of choice for the Beaux-Arts students who study at the venerable institution around the corner, and young couples who steal kisses in the wonderfully preserved art deco back room decorated with illustrations. Grab a spot on the leafy terrace if you can.

Pizza Chic

NEW *13 rue de Mézières, 6th (01.45.48.* *30.38, www.pizzachic.fr). M° St-Sulpice.* **Open** 12.30-2.30pm, 7.30-11pm Mon-Thur; 12.30-2.30pm, 7.30-11.30pm Fri, Sat; 12.30-2.30pm, 7.30-10pm Sun. **€€.** **Pizza.** Map p131 B3 ㉑
Despite the name, this contemporary, polished pizzeria isn't the least bit ostentatious and the pizzas are among the best in Paris. White (no tomato base) or red, the pizzas are beautiful as well as delicious: tuck into the luxurious spiciness of the *carciofi* (artichoke cream, raw artichokes, rocket, aged parmesan) or the simplicity of the *aurora* (tomato, mozzarella, fresh basil).

Prescription Cocktail Club

23 rue Mazarine, 6th (01.46.34.67.73, *www.prescriptioncocktailclub.com).* *M° Odéon.* **Open** 7pm-2am Mon-Thur; 7pm-4am Fri, Sat; 8pm-2am Sun. **Bar.** Map p131 C2 ㉒

This stylish 1930s-style speakeasy has a retro Prohibition feel but remains severely Left Bank, with crowds of well-dressed people sipping cocktails by candlelight. It's always busy and almost impossible to navigate at weekends.

Le Restaurant

L'Hôtel, 13 rue des Beaux-Arts, 6th *(01.44.41.99.01, www.l-hotel.com). M°* *St-Germain-des-Prés.* **Open** 7-10.30am, 12.30-2pm, 7.30-10pm Tue-Sat. **€€€.** **Haute cuisine.** Map p131 C2 ㉓
L'Hôtel's restaurant is a wonderfully atmospheric spot for lunch or dinner. You can choose from a short seasonal menu with such dishes as pan-fried tuna, John Dory or suckling pig. But for the same price you can enjoy the marvellous four-course *menu dégustation* or, even better, the *menu surprise.* Past highlights have included smoked Somme eel with horseradish and lime.

Le Rostand

6 pl Edmond-Rostand, 6th (01.43.54. *61.58). RER Luxembourg.* **Open** 8am-midnight daily. **Bar.** Map p131 C3 ㉔
Le Rostand has a truly wonderful view of the Jardin du Luxembourg from its classy interior, decked out with oriental paintings, a mahogany bar and wall-length mirrors. Perfect for a civilised drink after a stroll round the gardens.

Le Select

99 bd du Montparnasse, 6th (01.45. *48.38.24). M° Vavin.* **Open** 7am-2am Mon-Thur, Sun; 7am-4am Fri, Sat. **€. Café.** Map p131 B5 ㉕
For a decade between the wars, this area was where Man Ray, Cocteau and Lost Generation Americans hung out in the vast, glass-fronted cafés. Eight decades on, Le Select is the best of these inevitable tourist haunts.

Shu

8 rue Suger, 6th (01.46.34.25.88, www. *restaurant-shu.com). M° St-Michel or* *Odéon.* **Open** 6.30-11.30pm Mon-Sat. **€€€. Japanese.** Map p131 C2 ㉖

Shu specialises in *kushi-agué* – a sort of Japanese kebab, with different ingredients breaded and fired on sticks. But where it really excels is in the starters, often more refined than at the purest *kaïseki* bar. Despite the price, opt for the more expensive menu, which represents better value for money: €58 for an *amuse-bouche*, a delicious assortment of incredibly fresh sashimi, three seasonal dishes, nine *kushi-agué* and a choice of *ochazuké* (rice with green tea and condiments) or *inaniwa* (fine udon noodles) served cold with their own cooking liquor. There are some very good sakes on the wine list and the service is impeccable.

Le Timbre

3 rue Ste-Beuve, 6th (01.45.49.10.40, www.restaurantletimbre.com). Mº Vavin. **Open** noon-1.30pm, 7-10.30pm Tue-Sat. Closed Aug & 1wk Dec. €€.
Bistro. Map p131 B4 ㉗
Chris Wright's restaurant might be the size of the average student garret, but this Mancunian aims high. Typical of his cooking is a plate of fresh asparagus elegantly cut in half lengthways and served with dabs of anise-spiked sauce and balsamic vinegar. Mains are also pure in flavour – a slab of pork, pan-fried, comes with an accompaniment of petals of red onion.

Shopping

APC

38 rue Madame, 6th (01.42.22.12.77, www.apc.fr). Mº St-Placide. **Open** 11am-7.30pm Mon-Sat; 12.30-6.30pm Sun. **Map** p131 B4 ㉘
The look here is simple but stylish: think perfectly cut basics in muted tones. Hip without trying too hard, its jeans are a big hit.

Arty Dandy

1 rue de Furstemberg, 6th (01.43.54. 00.36, www.artydandy.com). Mº Mabillon. **Open** 10.30am-7pm Mon-Fri; 10.30am-7.30pm Sat. **Map** p131 C2 ㉙

Arty Dandy is a concept shop that thoroughly embraces the surreal, the tongue-in-cheek and the poetic – an R.MUTT sticker to create your own Duchampian loo, and the 'Karl who?' bag (which KL himself has been known to carry) are instant pleasers. More sublime offerings include Jaime Hayon's 'Lover' figurines.

Christian Constant

37 rue d'Assas, 6th (01.53.63.15.15). Mº Rennes or St-Placide. **Open** 9.30am-8.30pm Mon-Fri; 9am-8pm Sat, Sun.
Map p131 B4 ㉚
A master chocolate-maker and *traiteur*, Constant scours the globe for ideas. His *ganaches* are subtly flavoured with verbena, jasmine or cardamom.

Démocratie

NEW *14 bd St-Michel, 6th (01.56.24. 05.55). Mº St-Michel.* **Open** 11am-7.30pm Mon-Sat; 2-7pm Sun. **Map** p131 C2 ㉛
This multi-brand boutique has injected a hint of underground culture into the tourist district of Saint-Michel. Sisters Kimo and Diana took over the former music and bookshop Silly Melody, which had been run by Kimo and her father. They have since breathed new life and a new philosophy into the place, modernising it in the style of a London or Berlin concept store. On the ground floor, you'll find a selection of designer objects and accessories, books and magazines with a retro touch. Fashion for women and men is on the first floor, with a good selection of streetwear and brands such as Vans, Dunderdone and Be Street, but also ethnic print bags by Pendelton and trendy shoes by Jeffrey Campbell.

Gérard Mulot

76 rue de Seine, 6th (01.43.26.85.77, www.gerard-mulot.com). Mº Odéon. **Open** 6.45am-8pm Mon, Tue, Thur-Sun. Closed Easter & Aug. **Map** p131 C3 ㉜
Gérard Mulot rustles up stunning pastries. Try the *mabillon*: caramel mousse with apricot jam.

PARIS BY AREA

Hermès

17 rue de Sèvres, 6th (01.42.22.80.83).
Mº Sèvres Babylone. **Open** 10.30am-7pm
Mon-Sat. **Map** p131 A3 ⑬

If you thought that Hermès was about
horsey scarves and little else, a visit to
this shop should dispel the equestrian
rumours forever. Designed by Denis
Montel, the concept store is set in the
Hôtel Lutetia's former indoor pool. The
renovations have produced one of the
best-looking retail spaces on the Left
Bank. While the trademark scarves
and ties are all present and correct, the
three-floor store also focuses strongly
on homewares, from wallpaper and
carpets to sumptuous reproductions
of 1930s-era furniture by renowned
designer Jean-Michel Frank.

Hervé Chapelier

1bis rue du Vieux-Colombier, 6th (01.44.
07.06.50, www.hervechapelier.fr). Mº
St-Germain-des-Prés or St-Sulpice. **Open**
10.15am-7pm Mon-Sat. **Map** p131 B3 ⑭

Pick up a classic two-tone bag. Sizes
range from purses to weekend bags.

Huilerie Artisanale Leblanc

12 rue Jacob, 6th (01.44.07.36.58, www.
huile-leblanc.com). Mº St-Germain-des-
Prés. **Open** 11am-1.30pm, 2.30-7pm
Tue-Sat. **Map** p131 C2 ⑮

The Leblanc family started making
walnut oil before branching out to press
pure oils from hazelnuts, almonds, pine
nuts, grilled peanuts and olives. There
are vinegars and mustards too.

La Hune

170 bd St-Germain, 6th (01.45.48.
35.85). Mº St-Germain-des-Prés. **Open**
10am-11.45pm Mon-Sat; 11am-7.45pm
Sun. **Map** p131 B2 ⑯

This Left Bank institution boasts
a global selection of art and design
books, and a truly magnificent collection of French literature and theory.

Jean-Paul Hévin

3 rue Vavin, 6th (01.43.54.09.85,
www.jphevin.com). Mº Notre-Dame-
des-Champs or Vavin. **Open** 10am-7pm
Tue-Sat. Closed Aug. **Map** p131 B4 ⑰

Hévin specialises in the beguiling
combination of chocolate with potent
cheese fillings, which loyal customers
serve with wine as an aperitif.

Lefranc.ferrant

22 rue de l'Echaudé, 6th (01.40.21.
03.29, www.lefranc-ferrant.fr). Mº
St-Germain-des-Prés. **Open** 11am-7pm
Tue-Sat. **Map** p131 C2 ⑱

Béatrice Ferrant and Mario Lefranc
have a surreal approach to tailoring,
as in a strapless yellow evening gown
made like a pair of men's trousers –
complete with flies.

Marie-Hélène de Taillac

8 rue de Tournon, 6th (01.44.27.07.07,
www.mariehelenedetaillac.com). Mº
Mabillon. **Open** 11am-7pm Mon-Sat.
Map p131 C3 ⑲

Marie-Hélène de Taillac is a fine jeweller,
using diamonds and emeralds in simple
settings. This combination of precious
stones and modern styling has made her
popular with the fashion elite. They also
adore her Left Bank shop.

Marie Mercié

23 rue St-Sulpice, 6th (01.43.26.45.83,
www.mariemercie.com). Mº Odéon. **Open**
11am-7pm Mon-Sat. **Map** p131 C3 ⑳

Mercié's creations make you wish
you lived in an era when hats were de
rigueur. Step out in one shaped like
curved fingers (with shocking-pink
nail varnish and pink diamond ring)
or a beret like a face with red lips and
turquoise eyes. Ready-to-wear starts at
about €30; *sur mesure* takes ten days.

Patrick Roger

108 bd St-Germain, 6th (01.43.29.
38.42, www.patrickroger.com). Mº
Odéon. **Open** 10.30am-7.30pm daily.
Map p131 B2 ㉑

Whereas other *chocolatiers* aim for
gloss, Roger may create a brushed
effect on hens so realistic you almost
expect them to lay (chocolate) eggs.

Sonia Rykiel p140

Peggy Huyn Kinh

9-11 rue Coëtlogon, 6th (01.42.84.83.84, www.phk.fr). M° St-Sulpice. **Open** 11am-7pm Mon-Sat. **Map** p131 B3 ㊷

Once creative director at Cartier, Peggy Huyn Kinh now makes bags of boar skin and python, plus silver jewellery.

Pierre Hermé

72 rue Bonaparte, 6th (01.43.54.47.77). M° Mabillon, St-Germain-des-Prés or St-Sulpice. **Open** 10am-7pm Mon-Wed, Sun; 10am-7.30pm Thur, Fri; 10am-8pm Sat. Closed Sun in Aug. **Map** p131 B3 ㊸

Pastry superstar Hermé attracts connoisseurs from near and far.

Poilâne

8 rue du Cherche-Midi, 6th (01.45.48.42.59, www.poilane.com). M° Sèvres Babylone or St-Sulpice. **Open** 7.15am-8.15pm Mon-Sat. **Map** p131 B3 ㊹

Locals queue for fresh country *miches*, flaky-crusted apple tarts and shortbread biscuits.

Princesse Tam-Tam

52 bd St-Michel, 6th (01.40.51.72.99, www.princessetamtam.com). M° Cluny La Sorbonne. **Open** 1.30-7pm Mon; 10.30am-7.30pm Tue-Sat (closed 3-4pm Wed, Thur). **Map** p131 C3 ㊺

This fun, inexpensive underwear and swimwear brand has traffic-stopping promotions. Bright colours rule.

Sonia Rykiel

175 bd St-Germain, 6th (01.49.54.60.60, www.soniarykiel.com). M° St-Germain-des-Prés or Sèvres Babylone. **Open** 10.30am-7pm Mon-Sat. **Map** p131 B2 ㊻

This flagship store features a glamorous black and smoked glass look, perfect for narcissists. Menswear is located across the street, and two newer boutiques stock Sonia by Sonia Rykiel.

Vanessa Bruno

25 rue St-Sulpice, 6th (01.43.54.41.04, www.vanessabruno.com). M° Odéon. **Open** 10.30am-7.30pm Mon-Sat. **Map** p131 C3 ㊼

Bruno's mercerised cotton tanks, flattering trousers and tops have a Zen-like quality. She also makes great bags.

Yves Saint Laurent

6 pl St-Sulpice, 6th (01.43.29.43.00, www.ysl.com). M° St-Sulpice. **Open** 11am-7pm Mon; 10.30am-7pm Tue-Sat. **Map** p131 C3 ㊽

The memory of the founding designer, who died in 2008, lives on in this wonderfully elegant boutique, which was splendidly refitted in red in the same year. You'll find the menswear collection at 32 rue du Fbg-St-Honoré (8th).

Nightlife

Le Montana

28 rue St-Benoît, 6th (no phone). M° St-Germain-des-Prés. **Open** 11pm-5am daily. **Admission** free. **Map** p131 B2 ㊾

It's hard to believe that any place could out-hype Le Baron, but this exclusive club manages it. Revamped by über-cool graphic artist André, Le Montana is a VIP magnet – Lenny Kravitz, Vanessa Bruno and Kate Moss have all hit the floor here.

Arts & leisure

Le Lucernaire

53 rue Notre-Dame-des-Champs, 6th (01.42.22.26.50, www.lucernaire.fr). M° Notre-Dame-des-Champs or Vavin. **Admission** €15-€30. **Map** p131 B4 ㊿

Three theatres, three cinemas, a restaurant and a bar make up this versatile cultural centre. Molière and other classic playwrights get a good thrashing.

Odéon, Théâtre de L'Europe

Pl de l'Odéon, 6th (01.44.85.40.00, bookings 01.44.85.40.40, www.theatre-odeon.fr). M° Odéon. **Box office** 11am-6pm Mon-Sat. **Admission** €6-€36. **Map** p131 C3 (51)

Recent hits have included *As You Like It* and *Cyrano de Bergerac*. The theatre also plays host to the annual Impatience festival for young theatre companies.

Institut du Monde Arabe p142

The Latin Quarter & the 13th

The Latin Quarter

To many first-time visitors – especially those from the States – the Latin Quarter can be a big disappointment. Countless books have led them to believe that the area is somehow the quintessence of Paris, and they come with their heads stuffed with expat writers – Orwell, Hemingway, Henry Miller – only to find a touristy jam of bad restaurants and uninspiring shops. However, many of the narrow, crooked streets (like the Marais, the Latin Quarter was another part of Paris largely untouched by Haussmann) are charming, and there are some real architectural glories.

Sights & museums

Arènes de Lutèce
Rue Monge, rue de Navarre or rue des Arènes, 5th. M° Cardinal Lemoine or Place Monge. **Open** Summer 9am-9.30pm daily. Winter 8am-5.30pm daily. **Admission** free. **Map** p143 B4 ❶
This Roman arena, where wild beasts and gladiators fought, could seat 10,000 people. It was still visible during the reign of Philippe-Auguste in the 12th century, then disappeared under rubble. The site now attracts skateboarders, footballers and boules players.

Eglise St-Etienne-du-Mont
Pl Ste-Geneviève, 5th (01.43.54.11.79, www.saintetiennedumont.fr). M° Cardinal Lemoine/RER Luxembourg. **Open** 8.45am-7.45pm Tue-Fri; 8.45am-noon, 2-7.45pm Sat; 8.45am-12.15pm, 2-7.45pm Sun. July, Aug 10am-noon, 4-7.45pm Tue-Sun. **Map** p143 B4 ❷
Geneviève, patron saint of Paris, is credited with having miraculously saved the city from the ravages of Attila the Hun in 451, and her shrine has been a site of pilgrimage ever since. The present church was built in an amalgam of

Gothic and Renaissance styles between 1492 and 1626, and the interior is wonderfully tall and light, with soaring columns and a classical balustrade. The stunning Renaissance rood screen, with its double spiral staircase and ornate stone strapwork, is the only surviving one in Paris. At the back of the church (reached through the sacristy), the catechism chapel constructed by Baltard in the 1860s has a cycle of paintings relating the saint's life story.

Eglise St-Séverin

3 rue des Prêtres-St-Séverin, 5th (01.42. 34.93.50, www.saint-severin.com). M° Cluny La Sorbonne or St-Michel. **Open** 11am-7.30pm Mon-Sat; 9am-8.30pm Sun. **Map** p143 A3 ❸

Built on the site of the chapel of the hermit Séverin, itself set on a much earlier Merovingian burial ground, this lovely Flamboyant Gothic edifice was long the parish church of the Left Bank. The church dates from the 15th century, though the doorway, carved with foliage, was added in 1837 from the demolished Eglise St-Pierre-aux-Boeufs on Ile de la Cité. The double ambulatory is famed for its forest of 'palm tree' vaulting, which meets at the end in a unique spiral column that inspired a series of paintings by Robert Delaunay. The bell tower, a survivor from one of the earlier churches on the site, has the oldest bell in Paris (1412).

Eglise du Val-de-Grâce

Pl Alphonse-Laveran, 5th (01.40.51. 51.92, www.valdegrace.org). RER Luxembourg or Port-Royal. **Open** 2-6pm Mon-Sat; 9am-noon, 2-6pm Sun. **Admission** free. **Map** p143 A5 ❹

Anne of Austria, the wife of Louis XIII, vowed to erect 'a magnificent temple' if God blessed her with a son. She got two. The resulting church and surrounding Benedictine monastery – these days a military hospital and the Musée du Service de Santé des Armées – were built by François Mansart and Jacques Lemercier. This is the most luxuriously baroque of Paris's 17th-century domed churches. In contrast, the surrounding monastery offers the perfect example of Mansart's classical restraint. Phone in advance if you're after a guided visit.

Grande Galerie de l'Evolution

36 rue Geoffroy-St-Hilaire, 2 rue Bouffon or pl Valhubert, 5th (01.40.79.56.01, www.mnhn.fr). M° Gare d'Austerlitz or Jussieu. **Open** *Grande Galerie* 10am-6pm Mon, Wed-Sun. *Other galleries* 10am-5pm Mon, Wed-Fri; 10am-6pm Sat, Sun. **Admission** *Grande Galerie* €7; free-€5 reductions. *Other galleries* (each) €7; free-€5 reductions. No credit cards. **Map** p143 C5 ❺

Located within the Jardin des Plantes, this 19th-century iron-framed, glass-roofed structure has been modernised with lifts, galleries and false floors, and filled with life-size models of tentacle-waving squid, open-mawed sharks and monkeys swarming down from the ceiling. The centrepiece is a procession of African wildlife across the first floor that resembles the procession into Noah's Ark. Glass-sided lifts take you up through suspended birds to the second floor, which deals with man's impact on nature (crocodile to handbag). The third floor focuses on endangered species.

Institut du Monde Arabe

1 rue des Fossés-St-Bernard, 5th (01.40.51.38.38, www.imarabe.org). M° Jussieu. **Open** *Museum* 10am-6pm Tue-Thur; 10am-9.30pm Fri; 10am-7pm Sat, Sun. *Library* 1-8pm Tue-Sat (July, Aug 1-6pm). *Tours* 3pm Tue-Fri; 3pm & 4.30pm Sat, Sun. **Admission** *Museum* €8; free-€6 reductions. *Library* free. *Exhibitions* varies. **Map** p143 C3 ❻

One of Paris's most innovative museums reopened in 2012 after a three-year revamp. Collections from the 22 Arab countries that co-founded the museum can now be enjoyed once again, in an exciting and dynamic new interior. Some 600 items are on display, from places as diverse as Damascus,

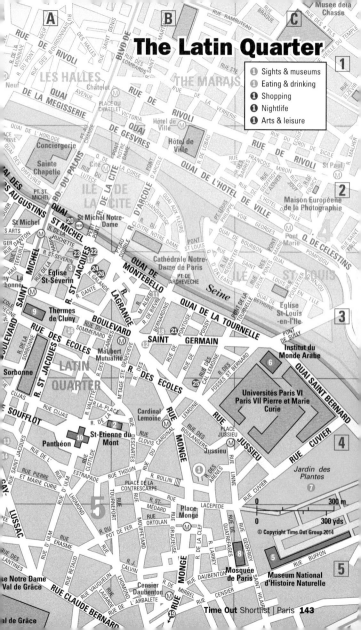

The Latin Quarter

- **1** Sights & museums
- **1** Eating & drinking
- **1** Shopping
- **1** Nightlife
- **1** Arts & leisure

Aleppo, Latakia, Amman, Kairouan and Manama, as well as the Musée du Louvre, the Musée du Quai Branly and the Bibliothèque Nationale de France. And where before the collection was limited to art, the new museum has widened its scope, showcasing the Arab world in thematic ways, covering its ethno-linguistic, historical, cultural, anthropological and geographical diversity. What's more, there's a lively events programme (exhibitions, film screenings, music and dance) and an excellent Middle East bookshop on the ground floor, and the views from the roof terrace (free access) are fabulous.

Jardin des Plantes

36 rue Geoffroy-St-Hilaire, 2 rue Bouffon, pl Valhubert or 57 rue Cuvier, 5th. Mº Gare d'Austerlitz or Place Monge (01.40.79.56.01, www.jardindesplantes.net). **Open** *Main garden* Winter 8am-5.30pm daily. Summer 7.30am-8pm daily. *Alpine garden* Apr-Oct 8am-4.40pm Mon-Fri; 1.30-6pm Sat, Sun. Closed Nov-Mar. *Ménagerie* 9am-6pm Mon-Sat; 9am-6.30pm Sun. **Admission** *Alpine garden* free-Nov-Mar; €2 Sat, Sun. *Jardin des Plantes* free. *Ménagerie* €11; free-€9 reductions. **Map** p143 C4 ❼

The Paris botanical garden – which contains more than 10,000 species and includes tropical greenhouses and rose, winter and Alpine gardens – is an enchanting place. Begun by Louis XIII's doctor as the royal medicinal plant garden in 1626, it opened to the public in 1640. The formal garden is like something out of *Alice in Wonderland*. There's also a small zoo and the terrific Grande Galerie de l'Evolution. Ancient trees on view include a false acacia planted in 1636. A plaque on the old laboratory declares that this is the spot where Henri Becquerel discovered radioactivity in 1896.

La Mosquée de Paris

2 pl du Puits-de-l'Ermite, 5th (01.45.35.97.33, tearoom 01.43.31.38.20, baths 01.43.31.18.14, www.mosquee-de-paris.net). Mº Monge. **Open** *Tours* 9am-noon, 2-6pm Mon-Thur, Sat, Sun (closed Muslim hols). *Tearoom* 10am-11.30pm daily. *Restaurant* noon-2.30pm, 7.30-10.30pm daily. *Baths* (women) 10am-9pm Mon, Wed, Sat; 2-9pm Fri; (men) 2-9pm Tue, Sun. **Admission** €3; free-€2 reductions. *Tearoom* free. *Baths* €15-€35. **Map** p143 C5 ❽

This vast Hispano-Moorish construct is the spiritual heart of France's Algerian-dominated Muslim population. In plan and function it divides into three sections: religious (grand patio, prayer room and minaret, all for worshippers and not curious tourists); scholarly (Islamic school and library); and, via rue Geoffroy-St-Hilaire, commercial (café and domed hammam). La Mosquée café is delightful – a courtyard shaded beneath green foliage and scented with the sweet smell of sheesha smoke.

Musée National du Moyen Age – Thermes de Cluny

6 pl Paul-Painlevé, 5th (01.53.73.78.00, www.musee-moyenage.fr). Mº Cluny La Sorbonne. **Open** 9.15am-5.45pm Mon, Wed-Sun. **Admission** €8; free-€6 reductions. **Map** p143 A3 ❾

The national museum of medieval art is best known for the beautiful, allegorical *Lady and the Unicorn* tapestry cycle, but it also has important collections of medieval sculpture and enamels. The building itself, which is commonly known as Cluny, is also a rare example of 15th-century secular Gothic architecture, with its foliate Gothic doorways, hexagonal staircase jutting out of the façade and vaulted chapel. It was built from 1485 to 1498 – on top of a Gallo-Roman baths complex. The baths, built in characteristic Roman bands of stone and brick masonry, are the finest Roman remains in Paris. The vaulted *frigidarium* (cold bath), *tepidarium* (warm bath), *caldarium* (hot bath) and part of the hypocaust heating system are all still visible. A themed garden fronts the whole complex.

PARIS BY AREA

Sweet treats

The cream of the capital's neo-pâtisseries.

Within a few days of **Aux Merveilleux de Fred** opening its latest branch (2 rue Monge, 5th, 01.42.27.86.63, www.aux merveilleux.com), it had a queue of sweet-toothed foodies stretching out of the door eager to try its *merveilleux* – a northern French combination of meringue, whipped cream and flakes of chocolate. Across the street, others lined up at **Ciel** (see p147) to sample Japanese chef Aya Tamura's heavenly angel cakes. Both are part of the current craze for specialist pâtisseries and the success of the blogosphere that makes the right cake the latest fashion accessory.

There seem to be two main schools of cake thought. On one side are the inventors, creating new cakes and rethinking old ones. Cyril Lignac, France's equivalent of Jamie Oliver, recently opened his second **Pâtisserie Cyril Lignac** (2 rue de Chaillot, 16th, www. lapatisseriecyrillignac.com) in an artfully distressed boutique opposite the Palais Galliera, where you can try his takes on old classics such as tarte au citron and millefeuille, baked in the 'laboratory' in the cellar.

Then there are the so-called 'monomaniacs', who take a single obsession to the extreme. The craze of the moment is decidedly choux-shaped, making macaroons look positively passé. Marais boutique **Popelini** (29 rue Debelleyme, 3rd, 01.44.61.31.44, www.popelini.com) sells round *choux à la crème* (profiteroles) and nothing but; Christophe Adam's **L'Eclair de Génie** (14 rue Pavée,

Ciel

4th, 01.42.77.85.11, www. leclairdegenie.com), which translates roughly as 'stroke of genius', is devoted to the eclair in every imaginable colour; **L'Atelier de l'Eclair** (16 rue Bauchaumont, 2nd, 01.42.36.40.54, www. latelierdeleclair.fr), serves up eclairs topped with everything from salted butter caramel to lemon meringue, plus savoury sandwich eclairs such as curried chicken or smoked salmon; and Christophe Michalak has teamed up with Alain Ducasse and designer Patrick Jouin at **Choux d'Enfer** (corner of rue Jean-Rey and quai Branly, 15th, 01.47.83.26.67), a streamlined kiosk where choux – Ducasse's 'memories of childhood' – are filled on the spot, as the craze for street food meets sweet food.

Le Panthéon

Pl du Panthéon, 5th (01.44.32.18.00).
M° Cardinal Lemoine/RER Luxembourg.
Open 10am-6pm (until 6.30pm summer)
daily. **Admission** €7.50; free-€4.50
reductions. **Map** p143 A4 ⑩

Soufflot's neoclassical megastructure
was the architectural *grand projet* of
its day, commissioned by a grateful
Louis XV to thank Sainte Geneviève
for his recovery from illness. But by
the time it was ready in 1790, a lot had
changed; during the Revolution, the
Panthéon was rededicated as a 'temple
of reason' and the resting place of the
nation's great men. The barrel-vaulted
crypt now houses Voltaire, Rousseau,
Hugo and Zola. New heroes are installed
but rarely: Pierre and Marie Curie's
remains were transferred here in 1995;
Alexandre Dumas in 2002. Mount the
steep spiral stairs to the colonnade
encircling the dome for superb views.

Eating & drinking

Atelier Maître Albert

1 rue Maître-Albert, 5th (01.56.81.
30.01, www.ateliermaitrealbert.com).
M° Maubert Mutualité or St-Michel.
Open noon-2.30pm, 6.30-11pm Mon-
Wed; noon-2.30pm, 6.30pm-1am Thur,
Fri; 6.30pm-1am Sat; 6.30-11.30pm Sun.
€€. **Bistro**. **Map** p143 B3 ⑪

This Guy Savoy outpost has slick decor
by Jean-Michel Wilmotte. The indigo-
painted, grey marble-floored dining
room with open kitchen and rôtisseries
on view is attractive but very noisy at
night. The short menu lets you have
a Savoy classic or two to start with,
including oysters in seawater gelée or
more inventive dishes such as the bal-
lotine of chicken, foie gras and celery
root in a chicken-liver sauce. Next up,
perhaps, tuna served with tiny iron
casseroles of dauphinoise potatoes, and
cauliflower in béchamel sauce.

Ciel

NEW *3 rue Monge, 5th (01.43.29.40.78,*
www.patisserie-ciel.com). M° Maubert-
Mutualité. **Open** 10.30am-11pm Tue-
Thur; 10.30am-1am Fri, Sat; 10.30am-
5pm Sun. €€. **Café**. **Map** p143 B3 ⑫

Macaroons, cupcakes and choux buns
have all had their food fashion moments
in Paris, and now it's the turn of the
angel cake – light, fluffy American
treats, here adapted by a Japanese
kitchen. There are six flavours on offer
at Ciel, a *salon de thé* entirely devoted
to angel cake: from the classic (rose,
chocolate and vanilla-caramel) to the
more unusual (lemon *yuzu* or green tea
matcha). In the evenings, the *salon de
thé* becomes a trendy bar, where fans
of Japanese whisky can indulge while
snacking on savoury dishes.

Le Crocodile

6 rue Royer-Collard, 5th (01.43.54.
32.37). RER Luxembourg. **Open**
6pm-2am Mon-Sat. No credit cards.
Bar. **Map** p143 A4 ⑬

Ignore the apparently boarded-up
windows at Le Crocodile; if you're here
late, then it's open. Friendly young
regulars line the sides of this small,
narrow bar and try to decide what to
drink – not easy, given the length of the
cocktail list: at last count there were 317
varieties. The generous €6-per-cocktail
happy hour (6-11pm Mon-Thur) will
allow you to start with a champagne
accroche-coeur, followed up with a
Goldschläger (served with gold leaf)
before moving on to one of the other 316.

Le Pantalon

7 rue Royer-Collard, 5th (no phone).
RER Luxembourg. **Open** 5.30pm-
1.45am daily. No credit cards. €.
Café. **Map** p143 A4 ⑭

Le Pantalon is a local café that seems
familiar yet is utterly surreal. It has the
standard fixtures, including the old
soaks at the bar – but the regulars and
staff are enough to tip the balance into
eccentricity. Friendly, funny French
grown-ups and foreign students chat
in a mishmash of languages; drinks
are cheap enough to make you tipsy
without the worry of a cash hangover.

Les Papilles

30 rue Gay-Lussac, 5th (01.43.25.20.79, www.lespapillesparis.fr). Mº Luxembourg. **Open** noon-2pm, 7-10.30pm Tue-Sat. **€€**. **Bistro**. **Map** p143 A4 ⑮

This quaint little bistro, which doubles as a wine shop and *épicerie*, is a safe bet in an otherwise touristy neighbourhood. Waiters rattle off the menu, then invite you to choose your bottle of wine from the wall. Wine aficionados will have a field day; wine amateurs, ask for help. A €7 corkage fee is applied to each bottle. On the plate, expect seasonal tastes such as carrot soup poured over crispy bacon and sour cream, cod with capers in a sizzling hot copper dish, and salted caramel and poached pear panna cotta. It gets crowded and the noise level picks up later on, but it's all part of the fun.

Le Pré Verre

8 rue Thénard, 5th (01.43.54.59.47, www.lepreverre.com). Mº Maubert Mutualité. **Open** noon-2pm, 7.30-10.30pm Tue-Sat. Closed 22 Dec-6 Jan. **€€**. **Bistro**. **Map** p143 A3 ⑯

Philippe Delacourcelle knows how to handle spices like few other French chefs. Salt cod with cassia bark and smoked potato purée is a classic: what the fish lacks in size it makes up for in rich flavour and crunchy texture, and smooth potato cooked in a smoker makes a startling accompaniment.

Ribouldingue

10 rue St-Julien-le-Pauvre, 5th (01.46.33.98.80, www.restaurant-ribouldingue.com). Mº St-Michel. **Open** noon-2pm, 7-11pm Tue-Sat. **€€**. **Bistro**. **Map** p143 A3 ⑰

This bistro facing St-Julien-le-Pauvre church is the creation of Nadège Varigny, who spent ten years working with Yves Camdeborde before opening a restaurant inspired by the food of her childhood in Grenoble. It's full of people, including critics and chefs, who love simple, honest bistro fare, such as *daube de boeuf* or seared tuna on a bed of melting aubergine. If you have an appetite for offal, then you might want to opt for the gently sautéed brains with new potatoes or veal kidneys with a perfectly prepared potato gratin.

Da Zavola

24 rue des Bernadins, 5th (01.46.34.66.97, www.dazavola.com). Mº Maubert-Mutualité. **Open** 10.30am-10pm Tue-Sat. **€**. **Café**. **Map** p143 B3 ⑱

Da Zavola is a contemporary café of the sort the Italians term a *gastronomia*, where you can taste gourmet treats from across Italy and get an outstanding espresso. The bar is open all day serving everything from prosciutto crudo and mozzarella to grilled aubergines and toasted foccacia, pasta at lunch and dinner, and *aperitivi* in the early evening. And for the perfect treat after *cannoli*, a traditional Sicilian dessert, order a *marocchino*, a lethal glass of syrupy liquid chocolate topped off with an espresso and a drop of frothy milk.

Shopping

Le Boulanger de Monge

123 rue Monge, 5th (01.43.37.54.20, www.leboulangerdemonge.com). Mº Censier Daubenton. **Open** 7am-8.30pm Tue-Sun. **Map** p143 B5 ⑲

Dominique Saibron uses spices to give wonderful flavour to his organic sourdough *boule*. Every day about 2,000 bread-lovers visit this boutique, which also produces one of the city's best baguettes.

Bouquinistes

Along the quais, especially quai de Montebello & quai St-Michel, 5th. Mº St-Michel. **Open** times vary from stall to stall, generally Tue-Sun. No credit cards. **Map** p143 A2 ⑳

The green, open-air boxes along the *quais* are one of the city's institutions. As well as the inevitable postcards and tourist tat, most sell a good selection of second-hand books – rummage through boxes packed with ancient paperbacks for something existential.

Diptyque

34 bd St-Germain, 5th (01.43.26.77.44, www.diptyqueparis.com). M° Maubert Mutualité. **Open** 10am-7pm Mon-Sat. **Map** p143 B3 ㉑

Diptyque's divinely scented candles are the quintessential gift from Paris. They come in 48 varieties and are probably the best you'll ever find. Prices aren't cheap, but with 50 to 60 hours' burn time, they're worth every euro.

Shakespeare & Company

37 rue de la Bûcherie, 5th (01.43.25. 40.93, www.shakespeareandcompany. com). M° St-Michel. **Open** 10am-11pm Mon-Fri; 11am-11pm Sat, Sun. **Map** p143 A3 ㉒

Unequivocably the best bookshop in Paris, the ramshackle Shakespeare & Co is always packed to the rafters with expat and tourist book lovers.

Nightlife

Caveau de la Huchette

5 rue de la Huchette, 5th (01.43.26. 65.05, www.caveaudelahuchette.fr). M° St-Michel. **Open** 9.30pm-2.30am Mon-Thur, Sun; 9.30pm-6am Fri, Sat. *Concerts* 10pm. **Map** p143 A2 ㉓

This medieval cellar has been a mainstay for 60 years. The jazz shows are followed by early-hours performances in a swing, rock, soul or disco vein.

Caveau des Oubliettes

52 rue Galande, 5th (01.46.34.23.09, www.caveaudesoubliettes.fr). M° St-Michel. **Open** 5pm-2am Mon, Tue, Sun; 5pm-4am Wed-Sat. *Concerts* 10pm Wed-Sun. **Map** p143 A3 ㉔

Atmosphere abounds in this former dungeon, complete with instruments of torture. There are various jam sessions in the week, and on Sundays.

Paradis Latin

28 rue Cardinal Lemoine, 5th (01.43. 25.28.28, www.paradislatin.com). M° Cardinal Lemoine. **Dinner** 8pm. **Show** 9.30pm daily. **Map** p143 B4 ㉕

This is the most authentic of the cabarets, not only because it's family-run (the men run the cabaret, the daughter does the costumes), but also because the clientele is mostly French, something which has a direct effect on the prices (this is the cheapest revue) and the cuisine, which tends to be high quality. Show-wise you can expect the usual fare: generous doses of glitter, live singing and cheesy *entr'acte* acts.

Arts & leisure

Studio Galande

42 rue Galande, 5th (01.43.54.72.71, www.studiogalande.fr). M° St-Michel. No credit cards. **Map** p143 A3 ㉖

Some 20 different films are screened in subtitled versions at this venerable Latin Quarter venue every week: international arthouse fare, combined with the occasional instalment from the *Matrix* series. On Friday and Saturday nights, dedicated fans of *The Rocky Horror Picture Show* turn up in drag, equipped with rice and water pistols.

The 13th

The construction in the mid-1990s of the **Bibliothèque Nationale de France** breathed life into the desolate area now known as the ZAC Rive Gauche, between Gare d'Austerlitz and the Périphérique. The long-term ZAC project includes a new university quarter, housing projects and a tramway providing links to the suburbs.

Sights & museums

Bibliothèque Nationale de France François Mitterrand

10 quai François-Mauriac, 13th (01.53. 79.59.59, www.bnf.fr). M° Bibliothèque François Mitterrand. **Open** 2-7pm Mon; 9am-7pm Tue-Sat; 1-7pm Sun. **Admission** *1 day* €3.50. *1 year* €38; €20 reductions. **Map** p151 E2 ㉗

PARIS BY AREA

Opened in 1996, the new national library, which houses over ten million volumes, was the last and costliest of Mitterrand's *grands projets*. Much of the library is open to the public: books, newspapers and periodicals are accessible to anyone over 18, and you can browse through photographic, film and sound archives.

Chapelle St-Louis-de-la-Salpêtrière

47 bd de l'Hôpital, 13th (01.42.16. 04.24). M° Gare d'Austerlitz. **Open** 8.30am-6pm Mon-Fri, Sun; 11am-6pm Sat. **Admission** free. **Map** p151 C2 ㉘

This austerely beautiful chapel, designed by Bruand and completed in 1677, features an octagonal dome in the centre and eight naves in which the sick were separated from the insane, the destitute from the debauched. Around the chapel sprawls the vast Hôpital de la Pitié-Salpêtrière, which became a centre for research into mental illness in the 1790s, when renowned doctor Philippe Pinel began to treat some of the inmates as sick rather than criminal; Charcot later pioneered neuropsychology here. Salpêtrière is one of the city's main teaching hospitals.

Docks en Seine

28-36 quai d'Austerlitz, 13th (www. paris-docks-en-seine.fr). M° Chevaleret or Gare d'Austerlitz. **Map** p151 D1 ㉙

The Docks en Seine belatedly opened its doors in 2012, transforming an industrial wasteland into a futuristic vision of culture and entertainment. A grassy terrace runs down to the water, there's a new restaurant on the roof (Moon Roof) and a bar/club (Wanderlust) on the first floor, and there are open-air screenings and exhibitions at the Cité de la Mode et du Design. The resurrection was completed with the opening of another club, Nùba, in late 2012. The Musée Art Ludique (www.artludique. com) opened here in late 2013, the world's first museum dedicated solely to entertainment art.

Manufacture Nationale des Gobelins

42 av des Gobelins, 13th (tours 01.44. 08.53.59). M° Les Gobelins. **Open** 11am-6pm Tue-Sun. **Admission** €6; free-€4 reductions. No credit cards. **Map** p151 B2 ㉚

The royal tapestry factory, which was founded by Colbert, is named after Jean Gobelin, a dyer who owned the site. Tapestries are still made here (mainly for French embassies), and visitors can watch weavers at work. The tour (in French; €7.50-€10) through the 1912 factory takes in the 18th-century chapel and the Beauvais workshops. Arrive 30 minutes before the start.

Eating & drinking

L'Auberge du 15

15 rue de la Santé, 13th (01.47.07. 07.45, www.laubergedu15.com). M° Les Gobelins. **Open** noon-2.30pm, 7.30-11pm Tue-Thur; noon-2.30pm, 7-11pm Fri, Sat. **€€. Brasserie. Map** p151 A2 ㉛

L'Auberge du 15 cultivates the air of a country brasserie, with Moroccan tiles lining the open kitchen and a hunting motif on the curtains. No more than ten tables fill the long room, waited on by hip young things. The seasonal menu echoes a farmhouse kitchen – soup from a tureen, cake sliced on its stand. You might get a silky *potage* of chestnuts and ceps poured over a scoop of crème fraîche. Then a hearty dish of tender veal with sweet vegetables and a cream and white wine sauce: pure indulgence.

Le Bambou

70 rue Baudricourt, 13th (01.45.70. 91.75). M° Olympiades or Tolbiac. **Open** 11.30am-3.30pm, 6.30-10.30pm Tue-Sun. **€. Vietnamese. Map** p151 C3 ㉜

The Vietnamese fare here is a notch above what is normally served in Paris. Seating is elbow to elbow and, should you come on your own, the waiter will draw a line down the middle of the paper tablecloth and seat a stranger on the other side. That

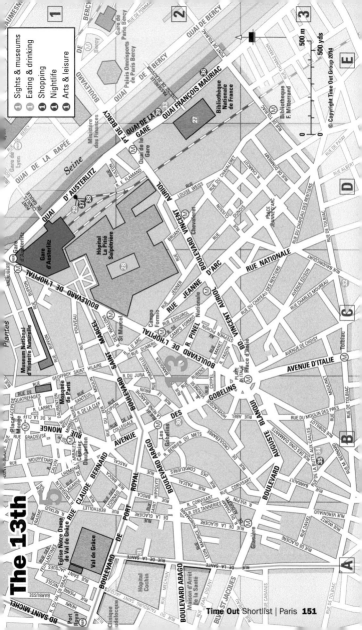

The 13th

Legend:
- **1** Sights & museums
- **1** Eating & drinking
- **1** Shopping
- **1** Nightlife
- **1** Arts & leisure

500 m
500 yds

© Copyright Time Out Group 2014

stranger might offer pointers on how to eat certain dishes, such as the no.42: grilled marinated pork to be wrapped in lettuce with beansprouts and herbs and eaten by hand, dipped into the accompanying sauce.

Petit Bain

7 port de la Gare, 13th (01.80.48.49.81, www.petitbain.org). M° Bibliothèque François Mitterrand or Quai de la Gare. **Open** 6.30pm-2am Wed-Sat; noon-5.30pm Sun (later in summer). **Bar.** **Map** p151 E2 ㉝

Petit Bain looks like a fluorescent green barge with a cubist wooden tree house plonked on top, and harbours an excellent line-up of concerts and exhibitions, plus a coveted terrace that doubles as a bar and restaurant. Below deck, a stage hosts gigs with everything from indie folk to rock on the eclectic playlist.

Sputnik

14 rue de la Butte aux Cailles, 13th (01.45.65.19.82, www.sputnik.fr). M° Place d'Italie. **Open** 2pm-2am Mon-Sat (from 5pm in winter); 4pm-midnight Sun. **Café. Map** p151 B3 ㉞

A hip crowd gathers in this rock bar, which doubles as a sports bar during important football and rugby fixtures, and trebles as an internet café at other times. Ever-changing art exhibitions add interest to the walls, and bands once a month draw an indie crowd.

Shopping

Les Abeilles

NEW *21 rue de la Butte-aux-Cailles, 13th (01.45.81.43.48, www.lesabeilles.biz). M° Corvisart or Place d'Italie.* **Open** 11am-7pm Tue-Sat. **Map** p151 B3 ㉟

This tiny boutique sells everything from candles to honey vinegar, honey mustard and speciality 'Miel de Paris', gathered by owner Jean-Jacques from his hives in Parc Kellerman. There's also a wonderful selection of honey pots and soaps.

Nightlife

Batofar

Opposite 11 quai François-Mauriac, 13th (09.71.25.50.61, www.batofar.org). M° Quai de la Gare. **Open** *Concerts* 7-11pm Mon-Sat. *Club* 11.30pm-6am Mon-Sat; 6am-noon 1st Sun of mth. **Map** p151 E2 ㊱

The current managers have helped revive Batofar's tradition of playing cutting-edge music, including electro, dub step, techno and dancehall nights featuring international acts. From June to September (noon-midnight), the bar sets up a temporary beach.

Nüba

NEW *36 quai d'Austerlitz, 13th (www.nuba-paris.fr). M° Chevaleret or Gare d'Austerlitz.* **Open** 11pm-5am Wed-Sat. **Map** p151 D1 ㊲

A vast terrace offers a superb view over the quays, along with DJs playing chill-out music, deckchairs, communal tables and table football. Inside, coloured lights reveal rooms done out in copper and stone. There are gigs in the evenings, punctuated by clubby electro sets and inventive dance shows from the House of Drama collective.

Wanderlust

32 quai d'Austerlitz, 13th (www.wanderlustparis.com). M° Quai de la Gare. **Open** 10pm-6am Thur; 11pm-6am Fri, Sat. **Map** p151 D1 ㊳

Spread across a huge space, Wanderlust includes a terrace for sunset drinks, an open-air cinema, art installations and a restaurant run by TV chef Benjamin Darnaud. Expect the cream of new-generation electronic dance music.

Arts & leisure

Piscine Josephine-Baker

Quai François-Mauriac, 13th (01.56.61.96.50). M° Quai de la Gare. **Open** times vary. **Map** p151 E2 ㊴

Moored by the Bibliothèque Nationale, the Piscine Josephine-Baker boasts a 25m main pool (with sliding glass roof).

Tour Montparnasse p154

Montparnasse

Montparnasse's heyday was short, but for a few years between the two world wars it was the emblematic 'gay Paree' district of after-dark merriment and fruitful artistic exchange. A great number of its most prominent figures were expats (including its finest chronicler, the Hungarian photographer Brassaï), and the late-night bars and artists' studios formed a bubble of cordial international relations that was irreparably popped in 1939. This is rich territory for art museums, but with the exception of the Fondation Cartier, they're all about past glories.

Sights & museums

Les Catacombes
1 av Colonel Henri-Rol-Tanguy, 14th (01.43.22.47.63, www.catacombes-de-paris.fr). Mº/RER Denfert Rochereau. **Open** 10am-5pm Tue-Sun. **Admission** €8; free-€6 reductions. **Map** p155 C3 ❶

This is the official entrance to the 3,000km (1,864-mile) tunnel network that runs under much of the city. With public burial pits overflowing in the era of the Revolutionary Terror, the bones of six million people were trans-ferred to the *catacombes*. The bones of Marat, Robespierre and their cronies are packed in with wall upon wall of their fellow citizens. The tour lasts approxi-mately 45 minutes.

Cimetière du Montparnasse
3 bd Edgar-Quinet, 14th (01.44.10. 86.50). Mº Edgar Quinet or Raspail. **Open** *16 Mar-5 Nov* 8am-6pm Mon-Fri; 8.30am-6pm Sat; 9am-6pm Sun. *6 Nov-15 Mar* 8am-5.30pm Mon-Fri; 8.30am-5.30pm Sat; 9am-5.30pm Sun. **Admission** free. **Map** p155 B2 ❷

This boneyard has literary clout: Beckett, Baudelaire, Maupassant, Sartre and Ionesco all rest here. There are also artists, including Brancusi, Frédéric Bartholdi and Man Ray. The impressive celebrity roll-call continues with Serge Gainsbourg, André Citroën, Coluche and Jean Seberg.

Fondation Cartier pour l'Art Contemporain

261 bd Raspail, 14th (01.42.18.56.50, www.fondation.cartier.fr). M° Denfert Rochereau. **Open** *11am-10pm Tue; 11am-8pm Wed-Sun.* **Admission** *€9.50; free-€6.50 reductions.* **Map** p155 C2 ❸

Jean Nouvel's glass and steel building, an exhibition centre with Cartier's offices above, is as much a work of art as the installations inside. Shows by artists and photographers have wide-ranging themes. Live events around the shows are called Soirées Nomades.

Fondation Henri Cartier-Bresson

2 impasse Lebouis, 14th (01.56.80.27.00, www.henricartierbresson.org). M° Gaîté. **Open** *1-6.30pm Tue, Thur, Fri, Sun; 1-8.30pm Wed; 11am-6.45pm Sat. Closed Aug & between exhibitions.* **Admission** *€6; €4 reductions; free 6.30-8.30pm Wed. No credit cards.* **Map** p155 A2 ❹

This two-floor gallery is dedicated to the work of acclaimed photographer Henri Cartier-Bresson. It consists of a tall, narrow *atelier* in a 1913 building with a minutely catalogued archive open to researchers, and a lounge on the fourth floor screening films. The Fondation opens its doors to other disciplines with three annual shows.

Musée Bourdelle

16-18 rue Antoine-Bourdelle, 15th (01.49.54.73.73, www.bourdelle. paris.fr). M° Falguière or Montparnasse Bienvenüe. **Open** *10am-6pm Tue-Sun.* **Admission** *free. Exhibitions €5; free-€3.50 reductions.* **Map** p155 A1 ❺

Sculptor Antoine Bourdelle (1861-1929), a pupil of Rodin, produced a number of monumental works, including the relief friezes at the Théâtre des Champs-Elysées. Set around a garden, the museum includes the artist's apartment and studios. A 1950s extension tracks

the evolution of Bourdelle's equestrian monument to General Alvear in Buenos Aires, Argentina, and his masterful *Hercules the Archer*. A modern wing houses bronzes.

Musée du Montparnasse

21 av du Maine, 15th (01.42.22.91.96, www.museedumontparnasse.net). M° Montparnasse Bienvenüe. **Open** *12.30-7pm Tue-Sun.* **Admission** *€6; free-€5 reductions. No credit cards.* **Map** p155 A1 ❻

Set in one of the last surviving alleys of studios, this was home to Marie Vassilieff, whose own academy and cheap canteen welcomed poor artists Picasso, Cocteau and Matisse. Shows focus on present-day artists and the area's creative past.

Tour Montparnasse

33 av du Maine, 15th (01.45.38.52.56, www.tourmontparnasse56.com). M° Montparnasse Bienvenüe. **Open** *Oct-Mar 9.30am-10.30pm Mon-Thur, Sun; 9.30am-11pm Fri, Sat. Apr-Sept 9.30am-11.30pm daily.* **Admission** *€13; free-€9.50 reductions.* **Map** p155 A1 ❼

Built in 1974 on the site of the old station, this 209m (686ft) steel-and-glass monolith is shorter than the Eiffel Tower, but better placed for fabulous views of the city. A lift whisks you up in 38 seconds to the 56th floor, where you'll find an upgraded café-lounge, a souvenir shop – and lots and lots of sky.

Eating & drinking

La Cerisaie

70 bd Edgar Quinet, 14th (01.43.20. 98.98, www.restaurantlacerisaie.com). M° Edgar Quinet or Montparnasse. **Open** *noon-2pm, 7-10pm Mon-Fri. Closed Aug & 1wk Dec.* **€€. Bistro**. **Map** p155 A1 ❽

Nothing about La Cerisaie's unprepossessing red façade hints at the talent that lurks inside. On the daily changing blackboard menu you might find *bourride de maquereau*, a thrifty take on the garlicky French fish stew, or *cochon noir de Bigorre*. *Baba à l'armagnac*, a variation on the usual rum cake, comes with great chantilly.

Cobéa

11 rue Raymond Losserand, 14th (01.43.20.21.39, www.cobea.fr). M° Gaîté or Pernety. **Open** 12.15-1.45pm, 7.15-9.45pm Tue-Sat. **€€€. Haute cuisine**. Map p155 A2 ⑨

Cobéa is a slick restaurant launched by Jerome Cobou and Philippe Bellissent, who won a Michelin star when he was head chef at L'Hôtel. The ethos here is gastronomy without the snobbery. Set in a renovated 1920s house with big windows overlooking a green space, it feels peaceful and cosy, while touches such as silverware and Bernardaud porcelain add a luxury feel. The set menus are a treasure chest of reworked classics, plus a daily-changing 'chef's surprise'. Each dish is accompanied by a well-sourced wine recommendation.

La Coupole

102 bd du Montparnasse, 14th (01.43.20.14.20, www.lacoupole-paris.com). M° Vavin. **Open** 8.30am-midnight Mon-Wed, Sun; 8.30am-1am Thur-Sat. **€€. Brasserie**. Map p155 B1 ⑩

La Coupole still glows with some of the old glamour. The people-watching remains superb and the long ranks of linen-covered tables, mosaic floor and sheer scale of the operation still make coming here an event. The set menu offers steaks, foie gras, fish and game stews, but the real treat is the shellfish.

Josselin

67 rue du Montparnasse, 14th (01.43.20.93.50). M° Edgar Quinet. **Open** 11.15am-3.15pm, 6-11.30pm Tue-Fri; 11.30am-midnight Sat; 11.30am-11.30pm Sun. Closed 1st wk Jan & Aug. **€**. No credit cards. **Crêperie**. Map p155 B1 ⑪

Josselin is the star *crêperie* of the area, and the one with the longest queues. The speciality is the Couple – two

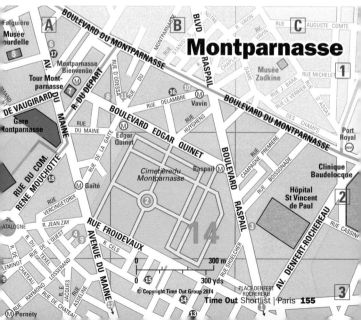

Bogato

layers of galette with the filling in the middle. Wash it all down with bowls of cider, of which the brut is best.

Severo

NEW *8 rue des Plantes, 14th (01.45.40. 40.91). M° Alésia, Mouton-Duvernet or Pernety.* **Open** noon-2pm, 7.30-10pm Mon-Fri. **€€**. **Bistro**. Map p155 A3 ⑫

Severo is all about well-bred meat selected by former butcher William Bernet and partner Hugo Desnoyer. On the menu, all sorts of piggy things to begin with, then mostly beef, from a modest *steak haché* with chips or green beans to a bloody entrecôte. Among the nursery-style desserts, go for the crème caramel or plum tart.

Shopping

Bogato

7 rue Liancourt, 14th (01.40.47.03.51, www.chez bogato.fr). M° Denfert-Rochereau. **Open** 10am-7pm Tue-Sat. **Map** p155 B3 ⑬

Everything here is about temptation, from the quaint furniture to pastry chef Anaïs Olmer's brightly coloured cupcakes, towering under glass bells on the counter like sugary art installations.

La Cave des Papilles

NEW *35 rue Daguerre, 14th (01.43. 20.05.74, www.lacavedespapilles.com). M° Denfert-Rochereau.* **Open** 3.30-8.30pm Mon; 10am-1.30pm, 3.30-8.30pm Tue-Fri; 10am-8.30pm Sat; 10am-1.30pm Sun. **Map** p155 B3 ⑭

You can't miss the yellow frontage of La Cave des Papilles. The owner is a lover of 'natural' wine and 80% of the 1,200 wines on offer are produced organically. It's not too outrageously priced either: with a choice of 60 to 80 bottles between €3 and €10.

Madame de

65 rue Daguerre, 14th (01.77.10.59.46, www.madamede.net). M° Denfert-Rochereau. **Open** 11am-7.30pm Tue-Sat. **Map** p155 B3 ⑮

This delightful second-hand shop only stocks pieces 'that are like new' – even better, the prices wouldn't look out of place in the sales.

Storie

20 rue Delambre, 14th (01.83.56.01.98, www.storieblog.com). M° Vavin. **Open** 11am-2pm, 3-8pm Tue-Sat; 5-8pm Sun. **Map** p155 B1 ⑯

A magical shop selling a mix of objects from around the world – from Korean coffee cups to wooden deer heads.

Nightlife

Mix Club

24 rue de l'Arrivée, 15th (01.56. 80.37.37, www.mixclub.fr). M° Montparnasse Bienvenüe. **Open** 11pm-5.30am Thur; 11.45pm-6am Fri, Sat. **Map** p155 A1 ⑰

The Mix Club has one of the city's biggest dancefloors. Regular visitors include Erick Morillo's Subliminal and Ministry of Sound parties.

Le Petit Journal Montparnasse

13 rue du Commandant-René-Mouchotte, 14th (01.43.21.56.70, www.petitjournalmontparnasse.com). M° Gaîté. **Open** 7pm-2am Mon-Sat. *Concerts* 9.30pm Mon-Thur; 10pm Fri, Sat. **Map** p155 A2 ⑱

Two-level jazz brasserie in the shadow of the Tour Montparnasse with Latin sounds, R&B and soul-gospel.

Arts & leisure

L'Entrepôt

7-9 rue Francis-de-Pressensé, 14th (01.45.40.07.50, www.lentrepot.fr). M° Pernety or Plaisance. No credit cards. **Map** p155 A3 ⑲

This multi-disciplinary arts centre and cinema is known for its leftfield documentaries, shorts, gay repertoire and productions from developing nations. Regular debates, poetry nights and concerts complete the programme.

PARIS BY AREA

Château de Versailles p162

Worth the Trip

North

Basilique St-Denis

1 rue de la Légion-d'Honneur, 93200 St-Denis (01.48.09.83.54). M° St-Denis Basilique/tram 1. **Open** *Apr-Sept* 10am-6.15pm Mon-Sat; noon-6.15pm Sun. *Oct-Mar* 10am-5pm Mon-Sat; noon-5.15pm Sun. **Tours** 10.30am, 3pm Mon-Sat; 12.15pm, 3pm Sun. **Admission** €7.50; free-€4.50 reductions.

Legend has it that when St Denis was beheaded, he picked up his noggin and walked with it to Vicus Catulliacus (now St-Denis) to be buried. The first church, parts of which can be seen in the crypt, was built over his tomb in around 475. The present edifice was begun in the 1130s. It is considered to be the first example of Gothic architecture. In the 13th century, mason Pierre de Montreuil erected the spire and rebuilt the choir nave and transept. St-Denis was the burial place for all but three French monarchs between 996 and the end of the *ancien régime*, so the ambulatory is a museum of French funerary sculpture. It includes a fanciful Gothic tomb for Dagobert, the austere effigy of Charles V, and the Renaissance tomb of Louis XII and his wife Anne de Bretagne. In 1792, these tombs were desecrated, and the royal remains thrown into a pit.

Château de Chantilly

Chantilly (03.44.27.31.80, www. chateaudechantilly.com). 40km N of Paris. Train from Gare du Nord, then taxi or bus. By car, A1 exit Chantilly. **Open** *Château* Apr-Oct 10am-6pm Mon, Wed-Sun (daily July, Aug). Nov-Mar 10.30am-6pm Mon, Wed-Sun. **Admission** Château & park €14; free-€5.50 reductions.

From the 14th century until 1897, the town of Chantilly was the domain of the Princes of Condé, the cousins of the French kings. Much of the cream-coloured château was destroyed during the Revolution, leaving the main wing to be reconstructed in the

19th century by Henri d'Orléans, the Duc d'Aumale. When the duke died in 1897, he bequeathed the Domaine de Chantilly to the Institut de France on the condition that the château be opened to the public as the Musée Condé, and that none of the artworks be moved or loaned to other museums. His remarkable collection includes three paintings by Raphael, and the *Très Riches Heures du Duc de Berry*, a medieval book of hours, containing the most exquisite colours imaginable. The collection is complemented by the surrounding park, landscaped by André le Nôtre (of Versailles fame).

Musée de l'Air et de l'Espace

Aéroport de Paris-Le Bourget, 93352 Le Bourget Cedex (01.49.92.70.00, www. mae.org). M° Gare du Nord, then bus 350/RER Le Bourget, then bus 152. **Open** *Apr-Sept* 10am-6pm Tue-Sun. *Oct-Mar* 10am-5pm Tue-Sun. **Admission** free. *With 1-3 animations* €8-€16; free-€12 reductions.

The impressive air and space museum is set in the former passenger terminal at Le Bourget airport. The collection begins with the pioneers, including fragile-looking biplanes and the command cabin of a Zeppelin airship. On the runway are Mirage fighters, a US Thunderchief, and Ariane launchers 1 and 5. A hangar houses the prototype Concorde 001 and wartime survivors.

East

104

5 rue Curial, 19th (01.53.35.50.00, www.104.fr). M° Riquet. **Open** noon-7pm Tue-Fri; 11am-7pm Sat, Sun. **Admission** free. *Exhibitions* prices vary. It's more than a century since tourist-choked Montmartre was the centre of artistic activity in Paris. But now the north-east of Paris is again where the action is, in a previously neglected area of bleak railway goods yards and dilapidated social housing. 104,

described as a 'space for artistic creation', occupies a vast 19th-century building on rue d'Aubervilliers that used to house Paris's municipal undertakers. There aren't any constraints on the kind of work the resident artists do – 104 is open to 'all the arts' – but they're expected to show finished pieces in one of four annual 'festivals'.

La Cité des Sciences et de l'Industrie

La Villette, 30 av Corentin-Cariou, 19th (01.40.05.70.00, www.cite-sciences.fr). M° Porte de la Villette. **Open** 10am-6pm Tue-Sat; 10am-7pm Sun. **Admission** €8; free-€6 reductions.

This ultra-modern science museum pulls in five million visitors a year. Explora, the permanent show, occupies the upper two floors, whisking visitors through 30,000sq m (320,000sq ft) of space, life, matter and communication: scale models of satellites including the Ariane space shuttle, planes and robots, plus the chance to experience weightlessness, make for an exciting trip. In the Espace Images, try the delayed camera and other optical illusions, draw 3D images on a computer or lend your voice to the *Mona Lisa*. The hothouse garden investigates developments in agriculture and bio-tech. The brilliant Cité des Enfants runs workshops for younger children.

Cité Nationale de l'Histoire de l'Immigration

293 av Daumesnil, 12th (01.53.59. 58.60, www.histoire-immigration.fr). M° Porte Dorée. **Open** 10am-5.30pm Tue-Fri; 10am-7pm Sat, Sun. **Admission** €6; free-€4.50 reductions. *Aquarium* €5-€7; €3.50-€5 reductions. No credit cards.

Set in the stunning Palais de la Porte Dorée, the collections trace more than 200 years of immigration history. There are thought-provoking images (film and photography), everyday objects (suitcases, accordions, sewing machines and so on) and artworks that symbolise the struggles immigrants had to face when integrating into French society. Don't miss the permanent Repères (bearings) exhibition that looks at why many immigrants chose France and the problems they faced upon arrival. One of the most moving areas is the Galerie des Dons – a collection of memorabilia donated by individuals whose families came from foreign countries.

Disneyland Paris/Walt Disney Studios Park

Marne-la-Vallée (www.disneylandparis. com). 32km E of Paris. RER A or TGV Marne-la-Vallée-Chessy. By car, A4 exit 14. **Open** Times vary, see website for details. **Admission** Prices vary, see website for details.

Young ones will get a real kick out of Fantasyland, with its Alice maze, Sleeping Beauty's castle and teacup rides. Walt Disney Studios focuses on special effects and the tricks of the animation trade. Thrill-seekers should head for the Twilight Zone Tower of Terror, which sends daredevils plummeting down a 13-storey lift shaft.

South

Maison de Jean Cocteau

15 rue du Lau, 91490 Milly-la-Forêt (01.64.98.11.50, www.jeancocteau. net). 60km S of Paris. RER D Maisse, then 7km taxi ride. By car, A6 exit 13. **Open** Mar-Sept 2-7pm Wed-Sun. Oct-early Nov 2-6pm Wed-Sun. *Early Nov-early Jan* 2-6pm Sat, Sun (Wed-Sun 19 Dec-1 Jan). Closed early Jan-Feb. **Admission** €7; free-€4.50 reductions.

Thanks to the hefty financial input of Pierre Bergé (partner of the late Yves Saint Laurent) and five years of refurbishment, Cocteau's old country house is now a fascinating museum. The living room is wonderfully flamboyant, with antique furniture and gold palm trees framing a Bérard painting of Oedipus. The bedroom, meanwhile, with its four-poster bed and a mural of a castle, boasts a fairytale quality

that's reminiscent of Cocteau's romantic fantasy *La Belle et la Bête*. Finally the study, with its leopard print walls and erotic memorabilia, offers the most intimate glimpse into the artist's creative process. The rest of the house has been converted into exhibition space with two galleries: one a collection of portraits of Cocteau by artists such as Picasso, Warhol and Modigliani; the other dedicated to temporary collections. Cocteau's body rests nearby, in Chapelle Saint-Blaise-des Simples (rue de l'Amiral de Graville, Milly-la-Forêt).

Musée Fragonard

7 av du Général de Gaulle, 94704 Maisons-Alfort (01.43.96.71.72, http:// musee.vet-alfort.fr). M° Ecole Vétérinaire de Maisons-Alfort. **Open** 2-6pm Wed-Sun. Closed Aug. **Admission** €7; free reductions.

In 18th-century French medical schools, study aids were produced in one of two ways. They were either painstakingly sculpted in coloured wax or made from the real things – organs, limbs, tangled vascular systems – dried or preserved in formaldehyde. Veterinary surgeon Honoré Fragonard (cousin of the famous rococo painter) was a master of the second method, and many of his most striking works are now on display here. *Tête humaine injectée* is a human head whose blood vessels were injected with coloured wax, red for arteries and blue for veins. *Cavalier de l'apocalypse* is a flayed man on the back of a flayed horse, inspired by a painting by Dürer.

Parc André Citroën

Rue Balard, rue St-Charles or quai Citroën, 15th. M° Balard or Javel. **Open** 8am-dusk Mon-Fri; 9am-dusk Sat, Sun, public hols.

This park is a fun, postmodern version of a French formal garden, designed by Gilles Clément and Alain Prévost. It comprises glasshouses, computerised fountains, waterfalls, a wilderness and themed gardens with different coloured

Curtain up

The Théâtre Paris Villette is back in the limelight.

The place to be for culture right now has to be La Villette in the 19th. In less than 30 years it's gone from abandoned abattoir district to lush modern park dotted with high-profile entertainment venues (including Zénith, Trabendo, Halle de la Chanson, La Grande Halle and Cité de la Musique), festivals galore, a contemporary circus (Espace Chapiteaux) and major museums (Cité des Sciences and Musée de la Musique). And in December 2013, it became home – for the second time – to one of the city's most avant-garde theatres, the **Théâtre Paris Villette** (www.theatre-paris-villette.fr), set amid the elegant arches of Villette's former abattoir sales hall, a neoclassical beauty built in the mid 19th century.

The previous Théâtre Paris Villette opened in the 1980s to promote contemporary theatre. The careers of several major modern playwrights were launched here, including Tony Award-winning Yasmina Reza (best known for

Art and *God of Carnage*). However, after a stream of financial concerns and poor ticket sales, the theatre closed its doors in 2012.

So imagine the joy and surprise when it reopened with everything new bar the name: a new look (a 70-seater all-white room and 200-seater auditorium), two new directors (Valérie Dassonville and Adrien de Van), and a new charter to bring avant-garde, contemporary theatre to '*la jeunesse*' – youngsters in the broadest sense of the word, from schoolkids to grown-up theatre virgins.

The new theatre promises an exciting line-up, mixing traditional productions with cutting-edge performances that use multimedia technology to enhance stage design and special effects. Tickets range from €10 to €22, and even if you don't fancy a show, come along for the bar – all vintage neo-pop with bold wallpaper and leather sofas. It's a fabulous spot to rub shoulders with the artists after the show.

plants and even sounds. The tethered Eutelsat helium balloon takes visitors up for panoramic views. If the weather looks unreliable, call 01.44.26.20.00.

West

Bois de Boulogne

16th. M° Les Sablons or Porte Dauphine. **Admission** free.

Covering 865 hectares, the Bois was once the Forêt de Rouvray hunting grounds. It was landscaped in the 1860s, when artificial grottoes and waterfalls were created around the Lac Inférieur. The Jardin de Bagatelle is famous for its roses, daffodils and water lilies. The Jardin d'Acclimatation is a children's amusement park, complete with miniature train, farm, rollercoaster and boat rides.

Château de Versailles

78000 Versailles (01.30.83.78.00, advance tickets 08.92.68.46.94, www. chateauversailles.fr). 20km W of Paris. RER C5 Versailles Rive-Gauche. By car A13 exit Versailles. **Open** *Apr-Oct* 9am-6.30pm Tue-Sun. *Nov-Mar* 9am-5.30pm Tue-Sun. **Admission** €15; free-€13 reductions.

Centuries of makeovers have made Versailles the most sumptuously clad château in the world. The famous Hall of Mirrors – a 73m (240ft) gallery overlooking the garden hung with 357 mirrors – was commissioned in 1678 by Louis XIV and decorated by Le Brun. The gardens sprawl across 8sq km and consist of formal parterres, ponds, elaborate statues and a spectacular series of fountains. Outside the château gates are the stables that now house the Académie du Spectacle Equestre, responsible for the elaborate horse shows by famous trainer Bartabas.

Musée Albert Kahn

10-14 rue du Port, 92100 Boulogne-Billancourt (01.55.19.28.00, www. albert-kahn.hauts-de-seine.net). M° Boulogne Pont de Saint-Cloud. **Open** 11am-6pm Tue-Sun (until 7pm May-Sept). **Admission** €4; free-€2.50 reductions.

The spectacular ten-acre *jardin* alone makes a visit here worthwhile: each section is modelled on a garden from around the world. Albert Kahn was an early 20th-century banker and philanthropist who financed 'discovery' missions across the world. His main legacy is 'Les Archives de la Planète' on show here – a fascinating collection of film and snapshots brought back from missions in over 60 countries.

Musée Belmondo

14 rue de L'Abreuvoir, 92100 Boulogne-Billancourt (01.55.18.54.40). M° Boulogne Jean Jaurès, then bus 123. **Open** 2-6pm Tue-Fri; 11am-6pm Sat, Sun. **Admission** €6; free-€4 reductions.

Jean-Paul Belmondo's father, Paul, was one of France's most important 20th-century sculptors, and one of the last to use neoclassical, academic techniques. The space, revamped by architects Chartier-Corbasson, is an interior designer's dream – the mix of stark white, black and timber materials lends a different mood to each section, and several rooms harbour alcoves in which Belmondo's sculptures sit enticingly.

Musée Marmottan – Claude Monet

2 rue Louis-Boilly, 16th (01.44.96.50.33, www.marmottan.com). M° La Muette. **Open** 10am-6pm Tue, Wed, Fri-Sun; 10am-8pm Thur. **Admission** €10; free-€5 reductions.

This old hunting pavilion has become a famed holder of Impressionist art thanks to two bequests: the first by the daughter of the doctor of Manet, Monet, Pissarro, Sisley and Renoir; the second by Monet's son Michel. Its Monet collection, the largest in the world, numbers 165 works, plus sketchbooks, palette and photos. Upstairs are works by Renoir, Manet, Gauguin, Caillebotte and Berthe Morisot, a Sèvres clock and a collection of First Empire furniture.

Essentials

Hotels 164
Getting Around 182
Resources A-Z 186
Vocabulary 189
Index 190

Hôtel Chavanel p169

Hotels

After a slew of major hotel openings in the last couple of years, the big news during 2013 was all about closures, with two of the city's most famous palace hotels shutting their doors for major renovations. The Ritz and the Crillon will both be out of action until 2015, as they freshen up to try to contend with the influx of Asian super-luxury from the Shangri-La, Royal Monceau, Mandarin Oriental and, from summer 2014, Peninsula Paris. In the meantime, these new five-star arrivals have taken service and design to a different level, although the accompanying rack rates can be eye-watering.

For something a little less *luxe*, the city's burgeoning boutique hotel selection means that you can still afford good design, as long as you can make do without the uniformed doormen. You can be soothed by fine linen, marble baths and a dreamy pool and hammam at Le Metropolitan, walk through silk taffeta curtains to your own terrace at Le Petit Paris, gaze across the Marais rooftops from the cool Jules et Jim, and fraternise at the trendy cava bar of the Spanish-owned Banke.

Further down the scale, there is now a wide choice of moderately priced and even budget design hotels, especially around the hip east and north-east of the city, such as Mama Shelter, Standard Design Hotel, 20 Prieuré and Hôtel Crayon. And shoestring travellers should consider booking a bed at St Christopher's Inn on the Canal de l'Ourcq, whose façade is lit up like an art installation at night (or at their new outpost opposite Gare du Nord).

Classification

We've divided the hotels by area, then listed them in four categories, according to the standard prices (not including seasonal offers or

ESSENTIALS

discounts) for one night in a double room with en suite shower/bath. For deluxe hotels (€€€€), you can expect to pay more than €350; for properties in the expensive bracket (€€€), €220-€350; for moderate properties (€€), allow €130-€219; while budget rooms (€) go for less than €130.

In the know

All hotels in France charge a room tax (*taxe de séjour*) of around €1 per person per night, although this is sometimes included in the rate.

Champs-Elysées & Western Paris

Buddha Bar Hotel

NEW *4 rue d'Anjou, 8th (01.83.96. 88.88, www.buddhabarhotelparis.com). Mº Concorde or Madeleine.* €€€€.
Opened in June 2013, this latest instalment in the Buddha Bar empire is a wonderful mix of French style and neo-Asian extravagance set in a handsome 18th-century *hôtel particulier*. The Le Vraymonde restaurant is headed by acclaimed Senegalese chef Rougui Dia.

Four Seasons George V

31 av George V, 8th (01.49.52.70.00, www.fourseasons.com/paris). Mº Alma Marceau or George V. €€€€.
There's no denying that the George V is serious about luxury: chandeliers, marble and tapestries, over-attentive staff, divine bathrooms, and ludicrously comfortable beds in some of the largest rooms in Paris. The spa area includes whirlpools, saunas and treatments; non-guests can reserve appointments.

Hôtel le Bristol

112 rue du Fbg-St-Honoré, 8th (01.53. 43.43.00, www.hotel-bristol.com). Mº Champs-Elysées Clémenceau. €€€€.
Set on the exclusive rue du Faubourg St-Honoré, the Bristol is a luxurious 'palace' hotel with a loyal following of

S H O R T L I S T

Best newcomers
- Buddha Bar Hotel (see left)
- Hôtel Chavanel (see p169)
- Hôtel La Maison Champs Elysées (see p167)
- St Christopher's Inn Gare du Nord (see p175)

Best spa splurge
- Four Seasons George V (see left)
- Le Meurice (see p173)

Best alfresco breakfast
- Hôtel de l'Abbaye Saint-Germain (see p179)
- Mama Shelter (see p175)

Best bars
- Hôtel Plaza Athénée (see p167)
- Royal Monceau (see p168)

Best for fashion week
- L'Hôtel (see p179)
- Le Montalembert (see p179)

Best bathrooms
- Four Seasons George V (see left)
- Renaissance Paris Arc de Triomphe (see p168)

Best bargain beds
- Mama Shelter (see p175)
- St Christopher's Inn (see p175)

Chic sleeps
- Hôtel Concorde Opéra Paris (see p169)
- Hôtel Amour (see p173)

Lap of luxury
- Hôtel le Bristol (see left)
- Hôtel W Paris-Opéra (see p171)
- Shangri-La Paris (see p168)
- Royal Monceau (see p168)

ESSENTIALS

fashionistas and millionaires drawn by the location, impeccable service, larger than average rooms and a three Michelin-starred restaurant with Eric Frechon at the helm.

Hôtel Daniel

8 rue Frédéric-Bastiat, 8th (01.42. 56.17.00, www.hoteldanielparis.com). Mº Franklin D. Roosevelt or St-Philippe-du-Roule. €€€€.

This romantic hideaway is decorated in chinoiserie and a palette of rich colours, with 26 rooms (free Wi-Fi) cosily appointed in toile de Jouy and an intricately hand-painted restaurant that feels like a courtyard. At about €50 a head, the gastronomic restaurant is a good deal for this neighbourhood.

Hôtel Fouquet's Barrière

46 av George V, 8th (01.40.69.60.00, www.fouquets-barriere.com). Mº George V. €€€€.

This grandiose five-star is built around the fin-de-siècle brasserie Le Fouquet's. Five buildings form the hotel complex, with 81 rooms (including 33 suites), upmarket restaurant Le Diane, the U Spa, indoor pool and a roof terrace for hire. Jacques Garcia was responsible for the interior design, which retains the Empire style of the exterior while incorporating luxurious touches inside – flatscreen TVs and mist-free mirrors in the marble bathrooms. And, of course, it's unbeatable for location – right at the junction of avenue George V and the Champs-Elysées.

Hôtel La Maison Champs Elysées

NEW *8 rue Jean Goujon, 8th (01.40. 74.64.65, www.lamaisonchamps elysees.com). Mº Champs-Elysées Clémenceau.* €€€€.
See box p172.

Hôtel Plaza Athénée

25 av Montaigne, 8th (01.53.67. 66.65, www.plaza-athenee-paris.com). Mº Alma Marceau. €€€€.

This newly renovated palace is ideally placed for power shopping at Chanel, Louis Vuitton, Dior and other avenue Montaigne boutiques. Material girls and boys will enjoy the high-tech room amenities, such as remote-controlled air con, internet and video-game access on the TV via infrared keyboard, and mini hi-fi. Make time for a drink in the Bar du Plaza, a cocktail bunny's most *outré* fantasy.

Hôtel Square

3 rue de Boulainvilliers, 16th (01.44. 14.91.90, www.hotelsquare.com). Mº Passy/RER Avenue du Pdt Kennedy. €€€€.

This courageously modern hotel has a dramatic yet welcoming interior, and attentive service that comes from having to look after only 22 rooms. They're decorated in amber, brick or slate colours, with exotic woods, quality fabrics and bathrooms seemingly cut from one huge chunk of Carrara marble. View exhibitions in the atrium gallery or mingle with media types at the hip Zebra Square restaurant and DJ bar.

Les Jardins de la Villa

5 rue Bélidor, 17th (01.53.81.01.10, www.jardinsdelavilla.com). Mº Porte Maillot. €€€.

Behind a sober frontage, the 33-room Jardins de la Villa is a playful affair, with a couture theme and a penchant for fuchsia pink. It's dotted with surreal touches – not least a high heel-shaped couch in reception. The beautifully appointed rooms pair modern luxuries (Nespresso machines, free Wi-Fi, sleek flatscreen TVs) with old-fashioned attention to detail. The location is off the tourist trail, but close to the métro.

Jays Paris

6 rue Copernic, 16th (01.47.04.16.16, www.jays-paris.com). Mº Kléber or Victor Hugo. €€€€.

Jays is a luxurious *boutique-apart* hotel that trades on a clever blend of antique furniture, modern design and high-tech equipment. The marble staircase, lit entirely by natural light filtered through the glass atrium overhead, gives an instant feeling of grandeur, and leads to five suites, each with a fully equipped kitchenette and free Wi-Fi. A cosy salon is available.

Le Metropolitan

10 pl de Mexico, 16th (01.56.90.
40.04, www.radissonblu.com). M°
Trocadero. €€€.

This 40-room offering from Radisson Blu is sleek. The entrance is only a few metres wide, but inside the triangular structure opens out into a surprisingly large area, with a vast art deco-style fireplace, and cream leather and black granite reminiscent of New York in the 1930s. The first floor contains a swank insiders' cocktail bar, but the biggest surprise of all is the breathtaking view of the Eiffel Tower from the front façade, best enjoyed through the huge oval window while lying on the four-poster bed of the sixth-floor suite. Below ground are a sublime swimming pool and hammam reserved for guests.

Opéra Diamond

4 rue de la Pépinière, 8th (01.44.70.
02.00, www.paris-hotel-diamond.com).
M° St-Lazare. €€€€.

This sparkling Best Western Premier lives up to its name with a night-sky decor made up of black granite resin punctuated with crystals and LEDs. The 30 rooms are equally splendid, with Swarovski crystal touches to the furniture, black bathrooms and satin curtains that close to show a photomontage of a female nude crossed with architectural imagery. Executive rooms have iPod stations, Nespresso machines, and speakers in the bathrooms.

Renaissance Paris Arc de Triomphe

39 av de Wagram, 17th (01.55.37.55.37,
www.marriott.com). M° Ternes. €€€.

You can't miss it. This six-storey glass façade is like no other part of the area. All rooms are stylishly done out in pale greys, charcoals and dark wood, with Eames-style furniture. Nice high-tech touches include an iPod dock on the bedside radio and a flatscreen TV with Wi-Fi keyboard. Bathrooms are a glory of polished metal, tasteful tiles and gleaming glass. The Makassar restaurant serves delicious Franco-Asian fusion food.

Royal Monceau

37 av Hoche, 8th (01.42.99.88.00,
www.leroymonceau.com). M° Charles
de Gaulle Etoile. €€€€.

The Royal Monceau is a supremely classy retreat. This is a hotel that takes art appreciation seriously, with its own art agenda blog and an art concierge. Philippe Starck was in charge of the refit, and his cheeky touches are everywhere. The bedrooms are a studied jumble, with beds in the middle of the room, pictures leaned up against the wall, a guitar waiting to be strummed and a lampshade decked with scribbled notes. But beyond all this designer frippery there lie some gorgeous treats, including vast walk-in wardrobes, spacious bathrooms with twin sinks, and huge mirrors that magically transform into TVs.

Le Sezz

6 av Frémiet, 16th (01.56.75.26.26,
www.hotelsezz.com). M° Passy. €€€.

Le Sezz has 26 sleek, luxurious rooms and suites. The understated decor represents a refreshingly modern take on luxury, with black parquet flooring, rough-hewn stone walls and bathrooms partitioned off with sweeping glass façades. The bar and public areas are equally sleek and chic. Free Wi-Fi.

Shangri-La Paris

10 av d'Iéna, 16th (01.53.67.19.98,
www.shangri-la.com). M° Iéna. €€€€.

Pierre-Yves Rochon's design at the Shangri-La is an ode to French imperialism, with colonial-style paintings, knick-knacks and light fittings

Les Jardins de la Villa p167

mixed with century-old marble floors, stained-glass windows and thick fabrics. Half of the 81 rooms and suites look out on to Eiffel's filigree tower, and the top-floor Suite Panoramique provides what could be Paris's best panorama over the Left Bank. The mansion, built in 1896 by botanist Roland Bonaparte (Napoleon Bonaparte's great-nephew), drips in Napoleonic carvings and gilding; and there's a Louis XIV-style salon whose splendour rivals Versailles. Dining-wise, expect the best of France and Asia, including Shang Palace, a gourmet Cantonese.

Opéra to Les Halles

Hôtel Brighton
218 rue de Rivoli, 1st (01.47.03. 61.61, www.esprit-de-france.com). M° Tuileries. **€€**.
With several of the bedrooms looking out over the Tuileries gardens, the Brighton is great value. Recently restored, it has a classical atmosphere, from the high ceilings in the rooms to the faux-marble and mosaic decor downstairs.

Hôtel Chavanel
NEW *22 rue Tronchet, 8th (01.47.42. 26.14, www.hotelchavanel.com). M° Madeleine.* **€€€**.

Located just a few steps away from place de la Madeleine and the Palais Garnier opera house, the Chavanel is superbly positioned for high-end shopping and highbrow culture. Twenty-five rooms of differing sizes and shapes are arranged across five floors, with two suites in the eaves, including one with a circular bed. The exquisite bathrooms feature tiles by Porcelanosa that resemble crushed silk.

Hôtel Chopin
10 bd Montmartre (46 passage Jouffroy), 9th (01.47.70.58.10, www.hotel-chopin. com). M° Grands Boulevards. **€**.
Handsomely set in a historic, glass-roofed arcade next door to the Grévin museum, the Chopin's original 1846 façade adds to its old-fashioned appeal. The 36 rooms are quiet and functional, done out in salmon and green or blue.

Hôtel Concorde Opéra Paris
108 rue St-Lazare, 8th (01.40.08. 44.44, www.concorde-hotels.com). M° St-Lazare. **€€€**.
Guests here are cocooned in sound-proofed luxury. The 19th-century lobby with jewel-encrusted granite columns is a historic landmark: the high ceilings, walls and sculptures look much as they

have for over a century. Rooms are spacious, with double entrance doors and exclusive Annick Goutal toiletries; the belle époque brasserie, Café Terminus, and sexy Golden Black Bar were designed by Sonia Rykiel. Guests have access to a nearby fitness centre.

Hôtel Crayon

25 rue du Bouloi, 1st (01.42.36.54.19, www.hotelcrayon.com). M° Les Halles. €€.
Hôtel Crayon offers colour therapy with rooms painted top to toe in a choice of 16 hues. Each also features a life-size hand-drawn nude pencilled on the wall in a Matisse style, a white bathroom with colour accents where vintage furniture has been adapted to support contemporary sinks, silky smooth cotton bedlinen and random vintage holiday snaps collected from flea markets and mounted in frames. You can order a selection of meals via room service, and a copious breakfast is served in the vaulted breakfast room.

Hotel O

19 rue Hérold, 1st (01.42.36.04.02, www.hotel-o-paris.com). M° Palais Royal-Musée du Louvre or Les Halles. €€.
Hotel O is a sleek, 29-room venture that adds some welcome hip to the area's accommodation options. Rooms (styled by cool young design company Ora-Ito, hence the 'O' in the hotel's name) are small but exquisite, with retro-futuristic features that make you feel like you're on board a 1970s spaceship, with clean lines, gracious curves and blocks of pink, grey, purple and dark turquoise.

Hôtel W Paris-Opéra

4 rue Meyerbeer, 9th (01.77.48.94.94, www.wparisopera.fr). M° Opéra/RER Auber. €€€€.
The Starwood hotel group's latest venture took two and a half years to finish, but it was worth the wait, with 91 rooms that ooze NYC style from every nook and cranny. For an all-out treat, the 'Extreme Wow' suite will set

you back a whopping €2,300 (don't worry, standard doubles start at €340), but you'll get 88sq m of smart modern design all to yourself, and the feeling that you've walked on to the set of a James Bond movie.

Hôtel Westminster

13 rue de la Paix, 2nd (01.42.61.57.46, www.warwickwestminsteropera.com). M° Opéra/RER Auber. €€€€.
This luxury hotel has more than a touch of British warmth about it, no doubt owing to the influence of its favourite 19th-century guest, the Duke of Westminster (after whom the hotel was named; the current Duke reportedly stays here as well). The hotel fitness centre has an enviable top-floor location, with a beautiful tiled steam room and views over the city, and the cosy bar features deep leather chairs, a fireplace and live jazz at weekends.

InterContinental Paris Le Grand

2 rue Scribe, 9th (01.40.07.32.32, www.ihg.com). M° Opéra. €€€€.
This 1862 hotel is the chain's European flagship – the landmark establishment occupies the entire block (three wings, almost 500 rooms) next to the opera house; some 80 of the honey-coloured rooms overlook the Palais Garnier. The space under the vast *verrière* is one of the best oases in town, and the hotel's restaurant and elegant coffeehouse, the Café de la Paix, poached its chef, Laurent Delarbre, from the Ritz. For a relaxing daytime break, head to I-Spa.

Mandarin Oriental

251 rue St-Honoré, 1st (01.70.98. 78.88, www.mandarinoriental.com). M° Tuileries. €€€€.
Set in a 1930s building on rue St-Honoré, the MO has a wonderfully indulgent location – and the interior doesn't disappoint either, with 138 luxurious rooms, fusion restaurants, a vast interior garden, and a smart spa with pool and seven spa suites

Chic sleep

Maison Martin Margiela's stunning new hotel.

Belgian designer Martin Margiela, the Howard Hughes of fashion, vanished from his brand in 2009 leaving a strictly anonymous collective to continue his avant-garde work. It is this talented crew who are behind the design of Maison Martin Margiela's first couture hotel, the **Hôtel La Maison Champs Elysées** (see p167). Beyond the cream stone façade, in a quiet street located between the Grand Palais and Avenue Montaigne, awaits an *Alice Through the Looking Glass* world.

Black cabochons on the cream marble floor seem to have been scattered by the wind as you enter the lobby. To the right is the White Lounge with its grand piano, illusional mirrors, and rows of hanging bulbs and stuffed flamingos in a glass case. To the left is the cigar bar, which is done out in burnt black wood with leather chairs. Black-clad tailor's dummies line the way to the Table du 8 restaurant and the secret urban garden beyond.

The numerous young staff are professional but relaxed, making this hotel feel more like

Los Angeles than the Golden Triangle. Previously a Sofitel, the building was also once the private club of the 'Centraliens' (graduates of the Ecole Centrale des Arts et Manufactures), and a gilded staircase leads to a series of magnificent Napoleon III salons that can be booked for weddings or other gatherings.

The main building has 11 rooms and six couture suites. The black Curiosity Case suite hosts revolving exhibitions in its floor-to-ceiling glass cabinet; the Gilded Lounge suite features cunning Napoleon III reproduction mouldings on the walls and a library of classic literature just behind the bed. The other suites are more classic Margiela with visual puns on minimalist white. Through a silver corridor that feels like the entrance to an exclusive club are the other 40 'boutique' rooms offering fantastic all-white bathrooms and plenty of high-tech minimalist cool – all are equipped with Apple TVs, iMacs or Mac Minis and Nespresso machines. The only downside is working out how to switch off the lights.

with private hammams. Chef Thierry Marx's gastronomic offering is the Sur Mesure restaurant, an all-white affair with Asian-influenced delights.

Le Meurice

228 rue de Rivoli, 1st (01.44.58.10.10, www.lemeurice.com). M° Tuileries. €€€€.
With its extravagant Louis XVI decor, intricate mosaic tiled floors and clever, modish restyling by Philippe Starck, Le Meurice is looking grander than ever. All 160 rooms (kitted out with iPod-ready radio alarms) are done up in distinct historical styles; the Belle Etoile suite on the seventh floor provides stunning views from its terrace. You can relax in the Winter Garden to the strains of jazz; for some more intensive intervention, head to the spa complex.

Montmartre & Pigalle

Hôtel Amour

8 rue Navarin, 9th (01.48.78.31.80, www. hotelamourparis.fr). M° St-Georges. €€.
This boutique hotel is a real hit with the in crowd. Each of the 20 rooms (with free Wi-Fi) is unique, decorated on the theme of love or eroticism by a coterie of contemporary artists and designers such as Marc Newson and Sophie Calle. Seven of the rooms contain artists' installations, and two others have their own private bar and a large terrace. The late-night brasserie has a coveted outdoor garden.

Hôtel Banke

20 rue La Fayette, 9th (01.55.33.22.22, www.derbyhotels.com). M° Le Peletier. €€€.
The Banke may well have the most eye-popping lobby in the city, a huge two-storey space done in outrageous belle époque style, all crimson, black pillars and gold leaf beneath a whopping glass roof. After such opulence, the rooms are perhaps something of a let-down; but they are stylish and comfortably equipped. The mezzanine bar partakes of the lobby's *luxe*, and the Josefin restaurant serves nouvelle Med cuisine.

Hôtel Particulier Montmartre

23 av Junot, 18th (01.53.41.81.40, www.hotel-particulier-montmartre.com). M° Lamarck Caulaincourt. €€€€.
Visitors lucky (and wealthy) enough to manage to book a suite at the Hôtel Particulier Montmartre will find themselves in one of the city's hidden gems. Nestled in a quiet passage off rue Lepic, this sumptuous Directoire-style house is dedicated to art, with each of the five luxurious suites personalised by an avant-garde artist. Free Wi-Fi.

Hôtel Royal Fromentin

11 rue Fromentin, 9th (01.48.74. 85.93, www.hotelroyalfromentin.com). M° Blanche or Pigalle. €€.
Wood panelling, art deco windows and a vintage glass lift echo the hotel's origins as a 1930s cabaret hall; its theatrical feel attracted Blondie and Nirvana. Many of its 47 rooms have views of Sacré-Coeur. Rooms have been renovated in French style, with bright fabrics and an old-fashioned feel.

Kube Hotel

1-5 passage Ruelle, 18th (01.42.05. 20.00, www.kubehotel.com). M° La Chapelle. €€€.
The younger sister of the Murano Urban Resort, Kube is a more hip and affordable design hotel. Like the Murano, it sits behind an unremarkable façade in an unlikely neighbourhood, the ethnically diverse Goutte d'Or. The Ice Kube bar serves vodka in glasses that, like the bar itself, are carved from ice. Access to the 41 rooms is by fingerprint identification technology.

North-east Paris

Hôtel Garden Saint-Martin

35 rue Yves Toudic, 10th (01.42.40. 17.72, www.hotel-gardensaintmartin-paris.com). M° Jacques Bonsergent. €.
The shops, cafés and bars along the Canal St-Martin draw visitors to this hotel, where creature comforts are

LE MARCEAU BASTILLE ★★★★

Hôtel-Gallery
13 rue Jules César
75012 Paris
Tél: 00.33(0)1 43 43 11 65
Fax: 00.33(0)1 43 41 67 70
infos@hotelmarceaubastille.com
Géneral Manager: Christophe Diallo

Le Marceau Bastille – Hotel gallery is a charming and contemporary 4 stars hotel, located nearly a few steps away from the Bastille square, as well "Gare de Lyon" train station and the historic Marais neighbourhood. The hotel interiors denote a characteristically contemporary style.

Le Marceau Bastille Hotel offers 55 rooms of two kinds: First, the "urban" option guarantees a cozy and resolutely avant-garde type atmosphere swathed in vibrant color, still seeped in elegance. The "ecological" option provides calm and sunny rooms set off by bright yet soft tones, natural materials, organic forms and sleek lines. The furnishings are contemporary and combine delicacy with modern technology. The living room and the breakfast room walls are dedicated to the Art with the permanent collections of contemporary artists.

Hotel Facilities
General
Bar, 24-Hour Front Desk, Newspapers, Non-Smoking Rooms, Rooms/Facilities for Disabled Guests, Elevator, free Safety Deposit Box, Heating, Design Hotel, Luggage Storage, Air-conditioning, Fitness room.

Services
Massage, Room Service, Laundry, Dry Cleaning, Breakfast in the Room, Fax/Photocopying.
Free! All children under 2 years stay free of charge for cots.
Free! Wi-Fi is available in the entire hotel and is free of charge.
Free! Pets are allowed on request. No extra charges.
Extra beds are available on request only. Any type of extra bed or baby cot is upon request and needs to be confirmed by the hotel. Public parking is possible at a location nearby.

Hotel Policies
Check-in 13:00 & Check-out 12:00
Accepted credit cards
American Express, Visa, Euro/MasterCard, Carte Bleue, Diners Club, JCB
Area Information
Architect, Historic and Art Area.
Place de la Bastille - L'Opéra Bastille - L'Hôtel Sully - L'Hôtel Carnavalet - L'Institut du Monde Arabe et la Mosquée de Paris - Le Pavillon de l'Arsenal. Le Quartier du Marais - La Place des Vosges - Cour Saint - Emilion
Stroll and Walk Area
La Promenade Plantée - Le Port de Plaisance de Paris Arsenal - Le Jardin des Plantes and Muséum National d'Histoire Naturelle - L'Ile Saint Louis.

guaranteed at an excellent rate. No prizes will be won for the ordinary decor, but there is a very pleasant patio garden, and the staff are helpful.

Mama Shelter

109 rue de Bagnolet, 20th (01.43.48. 48.48, www.mamashelter.com). Mº Alexandre Dumas, Maraîchers or Porte de Bagnolet. **€**.

Philippe Starck's design commission is a stone's throw east of Père Lachaise, and its decor appeals to the young-at-heart with Batman and Incredible Hulk light fittings, dark walls, polished wood and splashes of bright fabrics. Every room comes with an iMac computer, TV, free internet access and a CD and DVD player; and when hunger strikes, there's a brasserie with a romantic terrace. If you're sure of your dates, book online and take advantage of the saver's rate.

St Christopher's Inn

159 rue de Crimée, 19th (01.40.34. 34.40, www.st-christophers.co.uk/paris-hostels). Mº Crimée, Jaurès, Laumière or Stalingrad. **€**.

If you don't mind bunking up with others, you could try this Paris branch of the English youth hostel chain. The decor in the bedrooms has a sailor's cabin feel, with round, colourful mirrors, bubble-pattern wallpaper and 1950s-inspired cabin furniture. The hostel really comes into its own in its bar, Belushi's, where the usual backpack brigade are joined by Parisians bent on taking advantage of the canalside setting, satellite sports, lunchtime brasserie and cheap drinks. A second branch, located next to Gare du Nord, opened in spring 2013.

The Marais & Eastern Paris

Le 20 Prieuré Hôtel

20 rue du Grand Prieuré, 11th (01.47. 00.74.14, www.hotel20prieure.com). Mº République. **€**.

This young, funky and affordable place benefits from particularly welcoming staff. Each room has a huge blow-up of a Paris landmark covering the entire wall behind the bed, giving you the illusion that you are sleeping halfway up the Eiffel Tower, or on Bir-Hakeim bridge as the métro speeds by. Bathrooms are mundane in comparison, but things brighten up again in the light-flooded breakfast room, with pop art portraits and a reworked 1970s look.

Auberge Flora

44 bd Richard Lenoir, 11th (01.47.00.52.77, www.auberge flora.fr). Mº Richard Lenoir. **€**.

Flora Mikula, the hugely talented chef behind Les Olivades and Les Saveurs de Flora, left the smart 8th for the more boho 11th to pursue her dream of creating this urban inn. The 21 rooms are themed around *bohème* (brocade throws, fringed lampshades, vivid colours), *potager* (aubergine-coloured walls, vast pumpkin pictures as headboards), and *nature* (stone sinks, mirrors framed with rounds of wood). As you'd expect, breakfast is a treat.

Grand Hôtel Jeanne d'Arc

3 rue de Jarente, 4th (01.48.87.62.11, www.hoteljeannedarc.com). Mº Chemin Vert. **€**.

The Jeanne d'Arc's strong point is its lovely location on a quiet road close to pretty place du Marché-Ste-Catherine. Refurbishment has made the reception area striking. The bedrooms are simple but comfortable.

Hôtel Bourg Tibourg

19 rue du Bourg-Tibourg, 4th (01.42.78.47.39, www.hotelbourg tibourg.com). Mº Hôtel de Ville. **€€€**.

The Bourg Tibourg has the same owners as Hôtel Costes and the same interior decorator – but don't expect this jewel box of a boutique hotel to look like a mini replica. Aside from its enviable location in the Marais and its fashion-pack fans, here it's all about

Jacques Garcia's decor – impressive and imaginative. Exotic, scented candles, mosaic-tiled bathrooms and luxurious fabrics in rich colours create the perfect escape from the outside world. There's no restaurant or lounge – posing is done in the bars. Free Wi-Fi.

Hôtel de la Bretonnerie

22 rue Ste-Croix-de-la-Bretonnerie, 4th (01.48.87.77.63, www.bretonnerie. com). Mº Hôtel de Ville. €€.

With a combination of wrought ironwork, exposed stone and ancient beams, the labyrinth of corridors and passages in this 17th-century *hôtel particulier* are full of atmosphere. Tapestries, rich colours and the occasional four-poster bed give the 29 suites and bedrooms individuality. Location is convenient too. Free Wi-Fi.

Hôtel Gabriel

25 rue du Grand Prieuré, 11th (01.47.00.13.38, www.gabrielparis marais.com). Mº République. €€.

Paris's first 'detox hotel' is a shrine to quality kip. The air-conditioned, pure white rooms are not short on techno wizardry: there's an iPod station; free Wi-Fi, of course; and the sine qua non

of sleep aids, the NightCove device. This white box is easily programmed to emit sounds and light that stimulate melatonin: choose between sleep, nap or wake-up programmes. If you're still feeling run down, then head downstairs for a detox massage. A partner gym, suggested jogging routes and green taxis complete the healthy vibe.

Hôtel Jules & Jim

11 rue des Gravilliers, 4th (01.44.54. 13.13, www.hoteljulesetjim.com). Mº Arts et Métiers. €€€.

Located in the heart of the Marais, this modern hotel is surrounded by two paved courtyards and has lovely roof-top views. Guest rooms are comfortable, with all mod cons, while a continental buffet breakfast is served in the chic dining area. Guests can enjoy cocktails at the bar or on the terrace.

Hôtel du Petit Moulin

29-31 rue de Poitou, 3rd (01.42.74. 10.10, www.hoteldupetitmoulin.com). Mº St-Sébastien Froissart. €€.

Within striking distance of the hip shops on rue Charlot, this listed, turn-of-the-century façade masks what was once the oldest *boulangerie* in Paris,

Mama Shelter p175

lovingly restored as a boutique hotel by Nadia Murano and Denis Nourry. The couple recruited Christian Lacroix for the decor, and the result is a riot of colour, trompe l'oeil effects and a savvy mix of old and new. Each of its 17 exquisitely appointed rooms is unique, and the walls in rooms 202, 204 and 205 feature swirling, extravagant drawings and scribbles taken from Lacroix's sketchbook. Free parking.

Murano Urban Resort

13 bd du Temple, 3rd (01.42.71.20.00, www.muranoresort.com). M° Filles du Calvaire or Oberkampf. €€€€.
Behind this unremarkable façade is a super cool and supremely luxurious hotel, popular with the fashion set for its slick lounge-style design, excellent restaurant and high-tech flourishes – including coloured light co-ordinators that enable you to change the mood of your room at the touch of a button. The handsome bar has a mind-boggling 140 varieties of vodka to sample, which can make the fingerprint access to the hotel's 43 rooms and nine suites (two of which feature private pools) a late-night godsend. Free Wi-Fi.

The Seine & Islands

Hôtel des Deux-Iles

59 rue St-Louis-en-l'Ile, 4th (01.43.26. 13.35, www.deuxiles-paris-hotel.com). M° Pont Marie. €€.
This peaceful 17th-century townhouse offers 17 soundproofed, air-conditioned rooms kitted out in toned-down stripes, *toile de Jouy* fabrics and neo colonial-style furniture. Its star features are a tiny courtyard off the lobby and a vaulted stone breakfast area.

Hôtel du Jeu de Paume

54 rue St-Louis-en-l'Ile, 4th (01.43.26. 14.18, www.jeudepaumehotel.com). M° Pont Marie. €€€.
With a discreet courtyard entrance, 17th-century beams, private garden and a unique timbered breakfast room

that was once a real tennis court built under Louis XIII, this is a charming and romantic hotel. These days, it is filled with an attractive array of modern and classical art, and has a coveted billiards table. A dramatic glass lift and catwalks lead to the rooms and two self-catering apartments, which are simple and tasteful.

The 7th & Western Paris

Le Bellechasse

8 rue de Bellechasse, 7th (01.45.50. 22.31, www.lebellechasse.com). M° Assemblée Nationale or Solférino/ RER Musée d'Orsay. €€€€.
This former *hôtel particulier* was transformed by Christian Lacroix into a trendy boutique hotel. Only a few steps away from the Musée d'Orsay, it offers 34 splendid – though small – rooms, in seven decorative styles. Book early, as the Bellechasse is very popular.

Hôtel Duc de Saint-Simon

14 rue de St-Simon, 7th (01.44.39. 20.20, www.hotelducdesaintsimon.com). M° Rue du Bac. €€€.
A lovely courtyard leads the way into this popular hotel on the edge of St-Germain-des-Prés. Of the 34 bedrooms, four have terraces over a closed-off, leafy garden. It's perfect for lovers, though if you can do without a four-poster bed there are more spacious rooms than the Honeymoon Suite.

Hôtel Eiffel Rive Gauche

6 rue du Gros-Caillou, 7th (01.45.51. 51.51, www.hotel-eiffel.com). M° Ecole Militaire. €.
The Provençal decor and warm welcome make this a nice retreat. All 29 rooms feature Empire-style bedheads and modern bathrooms. Outside, there's a tiny, tiled courtyard with a bridge. If this is fully booked, try sister hotel Eiffel Villa Garibaldi (48 bd Garibaldi, 15th, 01.56.58.56.58).

ESSENTIALS

Dear Mary,

I followed your advice and checked the ParisAddress website to look for an apartment. This place we booked is just amazing, it has everything we were expecting and even more !

> Instant availability
> Instant booking
> Easy process
> Prices all included,
  no hidden fees !
> Personal greeting
> Assistance 7/7

WWW.PARISADDRESS.COM

You wish to live like a true Parisian ?

Saint-Germain-Des-Prés, the Latin Quarter, St Louis Island, the Marais, Eiffel Tower and so many other great areas for you to discover !

To make your next trip in Paris an unique and unforgettable experience, rent an apartment and discover Paris from 'within'.

ParisAddress invites you to discover picturesque and fully furnished apartments !

www.parisaddress.com - booking@parisaddress.com - +33 1 43 20 91 57

Hôtel Lenox

*9 rue de l'Université, 7th (01.42.96.
10.95, www.lenoxsaintgermain.com).
Mº St-Germain-des-Prés.* €€.

Its location may be in the seventh
arrondissement, but this venerable
literary and artistic haunt is unmistak-
ably part of St-Germain-des-Prés. The
art deco-style Lenox Club Bar, which is
open to the public, features supremely
comfortable leather club chairs and an
array of jazz instruments on the walls.
Bedrooms, which are reached by an
astonishing glass lift, have traditional
decor and city views.

Le Montalembert

*3 rue Montalembert, 7th (01.45.49.
68.68, www.hotel-montalembert.fr).
Mº Rue du Bac.* €€€.

Grace Leo-Andrieu's impeccable
boutique hotel is a benchmark of
quality and service. It has everything
that *mode* maniacs could want:
bathrooms stuffed with Molton Brown
toiletries, a set of digital scales and
plenty of mirrors with which to keep
an eye on their figure. Decorated in
pale lilac, cinnamon and olive tones, the
entire hotel has Wi-Fi access, and each
room is equipped with a flatscreen TV.
Clattery two-person stairwell lifts are a
nice nod to old-fashioned ways.

Sublim Eiffel

*94 bd Garibaldi, 15th (01.40.65.95.95,
www.sublimeiffel.com). Mº Sèvres-
Lecourbe.* €€.

Some Barry White on your iPod is
essential for this luuurve hotel not far
from the Eiffel Tower. Carpets printed
with paving stones and manhole covers
lead to the rooms, where everything
has been put in place for steamy nights.
It's all to do with the lighting effects,
which include a starry Eiffel Tower or
street-scene lights above the bed and
sparkling LEDs in the showers, filtered
by coloured glass doors. All guests get
the use of the mini-gym and hammam,
and there is a massage room too. The
bar adds a bit of jazz.

Artus Hotel

*34 rue de Buci, 6th (01.43.29.07.20,
www.artushotel.com). Mº Mabillon.* €€.

The Artus is the ideal spot for a classic
taste of Paris – you couldn't be any
closer to the heart of the Left Bank
action. Inside the look is chic boutique,
with 27 individually designed rooms
ranging from cosy to capacious. Staff
are eager to help and full of local tips.

Le Clos Médicis

*56 rue Monsieur-le-Prince, 6th
(01.43.29.10.80, www.dosmedicis.com).
Mº Odéon/RER Luxembourg.* €€.

More like a stylish, private townhouse
than a hotel, Le Clos Médicis is located
by the Luxembourg gardens. The
hotel's decor is refreshingly modern,
with rooms done out with taffeta
curtains and chenille bedcovers, and
antique floor tiles in the bathrooms.
The lounge has a working fireplace.

L'Hôtel

*13 rue des Beaux-Arts, 6th (01.44.41.
99.00, www.l-hotel.com). Mº Mabillon
or St-Germain-des-Prés.* €€€.

Guests at the sumptuously decorated
L'Hôtel are more likely to be models and
film stars than the starving writers who
frequented it during Oscar Wilde's last
days (the playwright died in a room on
the ground floor in November 1900).
Under Jacques Garcia's restoration,
each room has a theme: Mistinguett's
chambre retains its art deco mirror bed,
and Wilde's tribute room is appropri-
ately clad in green peacock murals. In
the basement is a small pool, which is
wonderfully private – only two people
are allowed down here at a time.

Hôtel de l'Abbaye Saint-Germain

*10 rue Cassette, 6th (01.45.44.38.11,
www.hotelabbayeparis.com). Mº Rennes
or St-Sulpice.* €€€.

A monumental entrance opens the way through a courtyard into this tranquil hotel, originally part of a convent. Wood panelling, well-stuffed sofas and an open fireplace in the drawing room make for a relaxed atmosphere, but, best of all, there's a large garden where breakfast is served in the warmer months. The 43 rooms and duplex apartment are tasteful and luxurious.

Hôtel du Globe

15 rue des Quatre-Vents, 6th (01.43. 26.35.50, www.hotel-du-globe.fr). M° Odéon. €€.

The Hôtel du Globe has managed to retain much of its 17th-century character – and very pleasant it is too. Gothic wrought-iron doors open into the florid corridors, and an unexplained suit of armour super-vises guests from the tiny salon. The bedrooms with baths are somewhat larger than those with showers, and if you're an early booker you might even get the room with the four-poster bed.

Hôtel des Saints-Pères

65 rue des Sts-Pères, 6th (01.45. 44.50.00, www.espritfrance.com). M° St-Germain-des-Prés. €€.

Built in 1658 by one of Louis XIV's architects, this hotel has an enviable location near St-Germain-des-Prés' boutiques. It boasts a charming garden and a sophisticated, if small, bar. The most coveted room is no.100, with its fine 17th-century ceiling by painters from the Versailles School; it also has an open bathroom, so you can gaze at scenes from the myth of Leda and the Swan while you scrub.

Relais Saint-Germain

9 carrefour de l'Odéon, 6th (01.44.27. 07.97, www.hotel-paris-relais-saint-germain.com). M° Odéon. €€€.

The wood-beamed ceilings remain intact at the Relais Saint-Germain, a 17th-century hotel renovated by acclaimed chef Yves Camdeborde (originator of the *bistronomique* dining

trend) and his wife Claudine. Each of the 22 rooms has a different take on eclectic Provençal charm, and the marble bathrooms are positively huge by Paris standards. Another major plus: guests get first dibs on highly sought-after seats in the 15-table Le Comptoir restaurant next door.

The Latin Quarter & the 13th

Familia Hôtel

11 rue des Ecoles, 5th (01.43.54.55.27, www.hotel-paris-familia.com). M° Cardinal Lemoine or Jussieu. €.

This old-fashioned Latin Quarter hotel has balconies hung with tumbling plants and walls draped with replica French tapestries. Owner Eric Gaucheron extends a warm welcome, and the 30 rooms have personalised touches such as sepia murals, cherry-wood furniture and stone walls. The Gaucherons also own the Minerve next door – book in advance for both.

Five Hôtel

3 rue Flatters, 5th (01.43.31.74.21, www.thefivehotel.com). M° Les Gobelins or Port Royal. €€€.

The rooms in this stunning boutique hotel may be small, but they're all exquisitely designed, with Chinese lacquer and velvety fabrics. Fibre optics built into the walls create the illusion of sleeping under a starry sky, and you can choose from four fragrances to subtly perfume your room. Guests staying in the suite have access to a private garden with a jacuzzi.

Hôtel les Degrés de Notre-Dame

10 rue des Grands-Degrés, 5th (01.55. 42.88.88, www.lesdegreshotel.com). M° Maubert-Mutualité or St-Michel. €€.

On a tiny street across the river from Notre-Dame, this vintage hotel is an absolute gem. Its ten rooms are full of character, with original paintings, antique furniture and exposed wooden beams (nos.47 and 501 have views of the cathedral). It has an adorable restaurant and, a few streets away, two studio apartments that the owner rents to preferred customers only.

Hôtel Résidence Henri IV

*50 rue des Bernardins, 5th (01.44.41.
31.81, www.residencehenri4.com).
Mº Cardinal Lemoine.* €€.

This belle époque-style hotel has a mere eight rooms and five apartments, so guests are assured of the staff's full attention. Peacefully situated next to leafy square Paul-Langevin, it's just minutes away from Notre-Dame. The four-person apartments come with a mini-kitchen featuring a hob, fridge and microwave. Free Wi-Fi available.

Hôtel de la Sorbonne

*6 rue Victor-Cousin, 5th (01.43.
54.58.08, www.hotelsorbonne.com).
Mº Cluny La Sorbonne/RER
Luxembourg.* €€.

It's out with the old at this charming, freshly renovated hotel, whose new look is very much a modern take on art nouveau, with bold wallpapers, floral prints, lush fabrics and quotes from French literature woven into the carpets. Rooms are all equipped with iMac computers.

Le Petit Paris

*214 rue St-Jacques, 5th (01.53.10.29.29,
www.hotelpetitparis.com). Mº Maubert
Mutualité/RER Luxembourg.* €€€.

This new venture is a dynamic exercise in taste and colour. The 20 rooms, designed by Sybille de Margerie, are arranged by era, running from the puce and purple of the medieval rooms to the wildly decadent orange, yellow and pink of the swinging '60s rooms. Luxury abounds with finest silks, velvets and taffetas.

Montparnasse

Hôtel Aviatic

*105 rue de Vaugirard, 6th (01.53.63.
25.50, www.aviatic.fr). Mº Duroc
or Montparnasse Bienvenüe.* €€.

This historic hotel has masses of character. New decoration throughout, in steely greys, warm reds, elegant, striped velvets and *toile de Jouy* fabrics, lends an impressive touch of glamour.

Hôtel Aviatic

ESSENTIALS

Getting Around

Airports

Aéroport Roissy-Charles-de-Gaulle

39.50, www.adp.fr. 30km (19 miles) north-east of Paris.

The arrival airport for most international flights. The three main terminals are some way apart; check which one you need for your flight back. The terminals are linked by the CDGVAL free driverless train. The **RER B** line (36.58, www.transilien.com) is the quickest way to central Paris (30mins to Gare du Nord; 35mins to RER Châtelet-Les Halles; €9.25 single). RER trains run every 10-15mins, 4.56am-11.56pm daily.

Air France buses (08.92.35.08.20, www.cars-airfrance.com; €15 single, €24 return) leave every 20-30mins, 6am-11pm daily, and stop at Porte Maillot and place Charles-de-Gaulle (35-50min trip). Buses also run to Gare Montparnasse and Gare de Lyon (€16.50 single, €27 return) every 30mins (45-60min trip), 6am-10pm daily; a shuttle bus between Roissy and Orly (€19 single) runs every 30mins, 5.55am-10.30pm daily.

RATP Roissybus (32.46, www.ratp.fr; €10) runs every 15-20mins, 5.45am-11pm daily, between the airport and the corner of rue Scribe/rue Auber (at least 45mins); buy your tickets on the bus.

Paris Airports Service is a 24-hour door-to-door minibus service between airports and hotels, seven days a week. Roissy prices go from €27 for one person to €100 for eight people, 6am-8pm (minimum €43, 4-6am, 8-10pm); you can reserve a place on 01.55.98.10.80, www.parisairport-service.com. A **taxi** into central Paris from Roissy-Charles-de-Gaulle airport should take 30-60mins and costs €40-€50, plus €1 per luggage item.

Aéroport d'Orly

39.50, www.adp.fr. About 18km (11 miles) south of Paris.

Orly-Sud terminal is mainly international and Orly-Ouest is mainly domestic.

Air France buses (08.92.35.08.20, www.cars-airfrance.com; €11.50 single, €18.50 return) leave both terminals every 20-30mins, 6am-11.30pm daily, and stop at Invalides and Montparnasse (30-45mins).

The **RATP Orlybus** (32.46, www.ratp.fr) runs to Denfert-Rochereau every 15mins, 5.35am-11.40pm (30mins); buy tickets (€7) on the bus. High-speed **Orlyval** shuttle trains (www.orlyval.fr) run every 4-7mins (6am-11pm daily) to RER B station Antony (€11.30 to Châtelet-les-Halles); allow about 35mins for central Paris.

Orly prices for the Paris Airports Service (see left) are the same as for Roissy-Charles-de-Gaulle. A **taxi** takes 20-40mins and costs €16-€26.

Aéroport Paris Beauvais

08.92.68.20.66, www.aeroport beauvais.com. 70km (43 miles) north of Paris.

This is Paris's budget hub, used by the likes of Ryanair and Wizz Air. **Buses** (€16) to/from Porte Maillot leave 15-30mins after each arrival and 3hrs 15mins before each departure. Tickets from Arrivals or buy tickets on the bus.

Arriving by car

Options for crossing the Channel with a car include: **Eurotunnel** (08.10.63.03.04, www.eurotunnel.com); **Brittany Ferries** (08.25.82.88.28, www.brittanyferries.com),

P&O Ferries (08.20.90.00.61, www.poferries.com) and **My Ferry Link** (08.11.65.47.65, www.myferrylink.com).

Arriving by coach

International coaches arrive at **Gare Routière Internationale Paris-Galliéni** at Porte de Bagnolet, 20th. For tickets (in English) call Eurolines on 08.92.89.90.91 or visit www.eurolines.fr.

Arriving by rail

Eurostar from London St Pancras International (0044.8432.186186, www.eurostar.com) to Paris Gare du Nord takes 2hrs 15mins direct. You need to check in at least 30mins before departure. Fares start at £69/€88 return.

Cycles can be taken as hand luggage if they are dismantled and carried in a bike bag (check dimensions with Eurostar). You can also check them in at the EuroDespatch depot at St Pancras (Esprit Parcel Service, 0044.844.822 5822) or the Geoparts depot at Gare du Nord (01.55.31.58.33). Check-in must be done 24hrs ahead; a Eurostar ticket must be shown. The service costs £25/€29.

Maps

Free maps of the métro, bus and RER systems are available at airports and métro stations.

Public transport

RATP (32.46, www.ratp.fr) runs the bus, métro and suburban tram routes, as well as lines A and B of the RER express railway, which connects with the métro inside Paris. State rail **SNCF** (36.35, www.sncf.com) runs RER lines C, D and E for the suburbs.

Fares & tickets

Paris and its suburbs are divided into six travel zones, with 1 and 2 covering the city centre. RATP tickets and passes are valid on the métro, bus and RER. Tickets and *carnets* can be bought at métro stations, tourist offices and tobacconists; single tickets can be bought on buses. Retain your ticket in case of spot checks; you'll also need it to exit from RER stations.

A ticket is €1.70, a *carnet* of ten €13.30. A Mobilis day pass is €6.60 for zones 1 and 2 and €15.65 for zones 1-5 (not including airports).

Métro & RER

The Paris **métro** is the fastest way of getting around. Trains run 5.30am-12.40am Mon-Thur, 5.30am-1.30am Fri-Sun. Numbered lines have their direction named after the last stop. Follow the orange *Correspondance* signs to change lines. The five **RER** lines run 5.30am-1am daily across Paris and into commuterland. Métro tickets are valid for RER journeys within zones 1 and 2.

Buses

Buses run 6.30am-8.30pm, with some routes continuing until 12.30am, Mon-Sat; limited services operate on selected lines Sun and public holidays. You can use a métro ticket, a ticket bought from the driver (€2) or a travel pass. Tickets should be punched in the machine next to the driver; passes should be shown to the driver.

Night buses

The 47 **Noctilien** lines run from place du Châtelet to the suburbs (hourly 12.30am-5.30am Mon-Thur; half-hourly 1am-5.35am Fri, Sat);

ESSENTIALS

look out for the Noctilien logo or the N in front of the route number. A ticket costs €1.70 (€2 from the driver); travel passes are valid.

River transport

Batobus
08.25.05.01.01, www.batobus.com.
One-day pass €15 (€7, €9 reductions). River buses stop every 20-25mins at the Eiffel Tower, Musée d'Orsay, St-Germain-des-Prés (quai Malaquais), Notre-Dame, Jardin des Plantes, Hôtel de Ville, the Louvre, Champs-Elysées (Pont Alexandre III). Tickets are available from Batobus stops, RATP and tourist offices.

Rail travel

Versailles and Disneyland Paris are both served by the RER. Most locations out of the city are served by the SNCF railway; the TGV high-speed train is steadily being extended to all the main regions. Tickets can be bought at any SNCF station, SNCF shops and travel agents. If you reserve online or by phone, you can pay and pick up your tickets from the station or have them sent to your home. SNCF automatic machines (*billeterie automatique*) only work with French credit/debit cards. Buy tickets in advance to secure the cheaper fare. Before you board any train, stamp your ticket in the orange *composteur* machines on the platforms, or you might have to pay a hefty fine.

SNCF
36.35, www.sncf.com.
Open 7am-10pm daily.

Taxis

Taxis are hard to find at rush hour or early in the morning. Ranks are indicated with a blue sign. A white light on a taxi's roof means it's free;

an orange one means it's busy. You also pay for the time it takes your radioed taxi to arrive. Payment by credit card – mention when you book – is usually €15 minimum. Don't feel obliged to tip, although rounding up to the nearest euro is polite.

Alpha
01.45.85.85.85,
www.alphataxis.fr.
G7
36.07, www.taxis-g7.fr.
Taxis Bleus
36.09, www.taxis-bleus.com.

Driving

If you're planning to bring your car to France, you should bring its registration and insurance documents with you.

Bison Futé
08.00.10.02.00, www.bison-fute.
equipement.gouv.fr.
Infotrafic
08.92.70.77.66 (€0.34/min),
www.infotrafic.fr.

Breakdown services

Beaking down in France can be an expensive business, so it's advisable to take out additional breakdown insurance cover before you travel, for example with a company such as the **AA** (www.theaa.com) or **Green Flag** (www.greenflag.com). **Dan Dépann Auto** (08.00.25.10.00, www.dandepann.fr) operates a 24-hour breakdown service in the Paris area.

Parking

There are still a few free on-street parking areas in Paris, but they're often full. If you park illegally, your car may be clamped or towed away. Don't park in zones marked for deliveries (*livraisons*) or taxis. *Horodateurs*, pay-and-display machines, take a special card (*carte de stationnement* at €15 or €40, from tobacconists). Parking is often free at weekends, after 7pm and in August. For car parks, see www. parkingsdeparis.com.

Vehicle removal

If your car is impounded, you'll need to get in contact with the nearest police station. There are eight car pounds (*préfourrières*) in Paris; to find out where your car might be, visit www.prefecture-police-paris. interieur.gouv.fr.

Car hire

To hire a car you must be 25 or over and have held a licence for at least a year. Some agencies accept drivers aged 21-24, but a day fee of €20-€25 is usual. Take your licence and passport. Bargain firms may have a high charge for damage: read the small print before signing.

Ada
www.ada.fr.
Avis
08.21.23.07.60, www.avis.fr.
Budget
08.25.00.35.64, www.budget.fr.
EasyCar
www.easycar.com.
Europcar
08.25.35.83.58, www.europcar.fr.
Hertz
01.55.31.93.21, www.hertz.fr.
Rent-a-Car
08.91.70.02.00, www.rentacar.fr.

Cycling

In 2007, the mayor launched a municipal bike hire scheme – Vélib (www.velib.paris.fr). There are now more than 20,000 bicycles available 24 hours a day, at nearly 1,800 'stations' across the city. Just swipe your travel card to release the bikes from their stands. The mairie actively promotes cycling in the city and the Vélib scheme is complemented by some 400km (250 miles) of bike lanes snaking their way around Paris.

A free *Paris à Vélo* map can be picked up at any mairie or from bike shops. Cycle lanes (*pistes cyclables*) run mostly N–S and E–W. N–S routes include rue de Rennes, av d'Italie, bd Sébastopol and av Marceau. E–W routes take in the rue de Rivoli, bd St-Germain, bd St-Jacques and av Daumesnil. You could be fined if you don't use them, which is a bit rich considering the lanes are often blocked by delivery vans. Cyclists are also entitled to use certain bus lanes (especially the new ones set off by a strip of kerb stones). Don't let the locals' blasé attitude to helmets and lights convince you it's not worth using them.

Bicycle & scooter hire

Note that bike insurance may not cover theft: check the contract before you sign.

Freescoot
63 quai de la Tournelle, 5th (01.44.07.06.72, www.freescoot.fr). Mº Maubert Mutualité or St-Michel. **Open** 9am-1pm, 2-7pm daily; closed Sun Oct-mid Apr.
Bicycles (from €15 per day) and scooters (from €45 per day) available for hire.

Left Bank Scooters
06.82.70.13.82, www.leftbank scooters.com.
This company hires out vintage-style Vespas (from €70 per day), with delivery and collection from your apartment or hotel. Various tours are also available.

ESSENTIALS

Resources A-Z

For further information on travelling to France from within the European Union, including details of visa regulations and healthcare provision, visit the EU's travel website: http://europa.eu/travel.

Accident & emergency

In a medical emergency, you should call the Sapeurs-Pompiers, who have trained paramedics.

Ambulance (SAMU)	**15**
Police	**17**
Fire (Sapeurs-Pompiers)	**18**
Emergency	
(from a mobile phone)	**112**

Credit card loss

Call one of these 24hr services.

American Express *01.44.77.72.00*
Diners Club *08.20.82.01.43*
MasterCard *08.00.90.13.87*
Visa *08.92.70.57.05*

Customs

Non-EU residents can claim a tax refund or *détaxe* (around 12%) on VAT if they spend over €175 in one purchase and if they live outside the EU for more than six months in the year. At the shop ask for a *bordereau de vente à l'exportation*.

Dental emergencies

Look in the *Pages Jaunes* (www.pagesjaunes.fr) under *Dentistes*. For emergencies contact:

Hôpital de la Pitié-Salpêtrière
47-83 bd de l'Hôpital, 13th (01.42. 16.00.00). M° Gare d'Austerlitz.
Open 24hrs.
SOS Dentaire
87 bd Port-Royal, 13th (01.43.37.51.00). M° Les Gobelins/RER Port-Royal.
Open *by phone* 9am-midnight daily.

Disabled

General information (in French) is available on the Secrétaire d'Etat aux Personnes Handicapées website: www.handicap.gouv.fr.

Electricity

France uses the standard 220-240V, 50-cycle AC system. Visitors with 240V British appliances need an adapter (*adaptateur*). US 110V appliances need an adapter and a transformer (*transformateur*).

Embassies & consulates

Australian Embassy
4 rue Jean-Rey, 15th (01.40.59.33.00, www.france.embassy.gov.au). M° Bir-Hakeim. **Open** *Consular services* 9am-noon, 2-4pm Mon-Fri.
British Embassy
35 rue du Fbg-St-Honoré, 8th (01.44. 51.31.00, www.ukinfrance.fco.gov.uk). M° Concorde. Consular services 18bis rue d'Anjou, 8th. M° Concorde.
Open 9.30am-12.30pm Mon-Fri. British citizens wanting consular services (such as new passports) should ignore the queue at 16 rue d'Anjou and instead walk in at no.18bis.
Canadian Embassy
35 av Montaigne, 8th (01.44.43. 29.00, www.amb-canada.fr).

ESSENTIALS

*Mº Franklin D Roosevelt. Consular
services (01.44.43.29.02)*. **Open**
9am-noon Mon-Fri. *Visas 37 av
Montaigne, 8th (01.44.43.29.16)*.
Open 8.30-10.30am Mon-Fri.

Irish Embassy
*12 av Foch, 16th. Consulate 4 rue Rude,
16th (01.44.17.67.00, www.embassy
ofireland.fr). Mº Charles de Gaulle Etoile*.
Open *Consular/visas* 9.30am-noon
Mon-Fri. *By phone* 9.30am-1pm, 2.30-
5.30pm Mon-Fri.

New Zealand Embassy
*7ter rue Léonard-de-Vinci, 16th
(01.45.01.43.43, www.nzembassy.
com/france). Mº Victor Hugo*.
Open 9am-1pm Mon-Fri.

South African Embassy
*59 quai d'Orsay, 7th (01.53.59.23.23,
www.afriquesud.net). Mº Invalides*.
Open 8.30am-5.15pm Mon-Fri.
Consulate/visas (01.47.53.99.70)
9am-noon Mon-Fri.

US Embassy
*2 av Gabriel, 8th (01.43.12.22.22,
http://france.usembassy.gov). Mº
Concorde. Consulate/visas 4 av
Gabriel, 8th (08.10.26.46.26). Mº
Concorde*. **Open** *Consular services*
9am-12.30pm, 1-3pm Mon-Fri.
Visas 08.92.23.84.72.

Internet

Milk
*31 bd de Sébastopol, 1st (01.42.33.
68.17, www.milklub.com). Mº Châtelet
or Rambuteau/RER Châtelet Les Halles*.
Open 24hrs daily.

Opening hours

Standard opening hours for shops
are generally 9am/10am-7pm/8pm
Mon-Sat. Some close on Mondays,
some for lunch (usually 12.30-2pm)
and some in August.

Pharmacies

All *pharmacies* sport a green neon
cross. If closed, a pharmacy will have
a sign indicating the nearest one
open. Staff can provide basic
medical services like disinfecting
and bandaging wounds (for a small
fee) and will indicate the nearest
doctor on duty. The following
are all open late:

Matignon
*1 av Matignon, 8th (01.43.59.
86.55). Mº Franklin D Roosevelt*.
Open 8.30am-2am daily.

Pharmacie des Champs-Elysées
*84 av des Champs-Elysées, 8th
(01.45.62.02.41). Mº George V*.
Open until 2am daily.

Pharmacie Européenne
de la Place de Clichy
*6 pl de Clichy, 9th (01.48.74.65.18).
Mº Place de Clichy*. **Open** 24hrs daily.

Pharmacie des Halles
*10 bd de Sébastopol, 4th (01.42.72.
03.23). Mº Châtelet*. **Open** 9am-
midnight Mon-Sat; 9am-10pm Sun.

Police

The French equivalent of 999/911
is **17** (**112** from a mobile), but
don't expect a speedy response. If
you're assaulted or robbed, report
the incident as soon as possible.
Make a statement (*procès verbal*)
at the *point d'accueil* closest to
the crime. To find it, contact the
Préfecture Centrale (01.53.71.53.71)
or go to www.prefecture-police-
paris.interieur.gouv.fr. You'll
need to obtain a statement for
insurance purposes.

Post

Post offices (*bureaux de poste*)
are open 8am-8pm Mon-Fri;
9am-1pm Sat, apart from the 24hr
one listed below. All are listed in the
phone book: under *Administration
des PTT* in the *Pages Jaunes*;
under *Poste* in the *Pages Blanches*.
Most post offices have machines
that weigh your letter, print out

ESSENTIALS

a stamp and give change, saving you from queuing. You can also buy stamps at a tobacconist.

Main Post Office
52 rue du Louvre, 1st (36.31). M° Les Halles or Louvre Rivoli. **Open** 24hrs daily.

Smoking

Smoking is prohibited in all enclosed public spaces. Hotels can still offer smoking rooms.

Telephones

All French phone numbers have ten digits. Paris and Ile-de-France numbers begin with 01; the rest of France is divided into four zones, 02 to 05. Mobile phone numbers start with 06. Numbers beginning with 08 can only be reached from inside France. The France country code is 33; leave off the first 0 at the start of the ten-digit number. Most public phones use *télécartes* (phonecards). These are sold at post offices and tobacconists.

Time

France is one hour ahead of GMT and uses the 24hr system (for example, 18h means 6pm).

Tipping

A service charge of ten to 15% is legally included in your bill at all restaurants, cafés and bars. However, it's polite to round up the final amount for drinks, or to leave a cash tip of €1-€2 or more for a meal, depending on service.

Toilets

The city's automatic street toilets are not as terrifying as they first appear. Each loo is washed down and disinfected after use. If a space age-style experience doesn't appeal, you could always nip into the toilets of a café; although theoretically reserved for customers, a polite request should win sympathy with the waiter.

Tourist information

Office de Tourisme et des Congrès de Paris
25 rue des Pyramides (08.92.68.30.00, www.parisinfo.com). M° Pyramides. **Open** *Summer* 9am-7pm daily. *Winter* 10am-7pm daily. Info on Paris and the suburbs; tickets. **Other locations** *Anvers, 72 bd Rochechouart, 9th. Gare de Lyon, 20 bd Diderot, 12th. Gare du Nord, 18 rue de Dunkerque, 10th. Porte de Versailles, 1 place de la Porte de Versailles, 15th.*

Visas

European Union nationals do not need a visa to enter France, nor do US, Canadian, Australian, New Zealand or South African citizens for stays of up to three months. Nationals of other countries should enquire at the nearest French embassy or consulate before leaving home. If you are travelling to France from one of the countries included in the Schengen agreement (most of the EU, but not Britain or Ireland), the visa from that country should be sufficient.

When to go

In July and August, during the long school holidays, there are often great deals to be had on hotels and a good range of free events laid on by the city (such as Paris-Plages), but many family-run restaurants and shops close as the locals go off *en vacances*. Avoid October if you can, with its fashion week and trade show action.

Vocabulary

General expressions

good morning/hello *bonjour;* good evening *bonsoir;* goodbye *au revoir;* hi *salut;* OK *d'accord;* yes *oui;* no *non;* how are you? *comment allez-vous?;* how's it going? *comment ça va?/ça va?;* sir/ Mr *monsieur (M);* madam/Mrs *madame (Mme);* miss *mademoiselle (Mlle);* please *s'il vous plaît;* thank you *merci;* thank you very much *merci beaucoup;* sorry *pardon;* excuse me *excusez-moi;* do you speak English? *parlez-vous anglais?;* I don't speak French *je ne parle pas français;* I don't understand *je ne comprends pas;* speak more slowly, please *parlez plus lentement, s'il vous plaît;* good *bon/bonne;* bad *mauvais/mauvaise;* small *petit/petite;* big *grand/ grande;* beautiful *beau/belle;* well *bien;* badly *mal;* a bit *un peu;* a lot *beaucoup;* very *très;* with *avec;* without *sans;* and *et;* or *ou;* because *parce que;* who? *qui?;* when? *quand?;* what? *quoi?;* which? *quel?;* where? *où?;* why? *pourquoi?;* how? *comment?;* at what time? *à quelle heure?;* forbidden *interdit/défendu;* out of order *hors service (HS)/en panne;* daily *tous les jours (tlj)*

Getting around

where is the (nearest) métro? *où est le métro (le plus proche)?;* when is the next train for... ? *c'est quand le prochain train pour..?;* ticket *un billet;* station *la gare;* platform *le quai;* entrance *entrée;* exit *sortie;* left *gauche;* right *droite;* straight on *tout droit;* far *loin;* near *pas loin/près d'ici;* street map *le plan;* bank *la banque;* is there a bank near here? *est-ce qu'il y a une banque près d'ici?*

Accommodation

do you have a room (for this evening/for two people)? *avez-vous une chambre (pour ce soir/pour deux personnes)?;* full *complet;* room *une chambre;* bed *un lit;* double bed *un grand lit;* (a room with) twin beds *(une chambre à) deux lits;* with bath(room)/ shower *avec (salle de) bain/douche;* breakfast *le petit déjeuner;* included *compris*

At the restaurant

I'd like to book a table (for three/at 8pm) *je voudrais réserver une table (pour trois personnes/à vingt heures);* lunch *le déjeuner;* dinner *le dîner;* coffee (espresso) *un café;* white coffee *un café au lait/café crème;* tea *du thé;* wine *du vin;* beer *la bière;* mineral water *eau minérale;* fizzy *gazeuse;* still *plate;* tap water *eau du robinet/une carafe d'eau;* the bill, please *l'addition, s'il vous plaît*

Numbers

0 *zéro;* 1 *un, une;* 2 *deux;* 3 *trois;* 4 *quatre;* 5 *cinq;* 6 *six;* 7 *sept;* 8 *huit;* 9 *neuf;* 10 *dix;* 11 *onze;* 12 *douze;* 13 *treize;* 14 *quatorze;* 15 *quinze;* 16 *seize;* 17 *dix-sept;* 18 *dix-huit;* 19 *dix-neuf;* 20 *vingt;* 21 *vingt-et-un;* 22 *vingt-deux;* 30 *trente;* 40 *quarante;* 50 *cinquante;* 60 *soixante;* 70 *soixante-dix;* 80 *quatre-vingts;* 90 *quatre-vingt-dix;* 100 *cent;* 1000 *mille;* 1,000,000 *un million*

Index

Sights & Areas

7th arrondissement p122
13th arrondissement p149
104 p159

a

Arc de Triomphe p56
Arènes de Lutèce p141
Atelier Brancusi p100

b

Basilique St-Denis p158
Bateaux-Mouches p57
Bibliothèque Nationale de
 France François
 Mitterrand p149
Bois de Boulogne p162
bridges, the p118

c

Canauxrama p95
Catacombes, Les p153
Cathédrale Notre-Dame de
 Paris p118
Centre Pompidou (Musée
 National d'Art Moderne)
 p100
Champs-Elysées p56
Chapelle St-Louis-de-la-
 Salpêtrière p150
Château de Chantilly p158
Château de Versailles p162
Cimetière de Montmartre
 p87
Cimetière du
 Montparnasse p153
Cimetière du Père-Lachaise
 p101
Cinéaqua p57
Cité de l'Architecture et du
 Patrimoine p57
Cité Nationale de l'Histoire
 de l'Immigration p159
Cité des Sciences et de
 l'Industrie, La p159
Collection 1900, La p70
Conciergerie, La p120
Crypte Archéologique, La
 p120

d

Disneyland Paris/ Walt
 Disney Studios Park
 p160
Docks en Seine p150

e

Eastern Paris p100
Ecole Nationale Supérieure
 des Beaux-Arts (Ensb-a)
 p130
Eglise de la Madeleine p71
Eglise du Val-de-Grâce
 p142
Eglise St-Etienne-du-Mont
 p141
Eglise St-Germain-des-
 Prés p130
Eglise St-Louis-en-l'Ile
 p121
Eglise St-Séverin p142
Eglise St-Sulpice p130
Egouts de Paris, Les p122
Eiffel Tower p122

f

Fondation Louis Vuitton
 p63
Fondation Cartier pour
 l'Art Contemporain p154
Fondation Henri Cartier-
 Bresson p154
Forum des Halles p71

g

Galerie-Musée Baccarat
 p57
Galeries Nationales du
 Grand Palais p57
Gare du Nord p95
Grande Galerie de
 l'Evolution p142

h

Hôtel de Ville p101

i

Ile de la Cité p118
Ile St-Louis p121

Institut du Monde Arabe
 p142
Invalides & Musée de
 l'Armée, Les p124

j

Jardin & Palais du
 Luxembourg p130
Jardin des Plantes p145
Jardin des Tuileries p71
Jeu de Paume p71

l

Latin Quarter p141
Les Halles p70

m

Maison de Jean Cocteau
 p160
Maison de la Culture du
 Japon p124
Maison de Victor Hugo
 p101
Maison Européenne de la
 Photographie p101
Manufacture Nationale des
 Gobelins p150
Marais, The p100
Mémorial de la Shoah, Le
 p101
Mémorial des Martyrs de
 la Déportation p120
Montmartre p87
Montparnasse p153
Mosquée de Paris, La
 p145
Moulin Rouge p94
Musée Albert Kahn p162
Musée Belmondo p162
Musée Bourdelle p154
Musée Carnavalet p104
Musée Cognacq-Jay p104
Musée d'Art et d'Histoire
 du Judaïsme p101
Musée d'Art Halle St-Pierre
 p87
Musée d'Art Moderne de la
 Ville de Paris p57
Musée d'Orsay p126

ESSENTIALS

Musée de l'Air et de
l'Espace p159
Musée de l'Erotisme p88
Musée de l'Orangerie p74
Musée de la Chasse et de la
Nature p104
Musée de la Mode et du
Textile p74
Musée de la Musique p96
Musée de la Vie
Romantique p88
Musée de Montmartre p88
Musée des Arts Décoratifs
p71
Musée des Arts et Métiers
p104
Musée du Louvre p74
Musée du Montparnasse
p154
Musée du Quai Branly
p126
Musée Fragonard p160
Musée Jacquemart-André
p57
Musée Maillol p124
Musée Marmottan –
Claude Monet p162
Musée National Delacroix
p132
Musée National des Arts
Asiatiques – Guimet
p61
Musée du Luxembourg
p132
Musée National du Moyen
Age – Thermes de Cluny
p145
Musée National Gustave
Moreau p88
Musée National Jean-
Jacques Henner p61
Musée National Picasso
p105, p106
Musée National Rodin
p126
Musée Valentin Haüy
p127
Musée Zadkine p132,
p133

n

North-east Paris p95

o

Odéon p129
Odéon, Théâtre de
L'Europe p140
Opéra p70
Opéra National de Paris,
Bastille p115
Opéra National de Paris,
Palais Garnier p86

p

Palais de la Découverte p61
Palais de Tokyo: Site de
Création Contemporaine
p61
Palais Galliera p61
Palais-Royal p74
Panthéon, Le p147
Parc André Citroën p160
Parc des Buttes-Chaumont
p96
Parc Monceau p62
Pigalle p87
Place de la Bastille p106
Place de la Concorde p74
Place des Vosges p106
Place Vendôme p76
Promenade Plantée, La
p106

s

Sacré-Coeur p88
Sainte-Chapelle p120
Seine, The p116
St-Germain-des-Prés p129

t

Théâtre Paris Villette p161
Tour Montparnasse p154

v

Vedettes du Pont-Neuf
p116
Versailles p162
Viaduc des Arts, Le p106

w

Western Paris p56, p122

ESSENTIALS